D0418873

Esmond
The Lost Idol
1895-1917

Johnnie Astor & Alexandra Campbell

Helion & Company Limited

Helion & Company Limited
26 Willow Road
Solihull
West Midlands
B91 1UE
England
Tel. 0121 705 3393
Fax 0121 711 4075
Email: info@helion.co.uk
Website: www.helion.co.uk
Twitter: @helionbooks
Visit our blog http://blog.helion.co.uk/

Published by Helion & Company 2017
Designed and typeset by Mach 3 Solutions Ltd (www.mach3solutions.co.uk)
Cover designed by Paul Hewitt, Battlefield Design (www.battlefield-design.co.uk)
Printed by Henry Ling Limited, Dorchester, Dorset

Text © Johnnie Astor & Alexandra Campbell 2017
Images © Johnnie Astor unless otherwise credited
Maps drawn by George Anderson © Helion & Company 2017

ISBN 978-1-912174-02-7

British Library Cataloguing-in-Publication Data.
A catalogue record for this book is available from the British Library.

All rights reserved. No part of this publication may be reproduced, stored in a retrieval system, or transmitted, in any form, or by any means, electronic, mechanical, photocopying, recording or otherwise, without the express written consent of Helion & Company Limited.

For details of other military history titles published by Helion & Company
Limited contact the above address, or visit our website: http://www.helion.co.uk.

We always welcome receiving book proposals from prospective authors.

Dedicated to my daughter, Violet, named after my grandmother, without whom this book would not have been possible.

JJA

Contents

Foreword

Johnnie Astor and I share a great uncle in Esmond Elliot, a beguiling character whose life was tragically cut short in 1917, at the beginning of the Third Ypres campaign.

The youngest, most loved and treasured, of the five children of Rolly and Mary Minto, he led a gilded, happy and fascinating childhood travelling to distant parts of the Empire, at its zenith, and experiencing different cultures and traditions. By virtue of the fact that his father was successively Governor-General of Canada and Viceroy of India and that his mother belonged to the Queen's inner circle, he would, in his brief life, have met some extraordinarily influential people, at the same time developing a wide and eclectic group of friends and colleagues. Almost without exception, he touched all who came across him. Even decades later, as the book details, people he met invariably remembered Esmond as someone out of the ordinary, a young man with a certain aura who transformed their lives. He carried an exceptional ability to connect with people and approached his destiny with an unshakeable faith and a remarkably mature set of ideals.

Johnnie's task would have been impossible without our great grandmother's personal tribute to Esmond which she put together in 1919. Initially, she thought of writing his biography for the family and close friends, but it soon became apparent to her that her words would not fully convey Esmond's true character and experiences. Having kept most of what he had ever written to her, from when he was a little boy to just a few days before he died, she had it typed up, together with his wartime notebooks and all the condolence letters she received after 1917, and made two copies, one for herself and one for her children. This is the first time any of this has been published. Mary also commissioned a very beautiful bronze of her lost son in 1921 which would be a constant and comforting reminder of him.

While I am sure that there were many other remarkable individuals who were lost in that terrible war, in Johnnie's and my family it was Esmond who stood out at the time and who left a gap felt by successive generations. Johnnie and Alex have captured the essence of Esmond's character and what he meant to those who knew and loved him.

Timothy Elliot, 7th Earl of Minto

Acknowledgements

A great debt is owed to Lord and Lady Minto for allowing us to consult family papers and peruse photograph albums at their home in the Borders; together with Violet Astor's extensive collection, which first inspired this book, they complete the picture of our subject's brief but full life. It is not in any small measure that their survival is due entirely to Lord Minto's efforts; he has done a wonderful job of organising and safeguarding them, along with Esmond's personal effects which returned from Flanders. Handling keepsakes and belongings, letters and jottings, of someone we had grown to know and love was exceptionally moving and it intensified our connection with those who fought so bravely and died on the Western Front a hundred years ago.

We are also immensely grateful to Gavin and Philippa Tweedie and to Dommie and Jane Elliot for their involvement in and support for this project.

By gracious permission of Her Majesty the Queen, we were given access to King George V's remarkable collection of wartime photographs and allowed to reproduce two images included in the illustrations. Our thanks go to Alessandro Nasini for his friendliness and resourcefulness when dealing with our requests.

We are indebted to the distinguished historian Professor Sir Hew Strachan; the generosity with which he made his advice freely available to us has been hugely appreciated.

Major James Kelly, Regimental Adjutant of the Scots Guards and Sergeant Platt, in the Regimental Archives at Wellington Barracks, were also very generous with their time, giving us much assistance in the sourcing of information and photographs in their collection. Philip Wright, archivist of the Grenadiers was lovely to work with; with a good deal of charm and humour, he quickly grasped our objectives and it was thanks to his tireless efforts that we were able to uncover a number of fascinating and amusing anecdotes connected with Esmond's fellow Guards officers, lifting them from the category of 'mere mentions' to that of 'real people' who, to varying degrees, but all very courageously, fought the good fight.

We would like to thank Eleanor Hoare and Sarah Warren-Macmillan at Eton College for giving us access to records in the Archives and College Library, which also houses the Macnaghten Library with its collection of First World War books. Alexandra Churchill was a mine of information on Esmond's Eton contemporaries, having written a very detailed book on the school's contribution to the Great War.

Glyn Prysor at the Commonwealth War Graves Commission made some very helpful suggestions and we are grateful for the interest he took in our book. He was able to provide us with a file on Mary Minto, which included correspondence between her and the Commission in the 1920s and 30s and details of her various visits to Proven and other war cemeteries.

Heartfelt thanks go to Tracy Murrell who, in the course of putting the book together, rescued us many more times than we will ever own up to – her smile is the perfect cure for technology-related hypertension. We should also like to mention Kim McSweeney, responsible for typesetting and illustrations, who dealt with us, computer luddites, with the utmost patience and good grace.

Jilly Cooper's enthusiasm for the story spurred us on in the last furlong; her warmth, ready wit and kindness have been delightful. She welcomed us to her house which, coincidentally, was once the family home of one of Esmond's fellow officers, Lt Gerald Drummond, who sadly never returned to it from the war.

We are further indebted to Major-General Mungo Melvin, David Hill of the Hawick Museum and Anabel Loyd, amongst others, for their support and advice.

Not to be forgotten are Christopher and Diana Godfrey-Faussett whose kindness and seemingly effortless hospitality have made numerous research related excursions north of the border a total joy.

It goes without saying that no such list would be complete without reference to our families. Our thanks go to them for their immense tolerance, insights and unstinting encouragement.

JJA & AC
London 2017

Introduction

My great uncle, Esmond Elliot, a Lieutenant in the Scots Guards, was killed on 6 August 1917 at Steenbeek near Ypres aged just 22. He left a deep and lasting impression on all those who came into contact with him. Among the countless tributes received by his mother, Lady Minto, the one from his Platoon Sergeant stands out as the most telling and eloquent: "We have lost our idol, for we had set him on a pedestal in our hearts. He came to us and claimed our affections so that, now he has gone, we will miss him more than words can tell."

He was on the brink of manhood and with a life ahead of him full of promise; one can only guess at what he could have achieved had he survived. It was his character that marked him out: he had immense courage, intelligence and good humour. Combining extraordinary energy with a profound sense of duty and concern for others, he seemed to have understood his purpose in life, a rare concept in one so young. Many among his family and friends sought to preserve his memory; he even inspired a brother officer in the Scots Guards, Wilfrid Ewart, to write about their joint experiences in *Way of Revelation,* the post-war battlefront best-seller, published in 1921. One of the two protagonists, Eric Sinclair, was based on Esmond.

Each soldier's experience of fighting is unique and Esmond's is a fresh and spontaneous account of the conflict which, one hundred years on, continues to hold a fascination. It reveals the rapid transformation and maturing of a young officer exposed to a brutal war; taking up several notebooks, the story, in his own words, forms the kernel of this book. With vivid descriptions of battle come reflections on life in general, the affection felt for his platoon and the inevitable sadness at the loss of friends.

It is all the more precious because the Army forbade soldiers from keeping such records in case they fell into enemy hands and gave away vital intelligence. Cameras were also discouraged at the Front, but the newly released light and foldable Kodak could be carried in a pocket. Many officers had them and the Army increasingly turned a blind eye to their use. Esmond took many interesting, informal photographs which give a good overview of what life was like behind the lines.

Soon after the outbreak of war and scarcely out of his teens, Esmond decided to postpone his studies at Cambridge and he joined the Lothians & Border Horse Yeomanry. In February 1916, he was appointed ADC in France to General Sir

Geoffrey Feilding, commanding the Guards Division, who later described Esmond as possessing "all the coolness of an older man and the dash of a boy". At this stage, the Army was preparing for the Battle of the Somme. It was a period of learning, necessitating patience and diplomacy, where he was exposed to the routines and exigencies of senior commanders; he was afforded a very privileged insight into how the Army was organised and managed and the logistics involved. He came into contact with several British and French Generals and politicians. The Prince of Wales (later King Edward VIII) was attached to the Guards Division and, on his return to England, presented Esmond with his horses and saddlery.

However, not content with being a mere spectator and anxious to get closer to the Front, Esmond left his staff position and joined the Scots Guards in August 1916, a move which propelled him into action and the opportunity to display initiative and leadership.

During the bitter winter of 1916-17, he saw fierce fighting on the Somme, when his Battalion suffered terrible losses. Esmond's role was particularly important in the build up to 3rd Ypres in July 1917; he led a daring and strategically important raid across the Yser Canal into no man's land on the other side and discovered that the Germans were holding the line very weakly—almost not at all. Thanks to this raid, the Guards Division were able to get men across the canal to the enemy side before the opening attack on 31 July, to commence their offensive from a much more advantageous position. The canal was up to 70 feet wide and a serious obstacle.

In addition to detailed diary entries, family letters from the Front, upbeat, witty and thoughtful, reveal a shrewd observer of people and situations. In this respect, he was very like his mother, Mary Minto, who kept a journal continually throughout her life. She was a redoubtable force; blessed with an enviable combination of beauty, charm and a wicked sense of humour, she was a supportive companion to her husband and very close to her five children. Her good health and resilience enabled her to acclimatise to life in India, as Vicereine, with relative ease. More importantly, it helped her to cope with the losses in her life: her husband and two of her children predeceased her. She was nearly 82 when she died in July 1940, at the start of the Blitz.

She was also a close confidante and Lady-in-Waiting to Queen Mary, accompanying the King and Queen on many travels during and after the War. Born in the Norman Tower at Windsor when her father, General Sir Charles Grey, was Private Secretary to Prince Albert and later Queen Victoria, she was cradled as a baby in the arms of the monarch and could just remember the wedding in St George's Chapel of Prince Edward and Princess Alix, later King Edward VII and Queen Alexandra.

In other ways, Esmond was the continuation of his father, the 4th Earl of Minto, who held the two most exalted positions under the Crown, Governor General of Canada and Viceroy of India. Described by Kitchener as "the best, most gallant and most able administrator that Britain ever produced", Lord Minto was brilliant in his dealings with people. Through his warmth, tact and gentle humour, he commanded a following amongst those who served under him; his shrewdness and mental stamina, in particular, enabled him to navigate through a challenging, transformative period in the history of the Raj.

Added to this, Lord Minto was a distinguished sportsman and steeplechase jockey, riding at Aintree and winning the French Grand National. Whilst inheriting this spectacular confidence on horseback, Esmond was primarily a team player and at Eton he coxed the First Eight three years in succession, winning the Ladies Plate at Henley in record time in 1911.

Nurtured in such a vibrant, stimulating and loving home and school environment, Esmond grew into a secure, resolute, happy young man, able to bring out the best in others.

It is to Violet Astor, my grandmother and Esmond's sister, that I owe an enormous debt of gratitude for her safekeeping of so many of Esmond's jottings, letters, personal effects and photographs. It's a rich treasury indeed and one which, together with her own recollections, has made it possible for me to reconstruct his remarkable life. It must, at times, have been inexpressibly sad for her to remember her little brother. The two had been especially close; she was the nurturing older sister who regularly corresponded with him when his father's appointment as Viceroy in 1905 meant the start of a long separation from his parents. She kept a careful eye on him when she returned to England in 1909, as a newly married woman. Crucially for her, she was the last member of the family to see him alive. Shortly after daybreak on a late May morning in 1917, at the end of his final leave, she drove him in her little car to Victoria Station and said farewell to him. How many times must she have thought back to that moment.

She was herself no stranger to sorrow having been left fatherless and a war widow with two young children in 1914. In the late summer of 1916, she married my grandfather John Astor; two years later, around the time of their wedding anniversary and two months before the armistice, a shell exploded very near him and tore off half of his right leg. My father's arrival into the world must have been a huge consolation; conceived shortly after Esmond's death, he was given my great uncle's first name, Gavin.

It has been with a mixture of emotions that I have put this book together. Researching and writing Esmond's story has brought me much closer to understanding the extraordinary times lived in by my grandparents and great grandparents and how the First World War changed everything. I found it much easier to dwell on his irresistible vitality and all the things he loved to do, rather than on his tragic end: how his life, however brief, enriched the lives of others. Many of his friends and brother officers were entertaining characters and I have tried where possible to include amusing anecdotes about them. I'm sure that Esmond, with his great sense of the absurd and his generosity of spirit, would have approved of these additions.

Finally, I wish to include Robert Rider's extraordinary story, without which this tribute would be incomplete. In the spring of 1974, Rider, a senior lecturer at Goldsmiths College in London, was on a walking holiday in the Lake District. Whilst strolling around the lovely market town of Keswick, his eye was caught by the window of John Young & Son, a well-established antique dealer. Amid an assortment of pictures and clocks, old globes and humidors, was a strikingly beautiful bronze bust of a young First World War Army Officer. His features were perfectly captured: a calm, steady gaze; straight nose; half smile; hair neatly parted on the right. Rich in hue and very lustrous, it was detailed in its execution. The uniform included shoulder pips, a Sam Browne belt, the outline of three medal ribbons and a tie-pin. Rider was instantly captivated. The owner of the shop, Mr Young, knew very little about the bust's provenance, beyond the fact that it had been bought at auction in Carlisle. It was by a successful Galashiels-born sculptor, Thomas John Clapperton. In exchange for a cheque of £60, the bust was delivered to Rider at his office.

The quest to discover the identity of the soldier began immediately. The unmistakeable configuration of the buttons gave a clue to his regiment, the Scots Guards, and the two shoulder pips indicated his rank – Lieutenant. By contacting the War Office Records in Whitehall, Rider was able to draw up a list of 47 lieutenants in the Regiment who were either killed in action or died as a result of wounds. After some elimination, the list of possible officers was reduced to half a dozen names. Among them was the Honourable Gavin William Esmond Elliot.

Rider's decision to publish a photograph of the bust in *The Border Telegraph* in August 1974, asking if any readers could identify the soldier, led to the sculptor's daughter, Jean Mears, coming forward as a willing and helpful contact. Correspondence with Jean yielded precious nuggets, including her very vivid recollections of Mary Minto's visits to Clapperton. It emerged that the bust had been commissioned in 1921, as a result of the success of the Minto War Memorial, unveiled in the same year: a statue of a soldier in a greatcoat, ready for the enemy, modelled on Esmond's face. Mary was so struck by its beauty and lifelike quality that she wanted something which she could have with her as a constant reminder of her son. Once completed, it was brought down from Scotland to be with her at her home in Hydon End in Hambledon.

It was a complete mystery as to how the bust was lost and ended up with an auctioneer in Carlisle but, gradually, through perseverance and painstaking research, Rider was able to piece together a clear portrait of Esmond: his character, family background, school and war record. Naturally, it involved the study of press cuttings and various family biographies and histories of the War. It also meant an exchange of letters with Eton, the Commonwealth War Graves Commission and the Indian Institute of Advanced Study in Simla, amongst others, and several key meetings in the Borders.

In 1976, Rider came into contact with my father, who obviously knew a great deal about his uncle, from his many conversations with his mother. He wrote about him in his short history of the Elliots of Minto in 1983. I found the letter, with a picture of the bust, tucked away safely in a sheaf of my father's papers. In 2016, I was fortunate to find Robert Rider, now in his eighties, and listen to what he had to say about my great uncle. Memories of his findings forty years ago were completely undiminished.

Johnnie Astor

Minto Family Tree

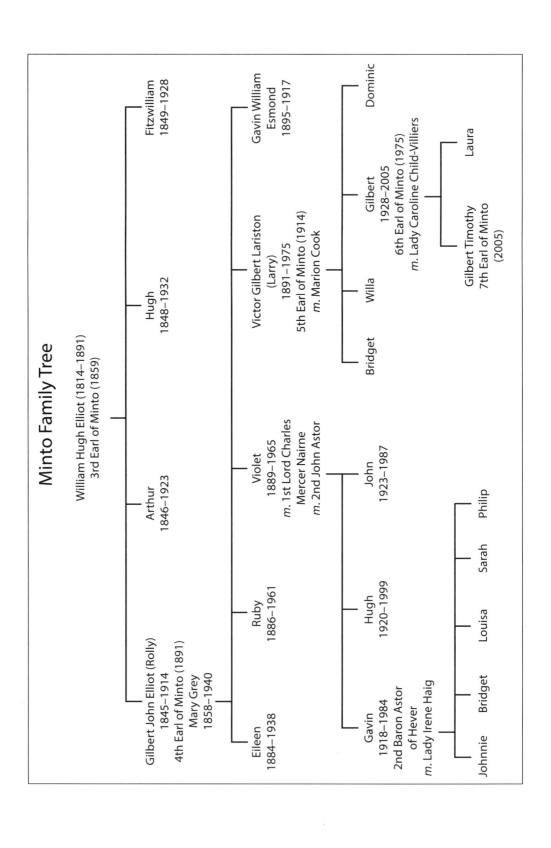

William Hugh Elliot (1814–1891)
3rd Earl of Minto (1859)

Gilbert John Elliot (Rolly)
1845–1914
4th Earl of Minto (1891)
Mary Grey
1858–1940

Arthur
1846–1923

Hugh
1848–1932

Fitzwilliam
1849–1928

Eileen
1884–1938

Ruby
1886–1961

Violet
1889–1965
m. 1st Lord Charles
Mercer Nairne
m. 2nd John Astor

Victor Gilbert Lariston
(Larry)
1891–1975
5th Earl of Minto (1914)
m. Marion Cook

Gavin William
Esmond
1895–1917

Gavin
1918–1984
2nd Baron Astor
of Hever
m. Lady Irene Haig

Hugh
1920–1999

John
1923–1987

Bridget

Willa

Gilbert
1928–2005
6th Earl of Minto (1975)
m. Lady Caroline Child-Villiers

Dominic

Johnnie

Bridget

Louisa

Sarah

Philip

Gilbert Timothy
7th Earl of Minto
(2005)

Laura

1

Family & Early Life

Everything depends on upbringing.
War and Peace, Tolstoy

Esmond Elliot was born on 25 April 1895 at 2 Portman Square, at the southern end of Marylebone. The baby, the fifth and last child of the Earl and Countess of Minto, was a delightful addition to an already very happy family unit. He was baptised Gavin, after his 17th Century ancestor Gavin Elliot of Midlem Mill in Roxburghshire, father of Sir Gilbert Elliot, first Laird of Minto; but he was also given two other names, William, after his paternal grandfather, and Esmond, inspired by a Thackeray novel his mother Mary was reading in the last months of her pregnancy. To her, he would always be known as 'Essy'.

By 1895, Esmond's father had already inherited the Earldom of Minto and established himself as a successful soldier and administrator. Better known as Mr Rolly, or simply Rolly, on account of his confident, rolling gait, he came from a long line of eminent diplomats and politicians. After returning from his first posting to Canada in 1885, he threw himself into the organisation of Volunteer forces; he was on the brink of a stellar career as a faithful servant of the Empire. His wife Mary was a renowned beauty with more than her fair share of intelligence and sparkle. They were devoted to one another and shared similar interests; both placing a high value on friendship and blessed with great energy and a positive outlook on life, they were a popular couple. What they loved most of all was their home at Minto, in the Scottish Borders, a scenic part of the country, steeped in history, in which the Elliots had played a significant and dramatic role, concurrently risking and safeguarding their lives, through skilful political manoeuvring during turbulent times. Set in idyllic parkland, Minto House, once regarded as one of Scotland's great houses, had been in the family for centuries. At the heart of it was a sixteenth century tower, but it had been transformed, most notably by William Adam, and had the unique characteristic of being V-shaped, which created striking perspectives and luminous interiors.

Rolly could count some interesting characters among his ancestors. Sir Gilbert Elliot, the first baronet, had imperilled himself supporting the Earl of Argyll and his rebel army in the attempted overthrow of James II in 1685. During the 1745 rebellion, Jean Elliot, daughter of the second baronet, kept a very cool head when she hosted some of Bonnie Prince Charlie's followers at Minto House without revealing that her father, openly hostile to the Jacobites, was in hiding in the nearby Minto Crags. Ten years later, she penned the lyrics to the exquisitely beautiful air, *Flowers of the Forest*, which lamented the terrible defeat of the Scots at Flodden in 1513.

Another Gilbert Elliot, Rolly's great-grandfather, who became First Earl of Minto, was Governor-General of India between 1807 and 1813. Having begun life as a lawyer and a Whig MP, he achieved fame and distinction through delicate missions abroad during the turbulent period of the Napoleonic wars. He was Commissioner in Toulon in 1793 and, the following year, became Viceroy of Corsica in response to the islanders' request for protection against the French. Having become President of the Board of Control of the East India Company in 1806, Lord Minto was appointed Governor General of Bengal in 1807. In this role, he had the difficult task of countering Napoleon's Asiatic ambitions; he was successful in establishing good relations with Persia and Afghanistan and with the great Sikh power at Lahore. And in 1809, Minto gave protection to the Phulkian States from the encroachment of Ranjit Singh, something which the old Raja of Nabha would later bring to the young Esmond's attention in 1906. He was also famed for bringing the French islands of Bourbon and Mauritius peacefully into British hands and the conquest of Java with the help of Stamford Raffles. It was largely due to Minto's patronage that Singapore was later founded. His sunglasses, vital equipment for a widely-travelled Scotsman in the Mediterranean and the Far East, are preserved in their original case at Minto.

His wife and family paid a huge price for his illustrious career. After a separation of six years, the sixty-three-year-old Earl caught a chill and died in Hertfordshire on his return journey from India to Scotland and never saw the bonfires that had been lit in welcome or his wife waiting for him with her children "under the ash tree on the lawn in front of the house at their beloved Scottish home".[1] This tragic story struck a chord with Mary because she wrote about it in detail in her book *India, Minto and Morley 1905-1910* and throughout her husband's career, she was reluctant to leave his side, taking great pains over his health and wellbeing.

Charles Elliot, born in 1801 and a nephew of the First Earl, brought Hong Kong into the British Empire. When still only a Captain in the Royal Navy, he was sent to the Far East by Palmerston, as an envoy of the Government, to bring to an end the Opium Wars. As part of the negotiations, Elliot persuaded the Chinese to cede that eponymous piece of land to Britain. When he returned home, the extent of the Sovereign's sense of humour failure was made plain. Both the Queen and the Prime Minister regarded Hong Kong as little more than a barren rock and criticised the deal. Failing to recognise its strategic potential, Palmerston dismissed his envoy and persuaded the Cabinet to repudiate the Peace Treaty but, by this time, the British had already occupied Hong Kong and, as there was nowhere else for the garrison to go, they were obliged to stay there.

The undulating Border countryside was where Rolly's own generation of Elliots indulged their passions. They shot and hunted throughout the autumn and winter, skated and curled when the pools and streams froze and fished and swam in the summer months, when daylight seemed to last forever. Hunting came top of the list for the family; they were never happier than with their horses and, in her recollections of the period, Mary painted an idyllic picture of a busy outdoor life, with plenty of adventure, for her young brood. They would go for expeditions in a cart pulled by a white donkey called Pharaoh: "On Sundays and holidays he was decked out in gala harness, in which blue beads predominated. 'Pharaoh' was very big, strong and full of courage; he never resented the cart being over-loaded and, in addition, would cheerfully carry two or three children on his back. The stables had a great attraction for the children, who learned to ride almost as soon as they could walk. Another source of delight to the children was 'Tommy', a tiny dark brown Shetland pony; he became their constant companion, and would follow them about like a dog." Tommy was Esmond's first mount, whilst he was still in petticoats.[2]

The Mintos were warm and affectionate parents who delighted in spending time with their children; Rolly, himself a lover of history, would read them Border folktales and ballads and the tone and rhythm of his voice would echo in their memories down the years. *The Lay of the Last Minstrel* by Sir Walter Scott, was a family favourite.

Rolly was the eldest of four sons, all born between 1845 and 1849. His mother was hugely influential in his life and he adored her; in John Buchan's words, "No mother and son were ever in more frank and intimate accord. His mother's combination of a keen critical mind with the happy glow of romance and the warmth of love made her influence supreme, and her personality when alive, and after death her memory, were the chief shaping forces in his life."[3] Through her guidance, Rolly grew into a self-assured and happy young man, active and adventurous, with a wonderful sense of humour and a capacity for winning friends. At Eton, he was a keen oarsman and runner; he played harder than he worked at Cambridge and during his summer vacations, he took up mountaineering in Switzerland. He loved being on top of a mountain, with the prize of stillness and a view of the peaks at the end of an arduous climb; later on, when he became Governor-General of Canada, he went climbing in the Rockies. But, by far and away, his passion was the steeplechase. He won the French Grand National at Auteil in 1874 on 'Miss Hungerford' and rode at Aintree for four consecutive years between 1874 and 1877.

It was around this time, in the middle of the 1870s, that Rolly's beloved mother first introduced him to the girl who would become his wife, in the library at Minto House. Mary, then aged 17, was the youngest daughter of General Sir Charles Grey and granddaughter of Earl Grey, Prime Minister between 1830-34, responsible for the Reform Bill and immortalised through his association with tea. Thanks to her father's position at Court, as Private Secretary to the Prince Consort (and later to Queen Victoria), Mary had been born in the Norman Tower, at Windsor. In a short autobiographical sketch for a book edited by Margot Asquith, she recalled the spectacle of the wedding of the Prince of Wales, later Edward VII, at St George's Chapel in March 1863; she was only four at the time. Rolly, then in his last year at Eton, was also at the Castle on that day, having been excused his studies to watch the bridal procession.[4]

Charles Grey's death, when Mary was only eleven, hit her hard and it was only natural when, renewing her friendship with Rolly in the winter of 1882-83, she would become captivated by him, a man thirteen years her senior, dashing, chivalrous and protective. Their eventual courtship, lasting only a week, ended in a Whitsuntide proposal at Panshanger, an ivy-clad gothic gem in Hertfordshire.[5]

After three daughters, an heir was born in 1891, Victor Gilbert Lariston, Larry; he was baptised in the Chapel Royal and Queen Victoria was a godmother. Mary's mother had just died and the old Queen had allowed her to keep the apartment at St James's Palace to have her baby there. Another son arrived four years later, as Rolly was approaching fifty:

> From his babyhood, Esmond held a unique position in the family. He seemed born into the world expecting happiness, nor was he ever disappointed. His merry face and dancing eyes, framed by auburn curls, were the true reflection of his sunny nature. He was, as a brother officer afterwards wrote to his mother 'irresistible'. No one could feel depressed in his presence. Esmond was throughout his life invariably the central figure, although totally unconscious of the fact. He met life with a smile, and neither illness nor disappointment was able to dim his cheerful outlook: 'What's the use of making a fuss? Now, let's talk about something else', was the characteristic way in which he would treat a difficulty. As Esmond passed through the stages of his boyhood his strength of character developed. He never deviated from what he considered to be his duty. He had supreme contempt for anything like swagger. He never failed to do his best but was diffident to a fault.[6]

Striking glimpses of family life are offered in the memoirs of Ruby, Lady Cromer, one of Esmond's sisters. *Such Were These Years*, written in 1939, casts an affectionate backward glance at a golden period before 1914, when the family was still seven strong. She remembered the gardens of Portman Square, when Esmond was a baby, where she and her sisters and Larry would play rounders in the summer; in the winter months, they would give their pennies to a veteran of the Crimean War, who only had stumps for legs and eked a living as a road sweeper. Minto House between 1891 and 1898 seemed to be a place filled with laughter and entertainment. Her parents would throw magnificent parties, especially at Christmas, where there would be dressing up and dancing. Mary's warmth and vibrant spirit made her popular with everyone; she was expressive and witty and could be relied upon to introduce a bit of fun and colour into the proceedings. She was such good company that her absence would be keenly felt. A bold and stylish dresser, on skating expeditions in Scotland and Canada she would perform confident turns on the ice, revealing bright jewel-coloured petticoats under sensible tweed skirts. She had a penchant for high-heeled shoes adorned with buckles and in different hues. Her crowning glory was her wavy auburn hair. Irredeemably feminine, she was worshipped by Rolly, who could not bear to be separated from her. Their written exchanges whenever they were apart oozed attentiveness and affection – his letters nearly always began with "My Darling Girl". They also teased each other with abandon and handed on the tradition of the April Fool to their children. Every year, on this day, each one in the family would be braced for some trick or other to be played on them.

Of Mary's female friends, fondly remembered by the children and spied on through the balustrade of the staircase at Minto House, the ones who stood out for their beauty and vivacity were Ettie Desborough, Esmond's godmother, Violet Granby, later Duchess of Rutland and Lady Randolph Churchill with "her blue-black hair…We already knew of her brilliant son Winston and faint echoes travel through the past of certain letters he had written in captivity from a Boer camp and which, I think, his mother received while staying at Minto."[7]

On 4 November 1898, the Mintos travelled to Canada for the second time so that Rolly could take up his appointment as Governor-General, setting sail from Liverpool on SS *Scotsman*; the voyage to Quebec took 12 days: "Icebergs were sighted near the Straits of Belle Isle. Although but three years old, Esmond made friends with the sailors and was constantly to be seen on the bridge with the Captain. Because of this, he was called the 'Commodore', or 'Commy', a nickname which stuck to him throughout his life, and which was often used by his father."[8] It was a horrendous crossing for Mary for, while little Esmond was distracted on the bridge, Larry was fighting meningitis and very nearly didn't survive the journey. His godmother, the

Queen, was deeply concerned and sent for reports on his condition – luckily, he recovered.

To a family who loved the outdoors, Canada was a vast adventure ready to be embarked upon – parts of it similar to Scotland, but on a much grander scale. Mary had a link with the Dominion beyond that which she forged as a young bride with Rolly in 1883. Her own father, also whilst newly married, had been posted to Quebec in 1837, when in command of the 71st Highland Foot Regiment; his brother-in-law Lord Durham went to Canada in the same year as Governor-General. On his return, Sir Charles Grey became Secretary to Prince Albert, beginning the long association with the Court that was to continue with his children.

Rolly's first posting across the Atlantic had not been without excitement: when the Riel Rebellion broke out among the native Indians in the Spring of 1885, he was seconded as Chief of Staff to General Middleton, commanding the Canadian Militia, and was sent out to the Far West in great haste to quell the uprising. About this time, he was also charged with the rapid recruitment of several hundred Canadian Voyageurs to navigate the rapids of the Nile in the Gordon Relief Expedition under the command of General Wolseley. As Ruby Cromer pointed out: "With this early tradition, it was no small wonder that the love of Canada ran warm in our veins. The long passages at Minto had teemed with relics – beaded mocassins, and snowshoes, Red Indian trappings, fur pelts, arrow slings and beaded leather garments."[9]

The crisp and clear winter climate and the hot dry summers suited the children who made the most of the countryside pursuits on offer. When the snow was thick on the ground they would be driven about in a little sleigh, covered from head to toe in bearskins. The went on toboggans, skated and skied; Esmond became quite an expert at this, aged only four or five. "Another form of amusement, when the snow was deep enough, was taking a flying leap off the roof of the skating house. This was a considerable jump for so small a boy, but in spite of being so much younger, he was always able to hold his own with his brother and sisters in their adventurous escapades."[10]

Esmond's confidence as a child would sometimes land him in trouble. In August 1899, he attended his first review of the naval crews on the Plains of Abraham just outside Quebec City. He was standing beside Mary behind the saluting point, when he was suddenly overcome by the desire to join the sailors and the guns. With lightning rapidity, he darted forward and sped across the ground, as fast as his little legs could carry him. Two tall ADCs in uniform and cocked hats started to run in pursuit, managing to corral and finally catch him, to the detriment of their dignity, the amusement of spectators and the relief of his parents.

It is said that, as Governor-General, Rolly covered well over 100,000 miles, travelling all over Canada. As John Buchan observed, with his sense of Border history:

"Generations of Whig decorum had not killed in him the moss-trooping instincts of the Liddesdale; his love of adventure, often of the roughest kind, and of every description of sport, brought him very near to the heart of the country."[11] Quite often the children accompanied him on his travels. Soon after their arrival, in the summer of 1899, the Mintos spent a month at Stanley House, at the mouth of the Cascapedia River in Quebec, where Rolly fished for salmon. There they also went bathing, messed around in boats and rode horses. The following year, the entire family went on their first tour of the North West. The children made their summer base on the Island of Victoria, where in the back of the Governor-General's official train, they made numerous expeditions to Manitoba, Alberta and Saskatchewan, covering immense distances across swathes of lake-filled wilderness. On a visit to Winnipeg, they watched their father receiving a hero's welcome: "he was well-nigh mobbed by those who would shake hands again with one who had been a companion in arms, and who had joined with the foremost pioneers in the protection of their lands." They went on horseback through prairies hitherto unspoilt by railroads, where Rolly would show them scenes from his earlier skirmishes: Fish Creek and Batoche. He would get emotional remembering the past, as old soldiers are wont to do, and the children would hang on his every word:

> And of all times, it would be these carefree weeks under canvas to which we would most look forward. Cold already with the nip of autumn, we would huddle round the camp-fires at night. Our tents were of the most primitive nature, and yet boasted little stoves. I remember waking up one morning and seeing my father in his thick blanket coat getting our fire to burn. How different from those sumptuous camps we were to know later in India, which lacked nothing save simplicity, and the grandeur of which did a little away with the fun.[12]

By far the most thrilling moment of that summer trip was their encounter with the Blackfoot and Sioux. The Mintos were all too aware that the people on the Indian Reserves and their traditions would not be destined to exist forever. Their graceful bare-back riding, war-paint, immense plumed headdresses and tomahawks were greatly admired by the 'Great Queen's Representative' and his little tribe. The proud cavalcade of Chiefs came to a halt to "air what grievances they had and to listen in reply to the White Man's speech."[13]

The Canadian lakes and rivers in all their glory beckoned each summer and the Mintos wasted no time in taking advantage of the opportunities for enjoyment offered by them, whether canoeing, sailing or rowing. Rolly risked life and limb, shooting the lumber slides on the Chaudière Falls, when he rashly exchanged the usual simple raft for a lumberman's boat. "Arrangements were accordingly made and the Mintos, accompanied by the Drummonds and the Grenfells, embarked above the Falls, quite unaware of the extreme danger of the adventure. Once in the boat, it was too late to draw back. The lock gates were open, the river was exceptionally high, the current carried them off, and soon they were plunging down a drop of twenty feet into the surging rapids of the Falls. The nose of the boat was completely submerged and the two men who were attempting to guide her were powerless. The torrent took command and flung the boat like a cork first one way, then the other, till, with its drenched occupants, it was providentially carried into calmer waters."[14]

Another drama took place on the Ottawa River and, on this occasion, the five-year old Esmond demonstrated an ability to steer, which he would later perfect at Eton. He was out on a wide stretch of the river one evening in a small sailing boat with his father, when there was a sudden squall. The water became very choppy and it was impossible for one pair of hands to attend to the sails and the rudder. Rolly's only option was to put Esmond in charge of the helm. His father told him to try his best to keep a straight course, as swinging round broadside to the waves would have been extremely dangerous. Little Esmond kept his nerve and listened to instructions; together they weathered the storm and never forgot their adventure.

When the rivers and creeks froze, the skates came out, normally at night time when these natural outdoor rinks would be lit by bonfires and fairy lights. Against this romantic back drop, French-Canadian folksongs would accompany the punters at their weekly winter parties.

Bicycling was another favourite family pastime and Esmond was given wheels very early on. At Ottawa, in the summer months, everybody was encouraged to get pedalling. If the distances were too great, Esmond and his tiny bike would be chauffeured to a rendezvous in time for tea.

> In order to assist the children on these expeditions, one of the staff – Captain Morrison Bell – commonly called 'Cloche' – noted for his resourceful imagination, carried a rope, which by some ingenious contrivance was to tow a string of bikes in line. This was tried once or twice, with such disastrous results that the towing of more than one child at a time was prohibited.

Cloche also started bicycle polo, played for a short time with enthusiasm on a circular grass clearing in the grounds of the Governor's house; it soon led to so many casualties, among adults and children alike, that Rolly vetoed it on account of it being "too expensive a game to life and property."[15]

There was a serious life-threatening moment at Government House in April 1904, shortly before the Mintos' return to Britain. A fire broke out in the children's wing before dawn on Easter Sunday morning; Violet, the youngest of Esmond's three elder sisters and the one he was closest to, remembered the two of them being hurried from their beds and taking refuge in the stables, where they knelt in the straw near the corn bins and prayed intently for their mother to be spared – following a skating accident in which she had broken a leg, Mary was lying in her room, immobile and helpless. Their prayers were answered, the fire was contained and she was delivered to safety, without further injury, and the damage was limited to a few rooms in the house.

Whilst in Canada, the Mintos' interest in amateur dramatics blossomed. Regular visits by a theatrical company occasionally called for the family to fill in the gaps at performances. Many long winter evenings were taken up rehearsing for pantomimes. Esmond was a natural performer, having learnt the art of mimicry in the school-room. He had a lovely governess and tutor called Mademoiselle de Jaffa, whom he loved to imitate; Mary described her as: "a brilliant linguist, clever, possessed of a great sense of humour and determined to get as much enjoyment as possible out of life. She prepared Esmond for school. She taught him how to speak French fluently and from her he acquired an excellent Parisian accent, which he never lost."[16] Ruby Cromer remembered her little brother on stage:

> Esmond, still aged only four, would delight an audience to a frenzy and bring the house down with applause, as with military precision he would strut across the stage drilling others far larger than himself, giving words of command, dressed in the uniform of a diminutive general, his tiny chest plastered with my father's service medals.

In the autumn of 1901, on her own without Rolly, Mary chaperoned the Duke and Duchess of Cornwall and York, later King George V and Queen Mary, on their first visit to the country. The couple stayed at Government House and were enchanted by the six-year old Esmond who, smartly dressed in a white sailor suit, introduced himself to the Duchess by flinging himself down on one knee and covering her hand with kisses. "Je vous aime de tout mon coeur!" he announced. Although, the royal itinerary was planned entirely by the Governor-General, because the Canadian Government was inexperienced in such matters, it was decided to delegate as much as possible to the Lieutenant-Governors of each individual province, in order to reduce the fuss and formality. Mary replaced her husband as the official pilot with so much charm that she endeared herself to the Queen. Ten years later, when she hung up her spurs as Vicereine, she was snapped up as Lady-in-Waiting.

Earlier in 1901, Winston Churchill also paid a visit. He was staying with the Mintos in January when news of the Queen's death broke in the Canada.

The following year, in December, Marconi stayed at Government House and arranged for Rolly to send Christmas wishes back to Britain by using the latest wireless technology; it was "the first New Year family greeting ever sent by wireless telegraphy across the ocean." The Italian scientist and his wife kept in touch with the Mintos and saw them whenever they were in England.

Mary and Rolly twice crossed the border into the United States, in 1899 and 1903. On their first visit there, they made friends with Theodore Roosevelt, then a Colonel and Governor of New York State, who was surprised at how friendly, warm and unpretentious Rolly was and, as he later confessed to Mary, quite the opposite of what he expected a British peer to be, "wedded to a frock coat and a tall hat, who had rarely left the London pavements." The admiration was mutual; with typical verve Rolly summed Rooosevelt up as:

> Quite one of the most remarkable men I ever met, bubbling over with energy of mind and body; hardly ever stops talking, a great sense of humour and an excellent raconteur; I should think afraid of nothing, physically or morally, and absolutely straightforward. Though a great sportsman – the house is full of magnificent heads – he has much literary talent, and has written many books…and is considered to be in the running for the Presidency. He is rather fat and short, with a bulldog expression, and a way of gnashing his teeth when eager in conversation. I delighted in him.[17]

With so many memories of interesting people, extraordinary adventures and spectacular scenery, the Mintos sailed out of Quebec homeward bound on 18 November 1904, having extended their tenure by a year, at the request of the Colonial Office. It was testimony to how skilfully Rolly had handled his mission. Rumours of his being favoured as a successor to Curzon in India had been circulating in the corridors of power for over a year and there were many on both sides of the Atlantic who were prepared to vouch for him. However, as the most important appointment in the Empire, it was also the most strenuous one and Curzon himself had warned Mary that he didn't think anyone over the age of fifty should consider accepting it.

Rolly left many friends in Canada, among them the Premier, Sir Wilfrid Laurier, with whom he seemed to share the same values and moral code. There was opposition in Canada to involvement in the Second Boer War – as there would be after 1914 to involvement in the Great European War – and it was only because the Governor-General had fostered such good relations with the Government that the latter agreed to send a volunteer force to South Africa.

Christmas 1904 saw the family back in the Borders. Esmond had left Scotland as a three-year old and returned aged nine: his blissful and carefree childhood was drawing to a close and in the New Year, he would have to exchange the nursery for prep school. He had seen and done a great many more things than the average boy; he had enjoyed a rare closeness to his parents who seemed to have had as much time for their children as for their official life; he was a great companion to his older brother and was doted on by his three sisters. He also had the security of Nana, the faithful nanny who had been with the Mintos for years and throughout their time in Canada. He knew nothing but love.

1905 would be a significant year in terms of endings and beginnings. Indeed, change was to be the dominant theme, as was separation. At the end of January, Esmond's parents took him to London and saw him off at Victoria Station, as he boarded a train with ten other boys and a tutor bound for Rottingdean and his prep school, St Aubyn's. "Esmond did his best to keep a brave heart, but as he said goodbye the tears would come, and the blank his bright presence would leave in his home might well cause other tears to flow."[18]

2

India

I do so miss you now, I miss you all very much.
                                                    Esmond

It was before breakfast on Friday, 18 August 1905, that Rolly met a messenger with a letter for him on his walk down to Minto from Cleughhead. He was going to see how the works to the main house were progressing; after an absence of seven years, the place needed modernisation. The plumbing was being overhauled, electricity was making an appearance and a new wing was being added. Although he was expecting a letter, for he had been tipped off about it the previous day in a telegram from the Prime Minister's Private Secretary, John Sandars, he had no inkling about its contents. When he opened it, he found enclosed a telegram from Balfour to Sandars, informing him of Curzon's resignation and requesting that Lord Minto be asked to accept the Viceroyalty of India.

Mary was in the garden when Rolly broke the news to her:

> The greatest appointment I have ever hoped for, and still what a pang to leave this dear old place again, and all the difficulties about the children. Mary took it so well. I know she feels the same as I do, and it is a recognition of her good work in Canada quite as much as of anything I have ever done. But it is a very high trial.[1]

They had been back a mere eight months.

In Mary's words, the news was: "a bombshell, and to the boys a terrible blow. The prospect of being separated from their father and mother for five long years was a great sorrow to them, whilst their parents realised what an anxious responsibility it was leaving the care of their precious boys to others."

As the summer drew to a close, the family savoured their remaining precious moments together, knowing that soon there would be a separation. Esmond had his first day's cub hunting at St Boswells on Pat, the black pony his father had given him just before his tenth birthday. At the beginning of October, in an informal meeting at Balmoral, the King presented Rolly with the Star of India and the Order of the Indian Empire. It was a personal touch and a departure from formal protocol, underlining the extent of Edward VII's regard for his proconsul. The King made a further gesture of friendship by coming to 6 Audley Square, the Mintos' base in London, on the couple's last full day in England, to wish them "God-speed and the best of luck".

Esmond came home from St Aubyn's to say goodbye. The wrench seared itself on Mary's memory:

> On Sunday afternoon, 29 October, the whole family went to the Zoo. In the evening the two boys went with their parents to the service in Westminster Abbey. Their mother sat between them, and listened to the beautiful singing in the dim light of the flickering candles, and prayed that God in his mercy would guard her boys from danger, and keep them safe from harm during her absence. The next morning the farewells were said. A little figure in pyjamas flew into his mother's room almost before it was daylight, jumped into her bed, and sobbed his heart out in her arms; but yet there were smiles through the tears, and the joyful anticipation of going to India in a year's time helped the parting.

On his return to school, Esmond wrote immediately so that the post would catch his parents and sisters before they left: "I hope you all will have a good voyage. I do so miss you now, I miss you all very much…I do hope the year will go quickly before going out to see you."

The adjective Mary used to describe the parting was "shattering"; she was "thankful that our three girls, Eileen, Ruby and Violet, are with us, and though now we are nearing our journey's end, in spite of new scenes and experiences, I seem all the time, to see before me the lonely little figures of my two boys, left behind, with tearful eyes, struggling to be brave."

On 18 November 1905, exactly a year to the day from when they left Quebec, the family docked in Bombay on the SS *Peninsular*. Across the water two cruisers, HMS *Renown* and HMS *Terrible*, boomed out a welcome salute; travelling on one of them were the Prince and Princess of Wales on their first state visit to India.

Adverse currents had delayed the Minto's journey and after two weeks of books and bridge, they were all too ready to escape the overheated ship with its engines throbbing at full pelt to make up for lost time. "I think you arrived yesterday at Bombay", Esmond wrote "Do you like India as much as Canada? The native people, when they come to call on a white person, will not go until he tells them to will they? How many stoppages did you have on your way out I wonder?"

Once the vast plains had been crossed, the welcome in Calcutta was truly splendid. The pomp and splendour of the Viceroy's court and the magnificent displays of imperial pageantry revealed the Raj at the height of its powers. There to greet the Mintos on their arrival at Government House, along with Lord Kitchener and other officials, was the Viceroy's Sikh Bodyguard, a magnificent escort numbering over a hundred men with an average height of six foot two. Their beautiful gold and peacock blue, fan-shaped turbans made them appear even taller and their vermilion kurtas over white breeches gleamed in the sunlight. On state occasions, they would be mounted alongside an open carriage in which the Viceroy sat under the shade of the Golden Umbrella, the ancient symbol of royalty, for to all intents and purposes the King's representative was a legitimate successor to the Mogul dynasty.

Mary's journal describes the formalities surrounding her husband's accession: "The 'state' connected with a Viceroy is at first overwhelming. An atmosphere of holy awe surrounds his person, creating an unnatural *gêne*. I prayed that before long we might be able to break through this uncomfortable constraint." There were over six hundred Indian servants in the house, and over a thousand counting the outsiders, who included a tennis marker, two ball boys and two 'assistant tennis ball gatherers'. A small boy was assigned to groom and de-tick the family dog. Dandy was a Dandie Dinmont acquired as a puppy by Rolly two years before leaving Scotland for Canada; master and hound were inseparable, as was plain to see in the majority of photographs, whether official or private. This steely character was given full ceremonial treatment on official tours around the country:

> It was amusing to see Old Dandy's departure, lying at his ease on the soft mattress of a specially made wooden bedstead, which was carried by four coolies with four relief men and one man in a red uniform, fully armed and holding a sword at the salute, walking beside him to ensure he should not fall out. The coolies speak respectfully of the Viceroy's dog Dandy Sahib, who accepts their homage and seems quite aware of his importance.

There were countless punkah-wallahs whose duty it was to pull ropes that kept the fans circulating the air day and night; without these, the heat and humidity made it impossible to sleep. Often, one punkah-wallah would fall asleep and have to be woken up, so to keep the punkahs going was a two-man occupation.

To be a servant in the Viceroy's household conferred high status. The strict division of labour was proscribed according to 'caste' and no servant would trespass on his neighbour's duties: the person who placed a candle in a candlestick would be different from the one who lit it and someone charged with tidying a room would not condescend to making the bed.

Mary made a list of 'our establishment', a bewildering number of different occupations appear on it, among them: a billiard marker, a time keeper, a chicken cleaner, twelve cooks, seven dooley coolies (iron pan carriers), ten Massálchis (glass and china cleaners), 23 Kuidmatgárs (waiters) and, in the stables, no fewer than 52 grooms.

The lawns required constant attention and irrigation; a group would spread out on them, with a yard or two between each person, and proceed up and down on their hands and knees picking out weeds. From the adjoining Maidan, where the trees were full of flying foxes, the jackals could be heard at night, an unearthly, sinister cry for those unused to the sound.

At state banquets, behind each chair the length of a huge table, a barefoot servant would stand motionless, his hand raised to his forehead in salute until the Viceroy took his seat. Behind the Viceroy himself stood attendants bearing the traditional Indian emblems of royalty: the gold and silver sticks and maces, peacock fans and a whisk made from a yak's tail.

The vastness of their quarters was bewildering to Mary: "All the rooms are immensely high, about 30 feet. They have enormous brown and gold doors and electric light has been put in quite recently. It took us an hour and a half to go through three sides of the house; it is depressingly large, and I tremble at the thought of unpacking and arranging."

The house had many family associations; a full-length portrait of the 1st Lord Minto, Rolly's great-grandfather, hung in the Council Chamber and a precious collection of rose-coloured china ordered by his brother, Hugh Elliot, when Governor of Madras, was still in a display case in the drawing room.

Sixteen miles up the Hooghly River from Calcutta was Barrackpore, the Viceroy's country residence. It had wonderful exotic gardens, with luxuriant masses of acalipha, morning glory and bougainvillia, and an ancient banyan tree, in whose shade the Mintos would entertain their friends to lunch or dinner. Mary summed it up as a "fairyland…an enchanting haven of rest – one feels one has for the moment escaped the watchful gaze of the public, and can be oneself." It took her a while to get used to the fast-descending darkness that occurs in the tropics: "with this heavenly summer weather it seems strange to be in one's room with all the lights turned on before 6 o'clock." In the summer months, the family would retire to Simla where Viceregal Lodge commanded a spectacular panorama of the Himalayas. There the climate in the summer was similar to that of a mild English spring. It always amused Esmond that there were ten servants dedicated to keeping the monkeys out of the rose garden.

Within a fortnight of their arrival, Mary was organising a State Ball for seven hundred guests and, ahead of that, a small dance to celebrate Eileen's 21st birthday.

This, together with the imminent arrival of the Prince and Princess of Wales in Calcutta, meant that she had less time to ponder her separation from Esmond and Larry who were spending Christmas on the Isle of Wight with their uncle Arthur Elliot. A tragedy unfolded while they were there: their aunt Madeleine was struck by typhoid fever; she was bedridden, needing round-the-clock care. The boys were transferred to another house and Nana stepped into the breech. She packed Larry and Esmond off to Minto, sparing them the distress of witnessing Madeleine's final moments.

New Year was miserable and Esmond missed his parents terribly. The present of a bicycle which arrived with a puncture was of little comfort, although he appeared very grateful for it; just before returning to school he wrote to them: "The holidays were not half so nice as when you were there, the house was so horrid and quiet… It is so good to think we are going to see you at the beginning of November, it is a long time, though it is something to look forward to." A month later he wrote again: "There are only 299 more days until we arrive in Calcutta, and I do so hope the time will go quickly."

Violet was his most regular correspondent at this time; he loved receiving news from her and berated his other sisters for their silence: "Will you please tell those two lazy girls to write to me 16 pages… and they are not to repeat themselves", he joked with her at the end of January. He had heard that there was a pair of lively little ponies at their disposal at Barrackpore, named Creepy and Crawley, which he was longing to ride with her.

In the intervening months, Mary received letters from Esmond once a week, deluging her with questions about the family and telling her in great, often comic, detail about what was happening at school. He even contrived to catch her out on April Fool's Day, following Elliot tradition. Mary told him about all the things they were getting up to, including the fact that his father had shot two bears, which prompted him to write to Rolly, enquiring: "I wonder how you missed the third?" But his mother was careful to shield him from bad news. On one occasion, he remonstrated with her after Eileen told him of a hunting accident suffered by Violet, which left her with a large horseshoe-shaped bruise: "I hear from Eileen awful accounts of Vi tumbling in the ditch, awful marks on her back where her pony walked on her, and from you she was not hurt at all."

Accompanied by his aunt and uncle, Victoria and Lewis Dawnay, on the SS *Macedonia*, Esmond arrived in Bombay on 23 November 1906. During the long journey, he befriended a lady poet, a sensitive artist who regaled him with her life story and its many sad chapters. She was going through a difficult time and Esmond cheered her up. She had been asked by the Ship's Captain to entertain the other guests with a recitation of her verses, which she duly rehearsed in front of the young boy. He apparently advised her, put her at her ease and made her laugh; they kept in touch after saying goodbye in Bombay and he sent her letters from school.

Also on board the *Macedonia* was a cousin of the Elliots, Kitty Drummond, who was greatly entertained by Esmond's conversation on deck as they approached the Indian coast. She asked him whether he was looking forward to seeing his sisters again. He replied in the affirmative, eagerly adding: "You know they are all old maids!" This description of Lord Minto's three very attractive daughters, aged 16, 19 and 21 and who were known in India as 'the destroying angels', on account of their capacity for breaking hearts, came as something of a surprise.

Early on the morning of 26 November 1906, Esmond stood on the platform at Bhatinda, a small railway junction in Patiala State, waiting for the arrival of the quarter of a mile-long train carrying the Viceregal party, which included ten secretaries and a staff of 120. Smartly dressed in a linen suit and with a rolled-up sun umbrella tucked under his arm he waited patiently. The reunion was recounted by Mary:

> We reached Bhatinda at eight o'clock and had the happiness of seeing a small white figure awaiting us on the platform, and soon Esmond, my sister Victoria and Lewis Dawnay, were all bundled into our carriage and we found ourselves all talking at once. There was so much to hear that the whole morning passed in asking and answering questions. How we laughed when Esmond told us that a Guard of Honour was at the station awaiting their train at the frontier and, to his dismay, he found that, as the Viceroy's son, he was expected to get out and take the salute, which he did, a tiny figure almost hidden beneath his solar topee.

Barely able to conceal his surprise, he steadied his nerves and performed this duty in front of the Prime Minister and a host of Indian dignitaries. Being the son of the Viceroy, Esmond would be exposed to close scrutiny, but he was an immediate hit and his photograph soon appeared in all the papers. The staff loved him.

Later, after the War, one of the officials wrote to Victoria Dawnay to tell her how impressed he had been by her eleven-year-old nephew: "No one could meet him and not love him and admire his character. Do you remember how we always put him in the forefront of our railway journey to the Viceregal Camp when any deputations had to be received, and how gracious he was, as though he had been doing nothing else all his life?"

Another wrote:

> The impression Esmond made on me during his visit to India has never faded. One evening at Agra I remember especially, when Vi induced him to recite some

Scottish stories for my benefit. Accent, point, gesture, all were perfect. He never seemed bored. I saw him once deeply engaged in conversation with a, to me, uninteresting girl. Not so to Esmond, to such an extent that I felt I must find out the subject that was engaging his close attention. 'Oh', he replied, 'I was just asking her how many people had proposed to her.'

The Mintos had embarked on a tour of the Phulkian States in the Punjab and Esmond was to accompany them. Mary summed up what lay in store:

> The joy of meeting him was great, the excitement of hearing all his experiences was intense, and his impressions of India were very amusing…he witnessed the lavish magnificence of the Indian Princes when doing honour to the Representative of the Sovereign. He was present at Durbars, Reviews, and Cavalry Manoeuvres. He saw the illuminated cities of the East, and drove through streets lined with the mounted men wearing the picturesque chain armour of past centuries. The luxury of the camps was bewildering. Elaborate gardens stretched before each tent bordering the long avenues which led to magnificent Durbar halls. The cool spaces within were rich with the splendour of jewelled thrones and multi-coloured fabric. Maler Kotla, Jhind, Nabha and Patiala were visited in turn.

Maler Kotla, a tiny state which no Viceroy had ever visited before, was a Muslim enclave in the middle of Sikh country: "The Nawab had on ropes and ropes of splendid pearls, I am afraid their beauty caused me to break the 10th Commandment", Mary confessed.[2] Nabha retained its long held traditions and the old Rajah, a mesmerising, wiry-framed individual with a full white beard and piercing green eyes, always appeared in traditional costume with a stiff skirt like a ballet dancer's worn over long white breeches reaching to the ankle. Just before the Mintos' train pulled out of Nabha, he came to say farewell. He went up to Esmond and bending low so that he could see the little boy's face under his sun hat, he said to him in Punjabi: "Your father is kind to the Phulkian Confederation because God the Immortal has caused the noble spirit of his ancestor, who saved our forefathers, to pass into him. You must never forget this and must be kind to my grandchildren, as your father is to me. My sword is yours." Then, in a gesture sealing the solemn pronouncement, he held out his sword hilt for Esmond to touch.[3]

At Patiala Esmond had his first experience of riding on an elephant, in a gilded howdah kept only for ceremonial occasions, before attending a Review of two thousand troops of the Imperial Service, followed by a magnificent firework display. He met the Maharajah, a boy of 15, nearly six feet tall and rather solidly built; his pearl-encrusted velvet coat won Mary's admiration: "A parure of huge pear-shaped diamonds hung over his brow, and from his neck to his waist he wore ropes of gigantic pearls; he also wore a diamond necklace, originally the property of the Empress Eugenie with a single diamond which is the fourth biggest in the world."

On their return to Calcutta, the family stopped at Delhi where they visited the house of a political agent who had spent much of his career on the Afghan border. After a good lunch, he gave the Mintos a tour of his house; arranged in a wheel formation on one of the walls were eighteen long and fearsome daggers: "Every one of those blades has been used for murder, the 18 owners of the 18 daggers were all hanged by my order," he told them proudly.

Violet remembered, when she had visited the Khyber Pass earlier in the year with her parents, meeting another agent, who lived five days from any form of civilization on the border with Afghanistan, in the midst of two of the worst tribes. His two predecessors had been murdered, the last by his own sentry. In the preceding 14 months, there had been 17 attacks, including five on him.

In Delhi, Rolly narrowly escaped being injured in a road accident. He was due to be dining with the 18th Tiwana Lancers at their mess to which he was being taken in a splendid new motor belonging to a Rajah. Unfortunately, the Rajah thought that the duty of driving the Viceroy was far above the station of his fully trained chauffeur; his Sirdar, a high-ranking official who knew absolutely nothing about cars, would be a far better choice. The journey, which involved a considerable amount of stalling and grinding of gears and much meandering all over the road, ended abruptly when the car hit a lamp post.

That year, a party of forty-five sat down to a traditional Christmas dinner of turkey, mince pies and plum pudding, on tables decorated with holly and mistletoe, in a luxurious 'shamiana' erected under the banyan tree. It was an extraordinary meeting of East and West; guests invited to Barrackpore by the Mintos included Lord Kitchener, or Lord K as he was better known, and Major Geoffrey Feilding, an ADC to Rolly, who as a General was later to command the Guards Division in the War. Esmond found the latter a little intimidating, notwithstanding his intimacy with the family, and clearly remembered their first encounter when he ended up as his aide at the beginning of 1916. Lord K, on the other hand, he found quite approachable as, lubricated by all the champagne and fine wines provided by Rolly, the Commander-in-Chief dropped his usual shyness and threw himself unreservedly into all the party games.

After a day of golf, riding, tennis and croquet, the Viceroy's band struck up and dancers, magicians and snake charmers appeared. The night air was warm and thick with garden scents and innumerable candles flickered against the black backdrop of lawns stretching down to the river. After dinner, it was time for pulling crackers; these were filled with presents carefully chosen for each of the guests. Lord K feigned terror when a shirt stud in the shape of a spider fell out of one pulled with Esmond and was delighted to find himself on the receiving end of an assortment of penny porcelain ornaments, to add to his renowned china collection. After songs and Christmas carols, the evening finished off with dancing and a wild paper chase round the house. Esmond retired to bed with his favourite Christmas present – a pet mongoose, described by his mother as "a small snapping creature which terrified me".

Rolly enjoyed a good relationship with John Morley, the Secretary of State for India, a Liberal intellectual with whom he would later draw up the Morley-Minto Reforms of 1909, legislation to increase Indian involvement in the country's government. An area amounting to three fifths of the subcontinent was governed directly as British India, but the rest, another 600,000 square miles of territory was Indian India, made up of 565 states, self-governing but in 'perpetual Alliance and Friendship' with Britain. These states were ruled by a host of different princes including Maharajahs, Nizams, Nawabs, Khans, Maharawals, Jams and Rajahs. They were part of a complex hierarchy and dealing with their rulers necessitated a great deal of diplomacy, something which came as second nature to Rolly. With his charm and bonhomie, he succeeded in smoothing the many feathers which Curzon had ruffled; following an interview with him, one Sirdar exclaimed: "His Excellency rained gentlemanliness on me." Many anecdotes concerning notable figures are found in the Viceroy's letters to Morley, such as the one about the Begum of Bhopal:

> I must tell you of the following story which will amuse you; I am overwhelmed with conceit! I heard privately the other day that the Begum of Bhopal was a little sore about certain matters, insufficient notice of her troops, as she thought, and other small things, so I wrote her a letter which, on opening, she at once pronounced so charming that she fired off a salute of twenty-one guns! Twenty-one guns for a letter is really quite delightful!

It was a rare self-congratulatory moment. Rolly was a good listener and was prepared to consider making changes to practices which some princes found nonsensical and even at times offensive.

One particular visit which demanded the utmost tact and patience was that of Habibullah, the Amir of Afghanistan, in January 1907. Britain had long been concerned about Russia's potential designs on India and saw this savage northerly kingdom as a vital buffer. The Amir had been invited to India before by Curzon, but it had been more of a summons than an amicable invitation and so it was turned down. He told his people at a Durbar the previous August: "The attitude adopted by Lord Minto, however, is so friendly and free from motives that I cannot possibly hesitate to accept the invitation of His Excellency, which is couched in such terms of friendship expressing the desire for an interview between friends." Of course, the Viceroy's entreaty was not completely free from motives: "In the Amir, we have a neighbour whose friendship is absolutely necessary to us in its connection with the frontier tribes. He wrote to Morley in September 1906. In an appraisal during the visit itself he emphasised the point: "However good our relations with Russia may promise to be, if one thinks of our military position for a moment and remembers what a little thing may bring about a war, the risks we should run in India under the modern conditions of the frontier tribes, if Afghanistan were not friendly, are appalling."

The meeting with the Amir was held at Agra and involved several thousand people largely accommodated in camps set up in the outskirts of the city. The Amir's own elaborate quarters was described in Mary's journal: "The Durbar shamiana glittered with gold and silver: a large empty room with prayer carpets was set apart for his devotions: his bed was a silver four-poster with heavy embroideries in place of sheets: his bath was a large inlaid slab of marble." The family lunched with Sir John Hewett, the Provincial Governor who had decorated the grounds around his camp, situated in front of a lake with myriads of Japanese lanterns. "The camp is very luxurious," Mary recalled and, with her sound sense of economy, added "Sir John is very lavish in his ideas and I think the provincial government will find no difficulty in getting rid of any surplus there may be in the treasury."

The highlight of the Durbar was the investiture of the Amir with the Order of the Bath at a sumptuous evening reception in the historic Red Fort. An elaborate dinner was organised for a hundred people and the Viceroy made a speech wearing his beautiful dark blue velvet robe adorned with the Star of India. Esmond, dressed in cerulean silk embroidered with silver thread, was one of his Pages, alongside the younger brother of the Maharajah of Dholpur. The Maharajahs of Bikaner, Scindia and Nabha, Sir Pertab Singh and the Begum of Bhopal sat watching the ceremony in their splendid costumes, ornate headdresses and glittering jewels.

Arranged in honour of the Afghan ruler was a great military review with 30,000 troops on parade. Whilst impressed by the show, the Amir was left seething. Driving away from it, he collared his Commander-in-Chief and barked:

Look you! You told me that mine was the finest army in the world. You assured me that the Afghan soldiers greatly excelled the soldiers of the Indian Empire, or the soldiers of the Russian Empire. You almost persuaded me that my forces outweighed the Indian and the Russian forces combined. What you saw just now? Ha! You are dumb! Do Kabul troops look so? Do they march so? Do they drill so?

Yet this is not the Army of India. It is but a single division out of nine such. And the whole Army of India is, now I learn, but a fraction of the military strength of the British Empire; and the whole Army of the British Empire itself, I further find is one of the smallest of the Armies amongst the world's Great Powers. Have you nothing to say?

On his return to Kabul, the Commander-in-Chief paid the ultimate penalty for his deception and was executed by being blown out of a cannon.

Notwithstanding the brutality of his regime, the Amir came across as a pleasant enough guest, but he imposed himself on the Mintos for a full two months, travelling around and using them as a base. Mary observed that he had never before: "seen trains, motor cars, polo, social gatherings and all the modern inventions taken as a matter of course". Habibullah had taken over from his father Abdur Rahman in 1901 and, although the ruler of a country which was very poor and rather medieval in its customs, he was an Anglophile who appreciated modern comforts and Western clothes. He liked wearing tweeds, a Norfolk jacket and plus fours being his favourite attire when 'casual dress' was called for; he enjoyed 'English' weather and was never happier than when it rained. Rather bizarrely, he also sought the advice of an English doctor, a Major Robert Bird of the Indian Medical Service, as to how to achieve satisfaction in the bedroom: the cure recommended by Bird, which seemed to do the trick, was to avail himself of his harem as much and as often as possible.[4] But he soon grew bored and found other aspects of marriage irritating, such as shopping expeditions with all four wives: "I cannot buy the same stuffs for all or all will be disappointed; and if the stuffs for each are not of equal beauty and value, I shall get into serious trouble," he confessed to Mary. He had a roving eye and seriously considered the addition of a European beauty to his harem. Whenever he attended a party on his travels around India, a member of his staff would carry a bag of trinkets for nubile ladies who might appeal to the Amir.

For all his peccadillos, he endeared himself to the Mintos. Always extremely polite, he refused to smoke in front of Mary. He was generous with gifts and endeavoured to spend as much time as possible conversing with the Vicereine and her daughters, on one occasion teaching them Persian love songs. He played croquet with Esmond and his sisters at Barrackpore.

Rolly confessed to Morley: "There is a great deal to like in him. He is courteous, eager in manner and full of conversation, which he tries to carry on in English which is at present difficult to follow. He strikes me as quick and clever. He is an expert mechanic and fond of gardening. When he intends to be witty he prefaces his remarks with 'Now I make joke', an explanation some of one's acquaintances might usefully adopt!"

At the end of his tour, Habibullah bade the Mintos a tearful goodbye expressing his desire to continue to correspond with them. He was escorted to the frontier by Rolly's Military Secretary, Major Victor Brooke, who reported that the Amir's emotion on receiving the Viceroy's telegram of farewell was painful to witness: "He drew Sir Henry McMahon aside, put on his motoring goggles to hide the tears that were coursing down his face, but was too overcome to say one word. He finally jumped on his horse, spurred him into a gallop and disappeared through the mountain passes."

Much later, during the War, Habibullah refused to support the Turks and the Germans in their desire to invade India. At that point, in 1915, India's army was depleted; tens of thousands of troops (out of a total of 160,000) had been sent to Europe to fight on the Western Front, suffering significant losses at Neuve Chapelle, 2nd Ypres and Loos. Had he raised the frontier tribes, Britain may well have lost Northern India. Perceived to be too soft in his dealings with India, he was assassinated by his brother in 1919, but it was his son who seized power and succeeded him on the throne.

Another person who would remain engraved on Esmond's memory was the tiny Begum of Bhopal, whom he met in January at a garden party in Agra, covered from head to foot in a burka. He thought she looked like a castle from a chess set and didn't quite know what to make of the 'purdah lady'; he felt a little odd when she caressed his face tenderly wearing red cotton gloves and kissed him through her veil. Everywhere he went, he was met by kindness; people were impressed by his maturity, calm dignity and easy naturalness. He never complained about the exhausting schedules and seldom appeared bored. For him, this vibrant and culturally diverse country provided a feast for the senses.

He went on from Agra, where he witnessed his first total eclipse of the sun, to the historic city of Fatehpur Sikri with its beautiful mosques. Returning to Calcutta, he attended the Minto Fancy Fête, an event with side-shows, a raffle in which Lord K won a baby elephant, and massed bands, organised by Mary on the Maidan. Its object was to raise money for the Calcutta Hospitals and the Minto Nursing Association;[5] it was hugely successful and the collection at the end totalled a staggering £25,000;[6] a gold coin was struck to commemorate the Fête and for months afterwards, a recurrent topic of conversation among attendees was 'Lady Minto's Big Feet!'. While his mother went on her first tiger shoot in Assam, Esmond journeyed to Darjeeling, although the mist disappointingly prevented a clear view of the peaks.

In the middle of March Esmond, accompanied by his mother, Ruby and Eileen, left Bombay on the SS *Persia* homeward bound. Saying goodbye to his father was unbearably hard; he was not to see him for three and a half years and when they did meet again, Esmond would find him greatly changed. The constant demands placed on him by his position, the endless paperwork and information which he had to process and the delicate business of keeping everyone happy in a tense and rapidly changing political climate, increased Rolly's levels of stress. Several attempts would be made on his life. Other factors which did little to help were the hot climate and everyday family worries; while his daughters were becoming more independent and making important decisions about their futures, his sons were still very young and on the other side of the world. He was very fortunate in having a large and supportive circle of friends and relations who could keep an eye on Larry and Esmond and, of course, he was lucky to have an extremely resilient wife.

Violet remained behind with her father on this occasion and assumed temporary responsibility for her mother's ceremonial duties. Mary wrote: "It was quite dreadful saying good-bye to Rolly and Violet, and I fear they will be dreadfully lonely. Violet was splendid and cheered up everyone; she and Esmond have been quite inseparable for nearly four months, and I can't think what she will do without him".

On the crossing home Esmond caught a chill which later developed into pericarditis; he returned to prep school after the Easter break but was kept off games and Mary remained in England until July as she was concerned about his health. She received some amusing letters from him at this time: "There is a new maid here, she is absolutely disgusting. She had rather a bad cough the other day, and coughed all over the mutton. Considering I had to eat it, it was not very nice. She always sneezes in one's ear." He followed it up with a joke about his ears, which he thought stuck out and probably, in fairness, deserved to be receptacles for sneezes. Following one particular farewell, earlier in the summer term, he wrote: "I did so hate saying good-bye last Wednesday. … Yesterday you dined with the King. I hope he was nice to you. As Violet is learning to drive the motor don't let her really be a saffriget!"

A year would pass before Esmond would be reunited with Violet, when she returned to England for Ruby's wedding in the spring of 1908. She was now nineteen and had metamorphosed from the fun-loving tomboy, partner in crime with the shared passion for break-neck riding – very much her father's daughter, she had won the 1908 Calcutta Ladies Steeplechase Cup – to a serene and elegant beauty who could hold her own with her two older sisters. All equally good-looking and talented, Rolly's three 'destroying angels' had inevitably set pulses racing at Government House. Many of the young officers on the Viceroy's staff fell under their spell and diaries and letters reveal the anxiety felt by Mary in having to help mend broken hearts on both sides. Rolly's Military Secretary, Victor Brooke, who had been so skilled in his dealings with the Amir, had fallen head over heels in love with Violet and confided as much to Mary who handled the situation kindly and sympathetically; inside, however, she was consumed by worry and resorted to

Veronal to help her sleep. Victor's feelings were not reciprocated, but he kept a stiff upper lip and remained on Rolly's staff; he was far too good at his job for the Viceroy to replace him.

In the Autumn of 1908, Violet unhesitatingly accepted a proposal from Lord Charles Mercer Nairne, the younger son of the 5th Marquess of Lansdowne who, like Rolly, had been both Governor-General of Canada and Viceroy of India. The bride wanted to be given away by her father and so, on 20 January 1909, the wedding took place in Calcutta amid huge fanfare and celebration. Security was tight because of recent unrest; the police were aware that bombs were being manufactured in the city and so every precaution was taken. The streets were lined with troops and in the Cathedral plain clothes detectives mingled with wedding guests. Moments before the bride's arrival in the state carriage, a bomb was discovered in a flower pot by the main doors and swiftly deactivated. But there was no time to dwell on this close call and, after the ceremony, a lavish wedding breakfast took place in the grounds of Government House; the cake, a colossus measuring over six feet, was cut by the bride with Lord K's sabre. He proposed a toast to the couple: "Lady Violet has won many hearts, and I feel sure there are none present who do not deeply and sincerely regret her departure from among us. For this we hold Lord Charles responsible, but considering his temptation I think we must forgive him."

In a letter to Morley, later that day, Rolly confided: "Everything went off splendidly; it was really an impressive sight... I am glad it's all over, but I do not at all like losing my daughter, who has been my constant companion". With Violet's departure to England, Esmond would gain a 'second mother' who lovingly made it her duty to keep an eye on him in his first years at Eton.

Dramatis Personae

Amir of Afghanistan, Habibullah Khan. 1872-1919. Emir from 1909-1919. His was said to be a brutal regime. Because of his extended visit to the Mintos, he appears frequently in Mary's diary. One entry reads: "There are many stories current about him. One is that if his interpreter makes any mistake he at once cuts off one of his toes. Another that he refused to allow a certain marriage to take place, the couple consequently eloped, but were soon caught and brought into the Amir's presence. He said, 'If you are so fond of this lady you shall have her all to yourself,' and there and then he had her boiled, and a cup of the liquid was offered to the unfortunate husband, who was made to drink it before being put to death."

Begum of Bhopal. 1858-1930. The only female head of state in Asia but a very progressive ruler of Bhopal, a Muslim state. In power from 1901-1926, she was always concealed under a veil – a *burqa* – in the company of men. Her legacy was in the field of public health; she pioneered vaccination programmes and improved hygiene and sanitation.

Brooke, Major Victor CIE, DSO. 1873-1914. 9th Lancers, buried at Annel Communal cemetery, brother of FM Alan Francis, 1st Viscount Alanbrooke.

Curzon, 1st Marquess Curzon of Kedleston, KG, GCSI, GCIE, PC, George 1859-1925. Eton/Oxford. Viceroy of India 1899-1905. Later Foreign Secretary. He had three daughters, of which Irene 1896-1966, the eldest, later Baroness Ravensdale, was a friend of Esmond's.

Dawnay, Lady Victoria. 1853-1922. Lady Minto's eldest sister, she lived at Beningbrough Hall, North Yorkshire. Her husband Lieutenant-Colonel the Hon. Lewis Dawnay, 1846-1910, was MP for Thirsk and Malton 1880-1892. His descendant, Ivor Dawnay, said that he was 'a vile-tempered, hang'em all, horse whipping, cantankerous man. The rudest man in Yorkshire.'

Drummond, Kitty. Cousin of Rolly. Wife of General Laurence Drummond, Scots Guards, Military Secretary to Rolly when he was Governor General of Canada.

Feilding, Major, later Major-General Sir Geoffrey, KCB, KCVO, CMG, DSO. 1866-1932. Charterhouse. Coldstream Guards, mentioned in despatches seven times. ADC to the Viceroy and lived with the Mintos very much as part of the family. His Airedale coexisted happily with the Viceroy's Dandie Dinmont terrier, Violet's Jack Russell and Eileen's tiny black Tibetan dog. GOC Guards Division 1916-18.

Hewett, Sir John. 1854-1941. Winchester/Oxford. Governor of the United Provinces 1904-1913. Lady Hewett was one of three sisters who were nicknamed '*The World, the Flesh and the Devil*'. Lady Hewett was '*The Devil*.'

Kitchener, Field Marshal 1st Earl, 1850-1916 (on HMS *Hampshire* which hit a mine off the Orkney Islands). Won fame in 1898 for winning the Battle of Omdurman and securing control of the Sudan. As Commander-in-Chief, India, he enjoyed good relations with Esmond's father after the conflicts he had experienced with Lord Curzon. Secretary of State for War at the time of his death.

Lansdowne, Henry Petty-Fitzmaurice, 5th Marquess of. 1845-1927. Eton/Oxford. Charles Mercer Nairne's father. He served successively as Governor-General of Canada, Viceroy of India, Secretary of State for War and Secretary of State for Foreign Affairs. He was the author in 1917 of the Landsdowne Letter, which called for Britain to negotiate peace with Germany. Turned down by *The Times*, it was published in the *The Daily Telegraph* on the 29th November.

Mercer Nairne, Charlie. Major the Lord Charles, MVO. Eton/Royal Dragoons, Violet's husband and Equerry to the King. 1874 to KIA Klein Zillebeke 30 October 1914.

Rajah of Nabha, Sir Hira Singh. 1843-1911. Raised to the rank of Maharajah a fortnight before his death. A smaller Sikh State, Nabha flourished under his rule and in 1877 was raised to a salute of 13 guns from being an 11-gun state.

Maharajah of Patiala, Sir Bhupinder Singh. 1891-1938. Aged 15 he weighed over 14 stone. Patiala was the largest of the Sikh States. Bhupinder Singh succeeded his father as Maharajah at the age of 9. A council of regency ruled in his name until he took partial power on his 18th birthday. Lord Minto invested him with full powers just before he left India in November 1910. Bhupinder Singh served on the General Staff in France, Belgium, Italy and Palestine in the First World War and represented India at the League of Nations in 1925. He introduced many social reforms which bettered the lives of his subjects. He married five times and had numerous consorts, with which he sired 88 children.

Sandars, Rt Hon John Satterfield 1853-1934, Private Secretary to Arthur Balfour, 1892-1905.

Maharajah of Scindia, Madho Rao Scindia of Gwalior 1876-1925.

Singh, Sir Pertab, Maharajah of Idar, 1845-1922. Career British Indian Army officer, ADC to Edward VII, 1887-1910, close to George V and godfather to Earl Haig's son, Dawyck, born in 1918.

Additional Note

In March 1907, Violet received a written marriage proposal from Prince Ram Mookerjee. Below is an abridged version.

Ula Castle House, Zemindar, Bengal.

My worthy father-in-law,
Won't you accede with any of my proposals? I have no objection to be married with your unmarried daughter? I will like a fair young lady who will love me tenderly and will like me. I am not unhandsome or unlearned, though young by age. If you accede we will live peacefully together with my this little wife. This little wife has no objection. Let me know the address where I will meet you. Is there any prohibition? Do not you be so much reserve. What sum will you give me as marriage presents? How is she by appearance? How are you all? We are well and good.

I like such a match. From a few month or more I have made up my mind to marry one wife or a young lady more to look after my household affairs. I want a large sum of money I am married with your daughter, send her name and address. I will see her. I am white and crimson red in complexion, meritorious, learned and by temper sanguine and virtuous. Such virtuous generally borns but one in the million; by moral character I am next to a God. I want a beautiful and good lady to marry. Will I go or will you come to see me, as you will like, write me sharp. If I like your daughter, I will marry her in spite of objections of societies.

I master of the devine department called music. I know how to make amusements with harmonium, piano, clarionet, or decide my case of the re-births of His Majesty the King and Emperor Edward VII and Prince Albert Victor, who are born as my sons such they are doing on well. They are now reading books for beginners. Remember sirs I am writing by being guided by impulses. The Benares city non-eater and non-drinker sages and astrologers spoke and insisted me by their process of astrological calculations, methods and processes. They want but little. I without company will go to see you unexpectedly and will see your daughter if I like I will marry.

Violet was not amused.

3

Eton

And nothing in life shall sever the chain that is round us now.

From *The Eton Boating Song*

He appears to draw from a well inside. He acts as an antidote to all depression.

Hugh Macnaghten, Esmond's Housemaster

A new and important chapter in Esmond's life began in May 1908 with the start of his education at Eton. It became, just as it did for so many of its pupils, his extended family. It was his first experience of living and studying in a community which, with its code and traditions, and its vibrant and nurturing atmosphere, would significantly influence his development.

Duff Cooper, who left Eton in 1908, encapsulated the essence of the place in his memoirs, *Old Men Forget*:

> Eton had meant much to me; how much I hardly knew at the time. I have met few Old Etonians who did not enjoy their time there and feel for the school a sentiment hard to express. It has little to do with the place itself, although it is beautiful, or with the teaching, although it is excellent, or with the tradition, although it is splendid. It has more to do with the friendships formed there, which are the first friendships and in happier times often prove the longest. In my case, such friendships were hallowed, as they were brought, almost without exception, to an early end by death.

The bonds described by Cooper made laying down one's life for one's friends almost a natural instinct, particularly for Esmond's generation which left Eton on the eve of the outbreak of War.

One of the school's greatest strengths lay in its encouragement of individuality and independence of thought, which tended to turn out confident pupils. Esmond was no exception; at the same time, he had a modest and self-effacing side, something his Housemaster Hugh Macnaghten, remarked on in his reports. Commenting on Esmond's refreshingly straightforward character, Macnaghten wrote that he was "probably the most trustworthy boy in the school". His poise and equanimity were traits which were always to stand him in good stead; at Eton, it was principally on the river; later on, it was at the Front. But, above all, it was his sunny disposition and kindness which drew everyone to him. His zest for life won him many hearts.

Three Earls of Minto had been to Eton and Esmond relished the idea of following in his beloved father's footsteps, half a century on. He lapped up any amusing anecdote concerning Rolly at school and was quietly proud of the fact that he was the son of the man in the most senior position in the Empire after the King.

His first half there began shortly after Ruby's marriage to Rowland Baring which was celebrated at St Margaret's Westminster that April. It was where, 25 years before, the Mintos had exchanged vows. The Queen was present, as was the Dowager Empress of Russia, but Mary felt Rolly's absence, as he had no choice, as Viceroy, but to remain in India. With his mother's help, Esmond arranged his belongings in his new room – there were no dormitories at Eton – and tried to make it as comfortable as possible. He accompanied her to Windsor Station and waved her off with his handkerchief until the train was out of sight. He would not see her again for two and a half years – a cruelly long lapse of time at that age. The following letter shows how much he felt the parting, 3 May 1908:

> My most Darling Beloved Mother, there really was not anything so horrible than saying good bye to you about 30 minutes ago. I do HOPE and pray the time will go VERY VERY quickly, and I will work my hardest and best to get on here. I do wish, darling Mother, you were not going out to India quite alone, and I hope it won't be very hot or rough; but I must not be selfish, as poor darling Father has been alone all this very long time, and he must have been so very sad and lonely sometimes all by himself. Now I must stop, and I do so hope and pray you will have a very comfy journey, and I will pray for it, but I always do for you all. VERY VERY BEST LOVE and HEAPS and HEAPS and TONS of KISSES, EVER YOUR MOST ADORING ESMOND

Mary wrote that he was almost the smallest boy in the school, measuring only 4ft 6 inches and the lightest but one at 4 stone 6 lbs: "It was not till he was nearly seventeen that he began to shoot up, and then grew for a time at a rate of four inches a year."

Esmond's first letters reassured his parents that he was settling in ably and demonstrated his concern for his mother's safety travelling back to India.

16 May 1908:
I have made great friends with the Grosvenor boy, son of the late Duke of Westminster I think. He is in remove and talking to a third form boy is awfully nice of him. I was awfully amused today, as I was told you have to pay £2 a half for the hiring of your bed, writing thing and wash stand. And whenever you're tanned (beaten) you have to pay 7/6 – rather odd, isn't it? I hope to save you the 7/6. I believe you arrive in Bombay tomorrow. I do hope it will not be very hot crossing the plains.

Mary crossed the plains of India in temperatures hitting 119 degrees Fahrenheit, long before air conditioning was invented. Lord Ripon, Viceroy between 1880 and 1884, famously said that the plains were hotter than the furnaces of Nebuchadnezzar. One night, after his train had left Bombay, both the driver and the guard died of heat stroke; coffins were then requisitioned at every station in case any of the Viceregal party suffered a similar fate.

Esmond was very fortunate in having an intelligent and gentle Housemaster, someone who really understood him. Macnaghten gave him security and ensured that he remained calm and cheerful during the long separation from his parents. An Old Etonian, himself, he was gifted at communication and pastoral care and his House was greatly sought-after by new boys; it won a record number of academic and sporting accolades. Charming and approachable, he became affectionately known to the boys as 'Muggins'. Above all, he was an outstanding Classics teacher; one of his best pupils, Patrick Shaw-Stewart, said of him: "he opened the eyes of some of us to the true meaning of a classical education".[1]

For the first couple of years at Eton, before his parents returned from India, the most important person in Esmond's life was Violet, who acted as a surrogate mother to him. After her marriage to Charlie, she was in England and able to take responsibility for her little brother's wellbeing. In October 1909, she took him to see an orthopaedic specialist in London because his feet turned outwards when he walked. He was prescribed callipers to correct his gait, which he had to wear at night. It was a nuisance and very uncomfortable, but he bore it with stoicism.

17 October 1909, letter to Mary:
The things for my feet have all come. At night I have to wear a thing which straps round my foot with another strap just below my knee. These are joined by a steel thing which keeps my foot in one position all night. It's rather uncomfortable, but now I am getting used to them. My boots have got a prolonged heel and things inside. I am not allowed to wear shoes at all.

Violet was often at Minto during the holidays to welcome him home. They relished each other's company, sharing a passion for horses and the countryside. Her sweet nature, charm and sense of humour chimed with his, as did her straightforwardness. In winter they hunted and in the summer they fished, rode and went for long walks in the Minto Crags, once or twice camping in little tents nearby. As their mother recorded:

> Esmond was passionately devoted to his home; the wild Border country had an intense fascination for him. He loved its variety; the hills, the moors, the woods, the streams appealed to him as no other part of the world could ever do. He was proud to belong to the Clan and always hoped to prove himself a worthy member of it.

Minto was a refuge for Esmond. Once or twice he had to return there, either to avoid infectious illnesses circulating at school or to recover from them. The beginning of 1910 saw a serious outbreak of measles at Eton which claimed the lives of two boys in one house. Macnaghten, himself, was laid low with influenza and Violet insisted on Esmond returning home to Scotland. Having missed being infected with measles, however, he succumbed to very bad bronchitis on a walking tour of Wales during the Easter holidays – Macnaghten's reports showed his frustration at all the lessons missed.

Christmas 1908 was spent in Rome with Francis Rodd, a friend from prep school who followed Esmond to Eton. Francis Rodd was the eldest son of Sir Rennell Rodd, a well respected and seasoned diplomat; in 1915, he took part in negotiations to extricate Italy from the Triple Alliance and bring it into the War on the side of the Allies. This was the second Christmas Esmond was spending with the Rodds for he had been to stay with them in 1907 in Stockholm, at the end of Rennell's posting there as Minister. On Christmas Day itself, at a tea party hosted by the King of Sweden, he had been put next to Princess Merta, daughter of Prince Charles of Sweden. He had described her company in a letter to Rolly: "Everything she said was 'I don't know'. She bites her nails so Mother can't go on at me, as Royalty does it as well." Skiing and skating had been laid on and he was given generous presents, including skis, a beautiful riding crop and, every young boy's prerequisite, a tool case. But by far the most appreciated gift for this curious, intelligent twelve-year old was a Kodak camera, given to him by "a Swedish lady". It sparked a fascination for photography which remained with him for the rest of his life.

Travelling to Italy with Francis Rodd in December 1908, he stopped at the Embassy in Paris to dine with Sir Francis Bertie who had been to Eton with Rolly: "I was never so shy in all my life, and never so hungry, having had breakfast at 8.30. Sir Francis was most amusing and told me Father was always getting flogged."

Esmond wrote enthusiastically about all things he had seen in Rome. Towards the end of his stay a very powerful earthquake struck Messina, killing around 200,000 people, made worse by the terrible tsunami which followed. Esmond was concerned about the plight of the victims and described the inadequate response of the government; Esmond to Mary, 19 January 1909:

> The Central Committee are not giving anything now, but are waiting until all the other funds have given all their money away, Sir Rennell and Lady Rodd are working like slaves. Lady Rodd has sent full boxes of clothes down to Calabria. The majority of people only take clothes for women so the poor boys and men get nothing. They have got one of my suits but I don't suppose it will fit anyone.

1909 felt like a long year. Mary remained in India with Rolly as the political situation there became more and more delicate. Their regular correspondence became a lifeline: Esmond and his parents exchanged letters at least once a week. Short notes would alternate with longer, more descriptive missives. Always very affectionate and expressive, Esmond never held back from saying what he felt, unless he thought it might worry his mother and father. Very rarely did he let things get on top of him; if they did, he would be charmingly apologetic. In true Minto style, he injected humour into his news, wherever possible. Commenting on the staff management skills of Ruby, now Lady Errington, he opined to Mary and Rolly: "Ruby does have bad luck with her servants, having to sack her cook for hitting the kitchen maid with a red-hot poker."

Rolly, in turn, wrote to Esmond telling him of a catering shambles at an important Banquet in Baroda. "There was a long delay for the first course owing to the soup being stopped by two sentries with fixed bayonets! They said they had orders that no one should come that way without a pass. The Officer of the Guard was eventually fetched and the soup, by this time cold, was allowed free passage!"

Encouraged at Eton to take an interest in current affairs, he would discuss them in letters to his parents, the hot topics of the time being militant suffragettes and growing tensions in Ireland. In turn, Mary and Rolly kept him abreast of news on the Indian subcontinent, focusing more on humorous encounters, rather than near misses with anarchists. In November 1909, Violet had to inform Esmond, before the newspapers reported it, that their parents were safe after one particular assassination attempt. Driving through Ahmedabad, the Mintos had two bombs thrown at their carriage, which were deflected by a sword hilt and a servant's arm. They were profoundly shaken by the experience, as there had been a fatality – a water carrier was killed when he picked up one of the bombs destined for the Viceroy, thinking it was a coconut. Mary wrote in her diary, 13 November 1909:

It was an ordinary bomb that they make in India with a detonator, picric acid and nails. We cannot be thankful enough that the bomb was minus the bit of lead which it needs to make it explode easily; had it been otherwise the results would have been very different, but it does not do to dwell on these things, we have got to play our part, and we must take the fortunes of war"

It was her birthday and she reflected on the fact that she could have also lost her life that day: "a bomb is hardly a suitable birthday present." Once, Violet and Rolly found themselves in front of a kraite, a deadly snake, as they were entering a lift at Government House; it unfurled itself and darted towards them, but a quick-witted servant flung a rug over it and beat it to death. The snake had been put there deliberately.

Just before Mary and Rolly's return from India in December 1910, Esmond wrote to his mother with excitement about seeing them again, spelling out their lengthy time apart.

23 October 1910, letter to Mary:
Many, many, very happy returns for your birthday. I am so sorry I have not got anything for you, but I hope you won't mind a Christmas and birthday one together. It seems too wonderful to think that I should only have to write three more letters to you in India. I have got leave to come up and meet you, but as I will not have seen Father for 3 years, 9 months, you for 2 years, 7 and a half months, Eileen for 2 years and one and a half months, don't you think that I should <u>not</u> come back here for the rest of the half?

The days leading up to Christmas were filled with celebration for the Viceroy's safe return. On 15 December, before leaving London for Minto, Mary and Rolly lunched with the King and Queen at Buckingham Palace; Rolly was presented with the Order of the Garter and Mary was asked to be one of the Queen's Ladies-in-Waiting. For the first time in four years, the family was reunited in Scotland. Mary remembered it as being an emotional time and recorded the welcome received by her husband in the Borders:

I was quite amazed at the reception Hawick gave us; the town seemed one mass of wild enthusiasm. The streets were packed with people, and a ceaseless roar of cheering was kept up the entire time. It was a happy moment when I saw Rolly standing safe and sound once more under his own roof and I think everyone's heart was very full. His Viceregal career was certainly ended with a gratifying burst of applause, and I feel very proud of him. The old Scotch saying "Safe In" is full of meaning and brings a great sense of relief and thankfulness. The storm has been weathered, the haven reached. India now becomes a sealed book to us. Frontier wars, sedition, conspiracies, plague and famine are now no longer nightmares that disturb our peace of mind. The steering gear is in other hands, our ship is safe in port, where there is a great calm, and I hope we may long be spared to enjoy our well-earned rest.[2]

Esmond had the satisfaction on being able to look back happily on 1910. His reports from Macnaghten were all good and he was making many friends: "Esmond is as jolly and happy in the House as it is possible to be, and it is always a pleasure to go and see him in his room. He appears to draw from a well inside. He acts as an antidote to all depression." It was also the year he was discovered by the Captain of Boats, a serendipitous moment which would transform his time at Eton.

Thursday 9 June 1910, was the fateful day, described in a letter to his mother:

Yesterday the VIII went out to practise for Henley. The Captain could not find anyone on Rafts with their boat to cox it, so he made me do it. I was terrified when he told me, as I have never done an VIII in my life, and much less a racing VIII, so I hardly knew what to say. When it was once started, I loved it, and luckily did not run into anything. It was great luck coming in for it, and I shall, I am sure, <u>never</u> again get the chance of coxing another.

He was wrong – he would get many more chances. The following year, 1911, Esmond coxed the victorious VIII at Henley, something which Macnaghten had predicted would happen in his Lent half report:

I believe he steered extremely well in Trial Eights, and I imagine that he has a chance of steering the Eight at Henley. I always think that steering requires more coolness and nerve than any other part of wet bobbing. He is much appreciated in the house. I have never heard anyone say a word in his dispraise, and he adds quite considerably to the gaiety of his tutor's.

During the selection process, Mary, who was with the Queen at Windsor, was excited to be able to go down to Eton and see him get into the boat, looking absurdly small in the midst of an exceptionally tall crew.

He gave the word of command with immense decision, his voice was powerful and his shouts to clear the way could be heard echoing from the river long after the boat had disappeared. Esmond was still so small that he was obliged to carry two stone extra to qualify him as to weight.

Soon after, on 8 July, watched by Mary and Rolly, Larry and Eileen, Esmond coxed the Eton VIII which won the Ladies Plate in record time. The heat at Henley was tropical and his mother declared that she had never experienced anything like it, even in India. The paint of the family Rolls Royce started blistering in the sun as it stood in a field.

At the end of June, he had acted as Page to his father, one of the four Knights of the Garter, at George V's Coronation. And he was in attendance again at Holyrood during the royal visit to Edinburgh later in July. The splendid Thistle Chapel of St Giles Cathedral had been restored and was opened by George V on 19 July, with Esmond acting as one of two train bearers to the King, dressed in a green coat with gold braid and a white satin waistcoat and breeches. At Holyrood that evening the proceedings were livened up by one of the Archers, General Douglas; he was part of the Guard of Honour opposite the King and Queen, and he fainted, tumbling over like a skittle. A mountain of a man, it took several people to move him. Esmond, who had had to behave impeccably throughout the ceremonies, finally couldn't contain his laughter.

In his end of academic year report to Lord Minto Macnaghten remarked that neither his son's triumphs on the Thames nor his ceremonial duties at Westminster Abbey and at Holyrood had turned his head.

> I am convinced that Esmond is just as simple and natural as he was at the begin-
> ning of the half, and he has gone through a trying experience in such a way as to
> gain from it nothing but good. He keeps the level head and level mind in prosperity
> as I believe he would in adversity. Many boys miss the joy of life through their own
> fault. That is not so with Esmond; I rejoice in him.

In the summer of 1912, Mary and Rolly took a house at Old Windsor and watched Esmond as, for the first time, he coxed the ten-oar *Monarch*, in his 19th Century Admiral's uniform, in the Procession of Boats on the Fourth of June. He had attained a huge distinction in the Eton tradition and they were incredibly proud.

On 6 July, the King and Queen were present at Henley and had come up the river in the State Barge. Mary recorded the race:

> Esmond's family joined them on the raised stand as they watched the race for the
> Ladies Plate. Eton had beaten Magdalen College, Oxford on the previous day
> and had to row in the final against Jesus College, Cambridge, the firm favourites

to win. Eton had drawn the more difficult side of the river. Cambridge started with a slight lead which Eton gradually made up. The crews raced neck and neck throughout the course. As the two boats came opposite the Royal stand the excitement was tremendous. Esmond's face was crimson; he seemed to be making superhuman efforts to shove the boat along as he bent forward to every stroke. His stentorian voice echoed down the river – it looked as if the race must end in a dead heat, so furiously was it contested. Suddenly, with a mighty effort, Eton shot ahead, and with a frantic spurt the race was won by nearly a length.

The coach, Mr de Havilland, came out to Mary afterwards, saying that the victory was practically due to Esmond who had shown remarkable judgment.

A fortnight later, just before Long Leave, Esmond's parents went to the Brocas fields to see the final of the House Four Races. Macnaghten's crew, with Esmond coxing, won again with the greatest of ease in record time. Rolly and Mary were invited to the Sock Supper in honour of this victory. Mary recorded the evening's proceedings in her diary:

> Esmond had steered the winners for the last four years, a record for a cox. In his speech proposing the health of the guests, Macnaghten said they were proud to welcome Lord Minto, who had held important positions in various parts of the Empire, but added that his claim to fame was not founded on this alone. Apparently, when Rolly first arrived at Eton in the 1850's, he had written to his mother that he had come 72nd in the School Sculling race, which he thought was "not bad for a first try". This information caused much amusement. Rolly then rose to return thanks. He told the boys all he owed to the great Eton traditions; then he told them that it was quite true that he had been 72nd in the Sculling race in his first half, but that, before he left Eton, he had pulled up 71 places, as he ended by being 2nd in the School Sculling.

Esmond endeared himself to many people across different years. It was Miss Dempster, the school physiotherapist who treated him for various sporting injuries, who best described his charisma and empathy for others:

> He had an amazing knowledge of people; nothing escaped him … He had a remarkable sagacity for picking out the right person. His criticisms showed a most accurate knowledge of human nature. His extraordinary memory for facts and faces, and keen powers of observation, plus the gift of getting people to talk openly to him, probably accounted for the unique manner in which throughout his life friends depended on his strength of character – a fact of which he was not aware

himself. I have never known any boy so thoughtful for others as Esmond. No anniversary, joyous or sad, was ever forgotten. He was universally generous and extra scrupulous about paying the smallest debt.[3]

His closest friend was Bob, Viscount Wendover. They were born one day and one mile apart. It was with Bob that Esmond went to watch the procession of the Garter Knights in Windsor Castle, in which both boys' fathers took part, when the Prince of Wales was invested with the Order in June 1912. Prince Edward had met Esmond at Holyrood the previous summer, where they talked about Eton's winning streak on the river. Both had outgoing personalities and Esmond obviously left an impression on the young prince as, when their paths were to cross again in France four years later, he inherited Edward's horses and saddlery when the latter left the Western Front.

Mary's memories of the two years before the War were golden; no longer in another part of the Empire, she was near all her children and able to fulfil her motherly duties. It was also before the shadow of Rolly's ill health was "beginning to darken the hitherto cloudless horizon of family life." She was able to see, at closer quarters, the influence of Eton on her son. She was now frequently on duty at Windsor, which pleased Esmond, as he was able to make a dash up to the Castle to have tea with her.

The summer half of 1913, Esmond's last at Eton, was nostalgically remembered by Mary. His achievements on the river, and the honour of coxing the *Monarch* again on the Fourth of June, were trumped only by his election to Pop, the elite group of prefects. Macnaghten wrote to Rolly: "He is genuinely surprised and apparently shocked at getting into Pop – some boys think this is a pose. I know it to be genuine, but at the same time, as I have told him, it is utterly absurd. He ought to get into Pop, being one of the best fellows in the school, and he has steered the Eight for three years – I am thankful he has done so."

Mary's recollection of the last weeks of school were full of nostalgia:

> Every mother's heart must swell with pride as she walks with a son in his light blue blazer, conscious that he is a hero in the eyes of his school fellows. Esmond's mother was no exception to the rule as she watched him on the 4th June 1913, in the historic school yard at Absence in his admiral's uniform as cox of the Monarch before taking his place in the Procession of Boats. Later as they sat together admiring the splendid display of fireworks, both Esmond and his mother were keenly conscious that the Eton chapter was drawing to a close, and the knowledge that the happy, irresponsible schoolboy days were nearly over brought an indefinable sense of sadness.[4]

She described his maturing: "Esmond, almost unconsciously, had grown up with a knowledge of big, imperial questions; he had seen for himself many parts of the Empire, he realised its vastness and its glory. Although so young in appearance, he was old in mind beyond his years."[5]

He decided to apply to Cambridge, working out a strategy which would help him give the entrance exam his best shot. He knew he wasn't strong in Classics and argued the case for switching from Greek to German. As early as 1909, he had played with the idea of what to do after university; he contemplated a career in diplomacy, while not totally discounting the possibility of returning to Canada to live on a ranch.

Being in 'Pop' meant that he was taking part in more debates, with titles as wide-ranging as 'Should Trade Unions be repressed?', 'The Advantages and Disadvantages of the Channel Tunnel and Reciprocity', with which he would often enlist his parents' help. Once, Esmond had the chutzpah to ask a visiting Cabinet Minister to finish an essay for him; he then had to spend time toning it down to make it appear more authentic.

In his last report on 12 December Macnaghten wrote:

> His last half has been quite as good as the rest. He has made for peace and good-will in the House and has been friends with everyone. He has no illusions about the superiority of Pop to other mortals, and I am quite certain that there is not a boy in the House who does not like him he has always been natural and simple, cheerful and contented, and has always been a strong influence on the right side … He practices goodness himself and respects it in others.
>
>   I cannot be sufficiently grateful to him for his pleasantness as a table companion. Some of the best boys break down in this respect, and anyone who is natural and sensible in talk, and takes trouble to keep things going, is an asset at table not to be over-prized.

Esmond was looking forward to Christmas at Minto and the prospect of spending time in France in 1914, learning about its culture and perfecting its language, before taking his place at Trinity College in the autumn.

Dramatis Personae

Bertie, Sir Francis, GCB, GCMG, GCVO, PC. 1844-1919. Ambassador to France 1905-1918.

Miss Dempster. School Physiotherapist. Johnnie Astor remembers visiting her several times after a football injury and happily listening to her talk about his family.

Grosvenor, Lt. Lord Edward '*Ned*'. 1892-1929. Royal Horse Guards/RAF/MC. Very close friend of Esmond from Eton who later tended his grave. 9th son of 1st Duke of Westminster. Founded Grosvenor Challenge Cup in 1923 for light aircraft. Founded RAF Auxiliary 601 Squadron in 1925 at White's and became Squadron Leader.

Rennell Rodd, James, 1st Baron Rennell, GCB, GCMG, GCVO, PC. 1858-1941. Haileybury and Balliol. Ambassador to Italy, 1908-1919. His third son, Peter, married Nancy Mitford.

Shaw-Stewart, Lt Cdr Patrick. 1888-1917. Eton/Oxford. Best remembered for his poem '*I saw a man this morning*'. Fought at Gallipoli, killed near Cambrai on 30 December 1917, buried at Metz-en-Couture. Academically brilliant, he won a Double First in Classics at Oxford. He was elected a Fellow of All Souls, but instead chose to pursue a career in banking. He was one of the youngest ever Managing Directors of Barings.

Wendover, Viscount Albert Edward Charles Robert, '*Bob*'. 1895-1915. Esmond's closest friend at Eton. Royal Horse Guards. Died of wounds in Boulogne 19 May 1915. He was one of the last British soldiers to be repatriated.

Additional Notes

Eton terminology

Absence: a roll call. A check on whether any boy is absent without leave. On the Fourth of June, there is a grand formal Absence taken in School Yard, by the Head Master and a team of other masters.

Half: a term.

Pop: an elite group of prefects formally known as The Eton Society.

Rafts: principal school boathouse by Windsor Bridge.

Wet bob: a rower.

4

Prelude to War

The little Chief left this morning and the sun seems to have gone behind a cloud.

Rolly

Esmond's father tended to view the transition from one year to another with apprehension. He more than once confessed to feeling sad about saying farewell to years that held happy memories for him and contemplating what the future might hold. New Year 1914, his 69th, was a particularly hard one to see in as, for many months, he had been unwell. He returned from India worn out and never regained his earlier vigour; a hunting accident in the spring, where he feared he was "losing (his) power of gripping" marked the beginning of a steady decline. On 3 January, when the hounds met at Minto, Esmond, who was on Rolly's favourite hunter, made certain to pass by the West Lodge approach so that his father could see him from his bed.

As had been the plan, Esmond set off for Paris on 17 January where he was to learn French with a family called the Lelièvres who lived in Rue Chernoviz, a quiet street in the fashionable sixteenth arrondissement. He had his place at Trinity, he had been given the choice to sit the languages part of his entrance exam in either March, June or October and he had opted to prepare for the paper in the summer. Regular news and humorous descriptions of his time on French soil cheered his father up no end. The housekeeper was: "very anxious for me to eat a lot, but is very particular about what she buys, as she says pheasants and partridges may give one appendicitis, which seems mad."

It was a bitterly cold winter. On 23 January, he wrote:

> I cannot describe to you the cold of this country. It has been 4 or 5 below zero according to this way of counting every day. There is heaps of ice floating on the Seine. It is the coldest winter, I believe for twenty years. My name has been,

and is, the cause of much trouble. After two days of being called Monsieur Minto, I thought it was time to tell them. I began by talking about English names, and gradually worked round that father and Larry were not called by the same name as me. The news was a terrible shock for Mme Lelièvres, she threw up her hands and said: 'Vous n'êtes pas Monsieur Minto?' They suggested every sort of excuse for me not being Monsieur Minto. Was I adopted? Had you been married before? Today I had a shock. Mme Duménil wrote to me and began 'Cher Lord Elliot'.

Esmond was very enthusiastic about Paris; he wrote about people he met and inter-esting conversations, the golf and tennis he planned to play, eccentric new fashions and different protocols: "they even paint their lips in the street, bringing out mirrors with them", he said of the women, who appeared heavily made up with black kohl eyeliner, in the style of the 'The World's Most Beautiful Woman'.[1] He wasn't used to "the blaze of colour on the women's faces" and dyed hair in strange styles: "Tell Eileen the latest fashion is for women to do their hair tightly over the lower part of the ear, leaving just the top bit bare – quite hideous," he wrote on 1 February. To an 18-year old fresh out of school, this new independence abroad must have seemed very exciting. He wrote again on 26 January:

> I have now seen a certain amount of Paris. I rather enjoy the sightseeing as it is so interesting. I can't describe the gaiety of the Lelièvres. I have been here now seven days. They have had two parties and have taken me to two others. There are two things which really annoy me, one is the way they introduce me to their friends. They give my whole pedigree as if I were a show animal. The following is what they always say: 'Monsieur Esmond Elliot qui est chez nous, le fils de Lord Minto, qui était le Viceroi des Indes'. When it has been said five times in under a minute it become almost too much of a good thing. The other thing is that Lelièvres has only shaved once since my arrival. Today I discussed it at déjeuner. I began by asking him if he would like to have a beard. He says it hurts him to shave more than twice a week because the violin rubs him. I then proposed he should have grown a beard. He said that it would get in his way. I have now promised to give him a safety razor which will not hurt him.

He was due to spend a month with a tutor in Compiègne, along with another Eton friend Henry Field, son of Marshall Field, the Chicago millionaire, with whom he was going to share digs in Cambridge along with Eddy Hartington. On 8 February, however, he received a telegram telling him that he needed to come home. Rolly's condition had deteriorated and all the family were gathering at Minto; in the following two weeks, Esmond's efforts were focused on helping his mother. On 25 February Esmond and Violet sat with their father, held his hand and had their last conversation with him; on Sunday 1 March, just before four in the morning, Rolly slipped away. Accompanied by pipers of the Scots Guards, the Viceroy was buried in Minto Churchyard, overlooking Teviotdale and the Border hills beyond. Charlie Mercer Nairne and Esmond were among those who carried his coffin which was placed in a grave lined with violets.

Mary was crushed by Rolly's death and leant considerably on her younger son for consolation; they went to France together in the immediate aftermath. Together with a maid and a chauffeur behind the wheel of their Sunbeam, the two of them took a tour of the Loire in an attempt to forget the pain of the preceding weeks. Esmond began writing a diary and in it he remarked that his mother had packed far from lightly for the trip: in addition to clothes, rugs and pillows, she had also taken a number of 'religious books' with her. Her Christian faith had always been central to her and here it sustained her, along with the company of her boy, whose presence was "like sunshine" – even Rolly had felt that Esmond was a source of light, writing to Mary in 1913, after a parting with his son: "The little Chief left this morning and the sun seems to have gone behind a cloud."

Mother and son spent three weeks at Tours; she described their time together in her journal in the third person: "During that time his never-failing care and tenderness helped her over those first days of acute sorrow and loneliness. He assisted his mother with her letters, both private and public, answering many of them himself, and always insisted on taking her out in the motorcar when he thought she was tired or feeling extra sad." It was at this time that he learnt to drive – the wide and empty roads of the Loire were ideal for a learner and he took to it easily. In fact, it was a welcome distraction which stopped him dwelling on his loss. After visiting a chateau, they would often find a grassy knoll or glade where they could enjoy a picnic before making their journey home. They drove south as far as the Pyrenees and visited Lourdes, where Mary bought a medal of the Virgin, which she kept until July 1917, when she sent it to him in Flanders.

They talked a great deal. One day Esmond told his mother how much his heart was set on joining a cavalry regiment, but his fear was that he might not be able to afford the lifestyle that went with it. He thought he would have to consider another career. Mary revealed that Rolly had always regretted that Esmond had not shown any inclination to join the Army as he felt quite sure that his son would make a good soldier.

At the end of April Mary returned to England leaving Esmond in France. Soon Europe was heading for conflict. Esmond's journal takes up the story:

1 August 1914:

A very critical situation has arisen owing to Austria Hungary's demands from Serbia...there are grave fears of a European war. Russia and Germany have mobilised, France is mobilising tonight, and the whole country seems to be alive, as trains pass every few minutes. The British Fleet has left for the North Sea. All the men here have been given their orders. I hear from Mother that Larry's Division is the first one to leave England, it seems too terrible to be true. Personally, I myself should love to go to the war, if war is declared, but it is an awful thought to think of one's brother going. Poor Mother writes terribly worried. Eddy received a telegram this morning from his father telling him to leave for England at once, which he did an hour later. I'm so glad to think that I shall be living in the same lodgings as him at Cambridge. The house is curiously the same as the one father was in when he was at Cambridge.

A letter, dated 2 August, showed the crisis deepening: "The whole of France was mobilising last night and one sees no man about now between the ages of nineteen and forty-five. Train after train went by here yesterday. All communications have been cut off. One saw nothing but sobbing women." After Britain declared war against Germany on 4 August, Esmond only just managed to get across the Channel via Dieppe; he was told there would not be another boat for a fortnight, it was standing room only. At one in the morning on 6 August, he walked into his mother's room at Lancaster Gate, unexpectedly, but to her great relief.

The future for Mary, as for many other mothers, now looked very different from the one she had anticipated. With her grief overshadowing her existence, she now had to come to terms with the frightening possibility that her sons, the younger one barely out of school, might be caught up in the developing drama on the Continent. Although long feared, the conflict with Germany and her allies had unfolded in a much more serious and far-reaching way. Her journal describes those first weeks of war:

A period of great uncertainty followed. It was hard to realise what a European war meant, the horrors of it seemed to have burst so suddenly upon the country. Everyone longed to be up and doing. Esmond was offered a commission in the Special Reserve, 3rd Battalion Royal Scots. He was nineteen, but had started growing so late that his doctor thought that it would be madness, until he was stronger, to send him into the trenches.

Although always very active, Esmond had not been robust physically and this had somehow affected his growth; when he left Eton, he was only 5ft 6 and still growing.

Along with catching the usual childhood illnesses, such as 'flu, measles and mumps, he had suffered complications, such as pleurisy and pericarditis, from some of the more severe infections. His gait had been corrected by the wearing of calipers and Miss Dempster's physiotherapy at Eton had helped with sporting injuries, including those sustained whilst out hunting. The initial doctor's report was ignored and Esmond insisted on going up before the Medical Board at the War Office. Sir Arthur Sloggett, who had known his mother in India, was persuaded to have him examined by two more doctors, but it was no good, they concurred with the original opinion that he wasn't fit to fight. Esmond was indignant in the extreme; he hated seeing his friends go off to war and not being able to join them. The months ahead seemed filled with uncertainty and frustration.

He decided that Cambridge could wait, at least for a year. No one thought the war would last beyond Christmas – and he could make himself useful with immediate effect in Home Defence. Lord George Scott, Colonel of the Lothians and Border Horse Yeomanry applied for Esmond and, on 18 October, he was gazetted Second Lieutenant with the Regiment in Edinburgh.

The first three months of the war were devastating for the British Expeditionary Force; names of friends and friends' sons began to appear in the newspapers. Half a dozen of Esmond's exact contemporaries at Eton would be killed that autumn and eight old boys of Macnaghten's. The sad news of Victor Brooke's death, during the retreat from Mons, came through at the very end of August. Three of the Viceroy's other ADCs would be lost: Thomas Rivers Bulkeley in the Scots Guards, recently married and with a baby son; Arthur Annesley and Arthur Charrington.

At the end of October, the family was dealt two hammer blows. On the 28th, Eileen's fiancé Francis Scott was wounded in both legs; it took a while for confirmation to come through. More swiftly delivered, however, was the news of Charlie's death at Klein Zillebeke on the 30th. His children Margaret and George were aged just four and two. Esmond travelled down to London to be with Violet at the Memorial Service at St Margaret's Westminster, a place which held happier memories.

Such was the trauma that Mary was unable to continue writing her journal. When she finally resumed recording her thoughts the following April, she gave her reasons:

> Have written no journal since October 1914, have not had the heart to chronicle all the appalling tragedies that this war has brought about. The one that unites us is poor Charlie's death; he was killed by a shell on 30th Oct having been sent to put some horses in a place of safety. The shell hit him on the head and he was killed instantaneously near Ypres. Violet was at Bowood and the news was broken to her by Evie Devonshire. The Lansdownes are heartbroken and all the family loved

Charlie the most. I can't write about it. On 28th Oct, we heard that Francis was wounded, shot through both legs at Hagehook. We were without news for a week.

Esmond was now writing a diary on a regular basis whilst quartered at the Roxburgh Hotel in Charlotte Square, Edinburgh:

We drill every day for three hours in the morning and musketry and aiming practice in the afternoon. I don't think we shall have horses for some time yet. Today is the first time I have worn uniform. I have got the ribbon of the ridiculous Coronation Medal plastered on my bosom, and of course everybody thinks I am some hero from the front. I am so shy of it that I wore my mackintosh to hide it.

Knowing that Mary was advising the King about hospitals, he wrote:

There is an enormous hospital at Craigleith, where there are twelve hundred beds. I don't know if it is one of the Territorial Hospitals or not. I hear the Scots Guards have lost twenty-six officers. There is a man in the hospital who was in the Lincolns. They started out with twelve hundred men, four drafts of one hundred and ninety men were sent out to them, and just before he left only two hundred and fifty answered the roll call.

He added that the feeling in Edinburgh was that there would be an invasion of the British Isles and that they expected it to come soon.

Esmond spent the New Year alone at Minto. There was plenty of hunting on offer and he was temporarily selected to command his squadron, but he found life dull and undemanding. There was more going on in London: Mary was forced to let 95 Lancaster Gate, the large house Rolly had bought in February 1913, and move into a smaller place in Berkeley Square. On 11 February 1915, Eileen and Francis were married in the Guards Chapel; the groom was on crutches, still lame from his wounds. Esmond came down from Scotland for the wedding.

Later that spring, Esmond and his regiment left Edinburgh for The Haining, a camp ten miles from Minto. They spent several days trekking across country and finding billets in empty country houses and farm buildings. One house had perfectly adequate stabling for the horses, but had rooms which had been stripped of furniture and were teeming with rats. It was a different picture at a place called Dryfeholm in Lockerbie, from where Esmond wrote to Mary on 10 May:

We arrived here yesterday and could not be in a better place. It belongs to a man called Jardine. It has been beautifully looked after by a dear old house-keeper, who was intensely upset at not having been warned of our arrival so she could have had the rooms ready. We have all got rooms, a sitting room and bathroom. It is a big house. They are immensely rich people, being the Jardine Matheson family. In spite of the lady dying two years ago her two carriage horses are still here. This is glorious country, in a valley surrounded by hills. I danced round the kitchen table last night with the house-keeper and suggested we should have a small dance tonight. Her reply was, "I am very sorry sir, but I am afraid I shall not be able to have the parquet floor in the drawing room polished by then."

From The Haining, Esmond would frequently ride over to see Mary and take her out for a picnic by the Crags.

It was at the end of May that Esmond learnt about the death of his close friend Bob Wendover. He had been wounded near Ypres on the 13th and his parents, Lord and Lady Lincolnshire, had hurried to France to be with him, returning later to England with his body; he was their only son.[2] On the very same day that Bob was wounded, Julian Grenfell, the eldest son of Esmond's godmother Ettie, was hit in the head by shrapnel. Both the Desboroughs and the Lincolnshires found themselves holding vigils for their boys in Boulogne. Mary recorded in her journal: "Ettie tells me Bob Wendover was so brave. She went to the Station to meet the poor Lincolnshires who didn't know how bad he was. They found him being operated on and he died next morning at 6 a.m." Julian held on for nearly a fortnight, but infection set in and he died on the 26th, holding his mother's hand. The next day, his poem *Into Battle* appeared, for the first time, alongside his obituary in *The Times*. Two months later, on 30 July, very close to where Julian had been wounded, his younger brother Billy was killed, leading a charge at Hooge; he was 25. His body was never recovered and his name was later carved on the Menin Gate. In September, another son of a friend was killed: 21-year-old Dermot Browne, a Lieutenant in the Coldstream Guards; his mother, Lady Kenmare would later join Mary on two pilgrimages to Vermelles, where he was buried.

Mary's morale was understandably very low. She was haunted by vivid dreams of Rolly and his last illness; his memorial stone, a beautiful Celtic cross, had gone up in Minto Churchyard at the end of August. The family gathered around it for the first anniversary of Charlie's death, prompting Violet to return to Scotland for the first time in 18 months. Mary was on call for duties at Court; more frequently now she was accompanying the King and Queen on visits to the wounded in hospitals and her diary revealed how seeing such suffering was proving a great mental strain for George V.

The Lothians and Border Horse Yeomanry had left for Haddington in July, where the officers were quartered at Amisfield, a house belonging to Lord Wemyss, who was to lose two sons in the war. Mary's journal captured Esmond's mood:[3]

Esmond's departure was a great sadness to his family, although he was still able to pay occasional visits to Minto. He began to wonder if he was taking soldiering seriously enough. His own Troop, composed chiefly of Border men, was very efficient. He was therefore much put out at being transferred to another Troop in order to improve their standard, composed of men of whom he knew nothing. Most of his Eton contemporaries were already at the front. Esmond felt he was not doing his share and was getting tired of exercising horses, Haddington had no attractions for him and rumours were abroad that the Yeomanry were to be reduced to bicycles.

In November, Esmond persuaded Larry to scout for a car for him; he was given a little 15-20 h.p. Darracq which his mother nicknamed 'The Bijou'.

From beginning to end, the year 1915 was unremittingly sombre; there was little respite from the growing feeling of dread with the realisation that this war was set to last a while. Bad news flooded in. A string of unsuccessful battles in the Spring added to the sense stalemate on the Western Front; the Shell Crisis exposed the unpreparedness of the country for a war of this magnitude; the Government under Asquith seemed perpetually on the back foot. The venture in the Dardanelles, which divided military opinion, was now proving very costly indeed. The press flexed its muscles and began to be more critical and vociferous; everyone had an opinion, the country was becoming fully engaged in the war debate. The most disastrous battle, which saw the first mass deployment of the New Army, took place in September of that year at Loos. Mary echoed the nation's reaction: "The papers announce our first real success in conjunction with the French. I fear it means endless loss of life, but they say 4,000 yards have been gained." Commenting on Sir Douglas Haig's replacement of Sir John French, as Commander-in-Chief in December 1915, Mary wrote: "What will the result be I wonder? This absolutely hopeless government is being shown up more clearly every day." Confidence in French's leadership had been waning steadily throughout 1915; he was in poor health and perceived to have poor judgement. Mary had remarked on his abuse of promotions and honours at GHQ: "35 per cent of his staff have been honoured and 5 per cent killed, while only 5 per cent of the Army has been decorated and 35 per cent killed."

Mary's journal now became a repository for press cuttings. Occasionally, she allowed herself the odd indiscretion on paper about behaviour in political, Army and Court circles. Her characteristically relaxed humour gave way to cynicism and annoyance. She was disappointed by Asquith who, along with his wife Margot, an old friend of Mary's, smuggled whiskey into Windsor Castle, despite the King's ban on alcohol in his household for the duration of the war. It would not have been quite so egregious, had they not mocked the suspension and invited fellow guests to flout it and consume spirits with them.

Esmond spent Christmas at Haddington and went to a farewell lunch for Henry Dundas who was leaving for the front; he felt that his relatively carefree days were coming to an end and knowing how hard it had been for Mary to watch friends lose their sons, he sent her a poem by Maurice Baring about Julian Grenfell:

Because of you we will be glad & gay,
Remembering you, we will be brave & strong;
And hail the advent of each dangerous day,
And meet the great adventure with a song.
And, as you proudly gave your jewelled gift
We'll give our lesser offering with a smile,
Nor falter on that path where, all too swift,
You led the way and leapt the golden stile.
Whether you seek new seas or heights unclimbed,
Or gallop in unfooted asphodel,
We know you know we shall not lag behind,
Nor halt to waste a moment on a tear;
And you will speed us onward with a cheer,
And wave beyond the stars that all is well.

Very early in the New Year, 1916, Esmond received a telegram from General Feilding, who was commanding the Guards Division in France, offering to take him on as his ADC. He remembered Feilding from Calcutta and the splendid Christmas dinner at Barrackpore under the banyan tree. Having obtained permission from his CO to accept the offer, Esmond said goodbye to his squadron and went to London with his mother to prepare for his departure to France. He assembled his kit and was dragged unwillingly to the photographer Bassano to have his portrait taken. In the middle of February, he and Mary were in Pall Mall when they bumped into Feilding, who revealed that he had only just secured Esmond in time, as another General, Sir Frederick Maude, had requested the War Office to send him to join his staff in Mesopotamia.

The last week together was spent quietly; their attendance at the theatre and small, informal dances decreased as his departure approached and preparations were interrupted only by the occasional ride in Rotten Row. Mary recorded a significant conversation they had:

A code was arranged in the event of Esmond being taken prisoner. He had no misgivings, he said if there was still work for him to do, he would be spared to do it, but if he had completed his appointed task on earth he would not come back.

He begged his mother not to fuss unduly and added, 'so many poor fellows are not able to go to the front: imagine what a wonderful privilege it is to be allowed to go and fight for one's country'. He was radiant and all the time he was packing he was singing snatches of songs and whistling.

On Sunday 20 February, the two of them went to the early service at the Berkeley Chapel in Mayfair, a regular place of worship and one which the Mintos were familiar with from the time they were living in Audley Square. He left for France on 22 February; the night before, he made his will.

Dramatis Personae

Annesley, Captain the Hon. Arthur, '*Jack*' 1880-1914. KIA Ypres. He was a lover of Winnifred Bennett who later became FM French's mistress. It was after Annesley's death that French met her, consoled her and became devoted to her, calling her "My Little Darling" even though she was almost a foot taller than him.

Asquith, Herbert. 1852-1928 '*Squiffy*' (because he enjoyed fine wines). Liberal Prime Minister from 1908-1916. Senior officers believed he was completely uncomprehending of military matters. Lady Minto witnessed first-hand the King's despair at Asquith's weak leadership, lethargy and drinking during the First World War. Lady Tree's teasing question, asked at the height of the conflict; "Tell me, Mr Asquith, do you take an interest in the war?" conveyed a commonly held view. By 1916 his colleagues had decided that he was unable to lead the country to victory and he was replaced by Lloyd George in December. Created 1st Earl of Oxford & Asquith, KG, PC, KC, FRS.

Bassano, Alexander. 1829-1913. Leading Royal and high society portrait photographer. He retired in 1903 but his studio continued. It was responsible for producing the Lord Kitchener Wants You army recruitment poster and Esmond was photographed there in February and October 1916.

Desborough, Lady, Ethel Grenfell, '*Ettie*'. 1867-1952. Mother of Billy and Julian Grenfell (see below). Society hostess who lived at Taplow Court. She was a great friend of Mary and godmother to Esmond and also Lady-in-Waiting to Queen Mary.

Dundas, Lt. Henry. MC and Bar. 1897-1918. Eton/Scots Guards. Wounded. Accompanied Lt. Brodie to negotiate with the Germans on 18 January 1917. KIA 27 September 1918 Canal du Nord.

French, Sir John. 8th Royal Irish Hussars. 1852-1925. Commander-in-Chief BEF 1914 – December 1915 when he was replaced by Haig. Field Marshal and created Earl of Ypres, KP, GCB, OM, GCVO, KCMG, ADC, PC.

Grenfell, Capt. Hon. Julian DSO, Royal Dragoons, died of wounds Boulogne 26 May 1915, aged 27; 2nd Lt. Hon Gerald William (Billy) Grenfell, 8th Service Batt. Rifle Brigade, died Hooge 30 July 1915, aged 25.

Haig, Sir Douglas. 1861-1928. Clifton College. Commander-in-Chief from December 1915. Created Field Marshal January 1917, later Earl Haig, KT, GCB, OM, GCVO, KCIE, ADC. Founder of the Royal British Legion.

Hartington, Marquess of, Edward, *'Eddy'*. 1895-1950. Eton/Cambridge/Derbyshire Yeomanry. Eton friend of Esmond, who was due to share rooms with him at Trinity. MP for West Derbyshire 1923-38. Parliamentary Under Secretary of State Dominion Affairs 1936-1940, for India and Burma 1940-1942 and for Colonies 1942-1945. Later 10th Duke of Devonshire, KG, MBE, TD.

Maxwell, Helen Heron-Maxwell, daughter of Lt. Colonel William Heron-Maxwell. They lived at nearby Teviot Bank and all attended Esmond's Memorial Service at Minto in August 1917. The second of four daughters, she died a spinster in 1932.

Scott, Lord Francis. 1879-1952. Eton/Grenadier Guards. KCMG, DSO, Mentioned in Despatches. ADC to Viceroy of India 1905-11 and married his eldest daughter, Eileen in 1915. In September 1916, he survived a stampede of 50 horses who knocked him over and galloped over him after a shell landed near them. Seriously wounded later in the War and lost a leg. After the War, he moved to Kenya where he became a prominent politician. He and his wife established a remarkable estate, Deloraine.

Scott, Lieutenant-Colonel Lord George. 1879-1952. Eton/Lothians & Border Horse. Lived five miles from Minto.

Sloggett, General Sir Arthur, 1857-1929, was a doctor and British Army officer. He served as Director General Army Medical Services in 1914 and Director-General of the Medical Services of the British Armies in the Field during the War.

5

Staff Officer

God help the Staff – especially
The young ones, many of them spring
From our high aristocracy
Their task is high, and they are young.
      A Prayer for those on the Staff, Julian Grenfell, 1915

Mary and Violet took Esmond to Victoria Station on 22 February 1916, where he met General Feilding; as they waved goodbye to him on a train crowded with officers, they took comfort from Feilding's words of assurance: "I'll take care of him" and from the fact that Esmond was in high spirits. He was doing what he wanted to do, returning to France. Now the French were facing the German attack on Verdun, a battle so brutal and punishing that it would force the British Army to bring forward its planned offensive on the Somme.

Escorted by a destroyer, Esmond's ship left Folkestone for Boulogne, carrying new recruits and men re-joining their units. He was prone to seasickness and never sailed without his 'Zotos'.[1] A car was waiting to take Feilding and his new ADC on the slow, three-hour journey to Hazebrouck, where comfortable billets had been prepared for them in a large house in the central square:

> 23 February, diary:
> During the night I heard a series of loud explosions. At breakfast I was told that an aeroplane had bombed the town; the number of bombs being thrown being about 19. One fell on the conservatory of the billet where Clutterbuck, the other ADC, was staying.

He didn't mention any bombs in the letter he wrote to his mother on arrival. Instead, he said reassuringly: "I am in a wonderful sort of palace tonight and shall be very comfortable. I have seen nothing so far to remind one that we are at war."

The following, intensely cold morning, Feilding and Esmond, accompanied by Colonel Ruthven, set off for Brigade Headquarters at Chateau Esquelbecq, stopping in Wormhoudt to meet General John Ponsonby, commanding 2nd Brigade. They completed their journey to HQ on foot; located just south of Dunkirk, it was a forbidding place, moated and turreted, with metre-thick walls, and dating in places back to the 13th Century.

23 February, diary:
At twelve the General and I motored to the Chateau de Lovie to lunch with Corps Commander Lord Cavan. We motored on to Poperinghe to see the 1st Brigade, commanded by General Pereira, who succeeded the General. In Poperinghe, we met Desmond Fitzgerald.

25 February, diary:
Walked with the General to the Divisional Artillery HQ, Zegerscappel. After lunch, we motored to Watten to see an exhibition of the Stokes trench mortar. They are capable of doing the most extraordinary amount of damage with a range of 450 yards. Had tea on our return with General Ponsonby and Staff, and such a nice Staff it is. Beckwith-Smith and Cecil Green being particularly nice.

26 February, diary:
Met de Satgé, in the Square. He was an Eton master and taught me both French and German. He is attached to the Division as one of the interpreters. The staff is large, there are two messes, A and B. A mess consists more or less of the personal staff, and the B mess consists of the Provost Marshal's interpreters, chaplains etc. The A mess consists of Colonels Ruthven and Darrell Jeffreys, Davidson, Bulgy Thorne, Allston, Payne, Clutterbuck and two interpreters. The Belgian interpreter is a Count de Grunne; he is a brother of the man I met in London at the Belgian Embassy. The weather has been terribly cold, much snow, last night there were 18 degrees of frost.

One of the first people Esmond encountered at Esquelbecq was the Prince of Wales, whom he hadn't seen since before the War. Now in the Grenadier Guards, he was waging a long-running personal battle with the Palace to be allowed to play a greater part in the War. Later, it was a source of long-standing regret that he didn't do more and he recalled his experience with the Guards gratefully as a transformative one. Esmond was very similar in stature to the Prince (they were both 5ft 7) and when he first arrived at the chateau, the owner, Monsieur Bergereau, could barely tell the difference between them.

27 February, letter to Mary:

I lunched with Corps Headquarters, Lord Cavan. There were five Generals there and two ADCs, very frightening indeed. I find that all men holding important positions when driving in a motor or carriage take up about twice as much room as is necessary (like Father used to do), so I now, for comfort's sake, always place myself on the back seat. I am sending Violet a postcard of the castle. My room is the window next to the nearest tower, on the second floor, and I have my bath in the tower of the second floor. Will you please tell Auntie Tor how much I like her little book. I use it every day and have it always in my pocket with the one you gave me with all the photographs.[2] I like the General most awfully. I don't know whether I am giving satisfaction, for I do nothing, have written one letter, and go out always with him, but I expect later there will be more to do.

28 February, diary:

Left with the General for Zegerscappel where we picked up General Wardrop. Went to inspect some Brigades of the Divisional Artillery.

In the Division there are four Artillery Brigades, each being commanded by a Colonel. The Brigade consists of four Batteries, each commanded by a Major or Captain. In a Battery there are four 18 pounders, which in their turn are divided into two sections (two guns), each section being commanded by a Subaltern. These guns are capable of firing 25 shots a minute. On the gun carriage is attached the limber containing 24 shells. Each gun has 2 waggons, each holding 76 shells. Besides this there is the 'train', whose business it is to keep the guns supplied with sufficient ammunition. Usually a Battery consists of 6 guns, making three sections of 2 guns each. The Heavy Artillery and Howitzers are controlled by the Corps.

Yesterday at tea time, Walter Dalkeith and Claudie Hamilton came over. Later the Prince and Eddy Stanley turned up. I am so glad they are coming on the staff, as all the others are so much older than me, they will make just the whole difference.

29 February, diary:

The Prince came up directly after breakfast; he has been ordered home for good, and I believe goes to Egypt, much to his annoyance. He has given me his two chargers and saddlery. Rode with the General, met General Heyworth, rode on to HQ of 1st Grenadiers.

It didn't take long for Esmond to realise that he was not going to be stretched in his role, particularly as he was one of two ADCs, the other being Tom Clutterbuck, in the Coldstream Guards. However, he enjoyed the variety of duties; one moment, he would be meeting interesting people, many of whom were in very senior positions; the next, he would be dealing with mundane tasks, such as riding around the countryside to identify which roads and junctions needed signposts. Crucially, he was on the receiving end of strategic and tactical information and news about significant events, troop movements and numbers, attacks and casualties. As he admitted to Eileen in a letter on 29 February: "It's very interesting and I learn a lot and if two Generals begin talking and one puts on a sufficiently stupid face, one may hear things one is not supposed to hear."

2 March, diary:
We have won back the Bluff, the six hundred yards of trench lost in February. It was a very important position, and everyone seems satisfied, though our casualties were 700.

There appears to be a lull in the battle for Verdun. The German losses are estimated at 168,000. The authorities believe that the Verdun attack is not the real thing, but that their big push will come somewhere else. Where? Opinions differ; perhaps Champagne, Arras or Ypres?

Rode in afternoon to Ledringhem to see the Divisional Cavalry.

Colonel Ruthven has been appointed GSO1 (General Staff Officer Grade 1) to the 8th Corps, commanded by General Hunter-Weston. I am sorry he is leaving.

3 March, diary:
Went with the General and Colonel Ruthven to Calais. We left at 8.30 a.m. going via Dunkirk and reached the camp at 10 a.m., where we found the 1st Brigade. Saw two companies doing bombing attacks. They rushed from the British trench (two platoons at a time) to the German trench. When they have consolidated that they send a bombing party down the communication trench and try and take the second line of trenches. The bombing party consists of six men; two with bayonets, the Bomber, the NCO in charge and two spare men.

We lunched with General Pereira and Gort, his Brigade Major. News was brought in that there had been a bad bombing accident in which Desmond Fitzgerald had been seriously wounded, together with Nugent, Hanbury, Father Lane Fox and a private. Later news was brought that poor Desmond was dead. He was such a ripper. Although I hardly knew him he had been most awfully nice to me the only time I saw him out here.

We went to the Duchess of Sutherland's hospital where the wounded had been taken. It is near the station, beside the canal bank, in rather a nice situation, where there can be no noise. It is entirely composed of huts.

The Duchess told us that Desmond had never regained consciousness, and died two minutes after he arrived there. It appears that Father Lane Fox, the RC priest, brother in law of General Pereira, was trying to throw a bomb. The bomb burst as soon as it left Lane Fox's hand, a fragment going into Desmond Fitzgerald's eye and penetrating his brain. We hear that Lane Fox will certainly lose a finger, and probably an eye too.

We motored back to St Omer, the GHQ. Sir Douglas Haig went out riding while we were there. He has an escort of five men and one officer of the 17th Lancers.

4 March, diary:
At 11.30 Lord Cavan, accompanied by General Gathorne Hardy, arrived for a conference. Afterwards the General and I went with them to the 5th Brigade for luncheon. In the afternoon walked with the General and General Heyworth. They were both fairly optimistic; they thought the war must be decided on the Western Front, that the Germans would probably make an offensive somewhere else besides Verdun. They thought we would never get into Germany but that they would, after our big offensive, retire to the line of the Meuse, and then there would be cries for peace in Germany. I gathered that they were not at all satisfied with our second line positions at Ypres.

At luncheon Lord Cavan said it was the greatest mistake, the authorities at home forming all these new Divisions and not refilling the old ones: the result being there are some very good Divisions much under strength. And the new divisions come out totally inexperienced, commanded by officers inexperienced in this war. If they would only draft them to the old Divisions to fill up the gaps, the old men would carry the inexperienced soldiers through.

5 March, diary:
Rode with the General to the 1st Grenadiers to see some NCOs and men regarding commissions. Passed Walter Dalkeith on the road. On the way home the General told me that 200,000 men were coming from Egypt, troops relieved from Gallipoli. He thought we had a million men over here now, and, with the French, over two and a half on the Western Front. He thought Verdun would probably go, as it is of no importance from a military point of view, and the guns had long ago been removed. Of course, politically, it would be an enormous victory for the Germans.

It is said that the Germans are prepared to lose half a million men in order to break the French front. Apparently on Friday (Feb 25th) there was almost panic in the Senate in Paris when the first attack on Verdun was launched, and the French began to retire. A midnight sitting was called to kick out Briand and Joffre. In fact, Joffre's tactics were extraordinarily good. The Germans attacked on a 15-mile front; Joffre retired gradually decreasing their front till it was only 5 miles broad. He thereby got them into a salient, and had a cross fire on them. Their losses must have been appalling, with French 75s firing from both sides.

When the Ministers heard the true story, they said Joffre was the greatest man in France. The French have such faith in him that it is said that the Army would never have allowed him to go. He has practically the power of a dictator amongst the army and the people.

6 March, diary:
Was sent to Heayech to fetch Colonel de Crespigny, commanding the 2nd Grenadiers. On the way there the car got stuck in the mud, and two horses had to be fetched to pull it out.

7 March, diary:
Rode in a bad snow storm and met Guy Shaw-Stewart. All leave is now being stopped for some time, I believe chiefly because of the train service, and also for fear of an attack. When leave is allowed, it means about 30,000 men (two Divisions) out of the country.

General Feilding wrote to Mary to inform her of Esmond's progress. In his letter, he hinted at the heir to the throne's poor choice of friends.

8 March, extract from a letter to Lady Minto from General Feilding:
Esmond is a great success, everyone likes him very much, but there is very little to do at present, and there will not be much to do while we are in reserve. The Prince of Wales has left us, he was miserable going. He is a particularly nice boy, and has all the makings in him of doing well, but he should really have about him someone of character, and I think that is his danger. Claudie Hamilton is a very nice boy, but lacking in character. The result will be that the Prince will become narrow minded and surrounded by toadies. We all like him, but I fear he is inclined to take a narrow view. It seems a pity, as he is at an impressionable age.

Esmond announced to his mother that he had resumed writing a diary and, in his typical self-critical way, which he hadn't shaken off since Eton, he added that it was "the most awful concoction of rot and I hardly think it worthwhile to go on with it." He was aware that he was watching history being made and he wished to record it. Always very observant and interested in people, he liked to know how each one slotted into the great war puzzle.

8 March, diary:

In the evening the American representative, a Mr Lowry, arrived for the night. Such a nice man! He is looking after the prisoners and is attached to the American Embassy in London. After dinner, everyone either played cards or chess, and he was left with me. Personally, I thought it very rude. However, I enjoyed myself enormously, and asked him every conceivable question during my hour's talk with him. He told me that his staff at the Embassy had increased from 25 to 115, that they were using the Austrian and German Embassies as offices, and were considering taking the Turkish Embassy too. He said that the Government pays the prisoners; a Captain receives 4/6 per day and a Lieutenant 4/-.

At the end of the war the British and German governments will settle accounts, as they pay their prisoners the same rate. He told me that the German prisoners, both officers and men, live in greater comfort than the troops out here. The officers are allowed a certain amount of freedom, and can go on parole for a day, which means they can go to a neighbouring town, but accompanied by an officer. The officers have their own mess, and have a servant between three or four of them. Apparently, the men never complained, but the officers often do, usually quite unreasonably.

The rules for prisoners here and in Germany are supposed to be the same, but in detail are different. He implied that German prisoners were better treated than British officers and men in Germany. He had never visited the German camps, only the British ones, but had lately been in Berlin. He said that life was just the same as before – theatres and restaurants crowded, but the condition of the people in the country was pitiable. He said that the recent riots in Berlin had been very serious. He added that he would stake his fortune on the war being over by Xmas, and that there could be no possible doubt as to what the result would be.

9 March, diary:

In the afternoon rode with De Chesnaye to Bergeus. It is an old fortified town supposed to have been built by Vauban, surrounded by ramparts.[3] In one of the forts we saw several Algerian men, called Cuirassiers, who looked awfully picturesque in their native dress. I took two photographs of them, and immediately an NCO rushed out shouting 'Ca c'est défendu'.[4] He looked at all De Chesnaye's papers but not at mine. After a little humouring, he was quite nice.

The incident with the NCO was undoubtedly reported back to HQ as, that evening, an order was received to the effect that any officer or soldier being found in possession of a camera would be tried by Court Martial. Esmond ignored this and continued to use his Kodak, for which he and Mary used the codename 'paint box': "I'm so glad you made me bring out my paint box," he wrote to her, "yesterday in the snow, I did two little rough sketches, they are not quite finished yet. Of course, it is difficult to paint out here, and yesterday was the first day I tried."

Frustration was mounting at the absence of any action. In a letter to Mary on 9 March, he wrote:

> Am still doing absolutely nothing, but as yet it has not been hinted to me that I am to be Stellenbosched.[5] The General tells me he heard from you yesterday, in fact the letter is lying in front of me now; I would give anything to read it. What were you writing about? He told me 'London gossip.'
>
> I saw Leggs Gibbs the other day, he dined here. He said Evie is much more cheerful again.

Evie Gibbs had been on Rolly's staff in India and was a great favourite of the Mintos; he was taken prisoner in November 1914 and spent the rest of the war in captivity.

On duty as censor Esmond discovered the various nicknames chosen for him:

> The other day I had to censor a letter entirely about myself – rather embarrassing. I was alluded to as the 'Boss' and the 'Little Lad' which rather amused me.

11 March, letter to Mary:
Today, twelve French officers came to look at the Division. A sort of programme was arranged so that they could see the various Battalions doing different things. Two Battalions marched past the General standing in front to take the salute. I could not help thinking at the time how odd it was that I should be his ADC and how many times he must have been in exactly the same position as me, seeing Father take the salute in India.

I found myself walking with one of the French officers who knew no English. They were all so nice. I did not realise before how much they hated the Huns, they could hardly speak of them and told me of the most awful atrocities. They were reluctant to take any prisoners – you have to feed them, and after the war they return home and the whole thing starts again.

15 March, letter to Mary:
Today I lunched at the HQ of the French Army Corps. There is a great etiquette in the French Army, such as a junior officer cannot introduce a senior officer;

two senior officers introduce themselves. I was frightfully bad at putting in 'Mon Colonel' and 'Mon Commandant' etc, as I never can tell a French officer's rank. They are astoundingly polite.

10 March, diary:
Everybody seems to be generally more optimistic. I asked the General why we did not give up the Ypres Salient. Apparently, it is entirely owing to the Belgians, who want us to keep the last Belgian town. Rumour has it that the Belgians would no longer fight if we gave up Ypres; this would mean a loss of 40,000 men. When one thinks of the enormous casualties we have suffered in the Ypres Salient, one cannot help asking if it is not wrong to give way to sentiment, when so many lives are at stake. The General said that some time ago Smith-Dorrien and French had a big fight over this. As a result, Smith-Dorrien gave up his command, as he felt it so wrong keeping this death trap of a salient.

There is much feeling about the reduction in honours, which has been reduced for the whole Division to 125, one third of which is for 'special mentioned'; the remainder being 'mentioned in dispatches'. One hundred and twenty-five does seem few when one considers it covers between 15 and 20,000 men.

11 March, diary:
De Grunne, the Belgian interpreter, returned today from Paris. He says they are most optimistic; that the Germans are believed to have lost 85,000 men in dead alone, and that their casualties a day are estimated at an average of 10,000 a day. He said he saw a friend of his, a machine gun officer, back from Verdun who said the German losses were appalling. He was firing his machine gun at Douamont, and could not understand why they did not advance, but remained in mass formation. They discovered afterwards that there were such heaps of dead that, though killed, they remained upright.

Clemenceau is apparently trying to kick out Joffre and place Petain at the head of the army. Of course he will not succeed as the army would never accept it.

Went for a short ride with the General, returned for a rag football match – HQ against the Artillery.

13 March, diary:
A man called Law lunched. He is a Nationalist MP and is going round the Irish regiments. His son is in the Irish Guards, his Colonel being McCalmont, the Ulster MP. He said that Ireland had not done well recruiting, but feared a Secret Service called Sinn Fein had started again, being financed by German-American money.

Very good news from Verdun. The German artillery fire is diminishing, and the French claim to have silenced some heavy guns.

An amusing story was told by the General. Herbert Asquith came over to St Omer to see French. They filled him up with champagne, and towards the end of dinner, Asquith, who had had more than his share, leant across the table and said: "The extraordinary thing about this war is that it has never produced a first-class General" whereupon Henry Maxwell replied: "The thing that strikes me is that, though the Radical Government have been in power for 12 years, they have never yet produced even a second-rate statesman."

15 March, diary:
Went with the General to Rousbrugge to lunch with General Hely d'Oissel at HQ 26th Corps Armee Française. He is a most charming man; not the least alarming. He personally thought the war would last another year, but was perfectly confident of victory. His Chief of Staff thought that the war would be over in December. In his opinion German finances could not stand it. They were all very optimistic.

We went to the HQ and then on to Poperinghe to see General Heyworth, 3rd Brigade. He gave a most unsatisfactory report of the trenches we are taking over from the 6th Division. Apparently, there are no parapets, and the 2nd line hardly exists. They say it will take three weeks before the trenches can be got right, and we can only hope in the meantime that the Huns won't attack.

I believe we are still rather short of ammunition, and an order has been given to be economical with shells.

The General told me yesterday that the Germans are bringing over ten Divisions from Russia, which means 200,000 men. The thing which strikes everyone is their marvellous output of ammunition. The only disappointing thing in the day was that the French staff at Rousbrugge only estimated the German losses in proportion of two to one; but the General thinks they must be under-estimating it.

17 March, diary:
Rode in the morning. In the afternoon motored to Ypres with the General to see General Heyworth; he is in dug-outs on the Canal banks. We were firing a little the whole time, and whilst we were there the Germans started shelling for about 10 minutes, right behind us in the direction of Vlamertinghe.

The whole of Ypres is in ruins; there is not a house untouched. What must have been a beautiful Cathedral looked very fine in its ruins. Only two spires remain.

The dug-outs are dug in the bank, with enormous sand bags on top, which makes them more or less safe from shrapnel.

On our way through Poperinghe stopped at the "Fancies", an entertainment got up by the 6th Division – an excellent show.

On 18 March 1916, General Feilding and his staff were on the move, leaving Esquelbecq and staying temporarily in Poperinghe, 'Pop', on the Salient. 'Pop' was a busy hub for soldiers with time off. Those who needed to satisfy their spiritual needs gravitated to Talbot House, or 'Toc-H', set up by the Rev. 'Tubby' Clayton, which had a chapel in the attic, a garden and a library; those who needed physical comforts, instead of, or in addition to spiritual succour, had plenty of choice among the restaurants, hotels and brothels. The notorious Skindles, catered to every requirement. The *'Fancies'* was a show in which professional actresses performed, rather than the army norm of men dressed as women and, because of this, it was hugely popular.

In a letter to his mother from Poperinghe, Esmond played down the threat of shells:

19 March (Sunday), letter to Mary:
Friday was the first day I had been near any sort of shell fire. They fired only a very few shells and a long way from us. It was most interesting seeing the dug outs. We moved up here yesterday, an awful day of chaos, no-one knowing where anything was; I suppose we stay here for some time. We are considerably behind the firing line. I am in quite a good billet, in a deserted house, no furniture, but as I have my camp bed, I am all right. This is the noisiest town I have ever been in. Today I saw two air fights. They both fired at each other, but the shooting of both was bad, and nothing seemed to happen. All over this country little cemeteries are dotted. I am afraid I shall never find Charlie's grave.

19 March, diary:
Was sent out this morning to reconnoitre the country in the Vlamertinghe area for a house that would be suitable for our HQ. Poperinghe is considered to be too far away.

The General and Davidson went into the line. They had a very nasty time, they were shelled in the line; they waited 20 minutes, and were then shelled between Haymarket and Potijye, and had to run for it. When they got to Brigade HQ they were shelled there too.

All the supplies for the 14th and 5th Corps and the Canadians go through this small town, so I suppose they will soon be shelling us.

20 March, diary:

In the morning motored out nearly to Vlamertinghe where we found our horses. Then rode on to Machine Gun Farm and on to Burgomasters Farm. In the afternoon motored to Ypres, still being shelled, particularly the Canal Bank, where the 2nd Brigade's HQ is. General Heyworth is changing his HQ, as it has suffered the worst shelling since the 14th Corps was formed on January 3rd. A lot of damage was done and 30 wounded and 10 killed. They were absolutely blown to bits and unrecognisable.

On leaving the dug-out 2 shells came awfully near us, and the General said that, if we had not got into the ruined house in time, one of the shells would have got us.

4 bombs were dropped on us here at 6 a.m. doing little damage.

There are an enormous number of troops in Poperinghe; it seems to me to be mad, as we are bound to be shelled as soon as the Germans know of it, and there will surely be endless casualties. The reason the Intelligence give for the shelling is that the Germans are withdrawing from Ypres for Verdun, which they mean to take at any price, and the artillery fire is to try and bluff us that something is up.

21 March, diary:

I was given work in the HQ office all day. Went for a walk with Allston in the afternoon. Heywood, our new GSO1, arrived today. He has been at GHQ and says they are all optimistic about Verdun. It's touch and go whether it falls. It is the opinion at GHQ that the French don't mind losing Verdun as long as the Germans pay a high enough price for it. Their losses are estimated at 180,000 and the French about half that number.

23 March, diary:

The Commander-in-Chief came in the afternoon. I met him at the door. He looked most awfully nice. He motors in a Daimler, and a Rolls Royce follows him for fear his car breaks down. He had an ADC, Major Thompson of the 17th Lancers, and his bodyguard Officer, also of the 17th Lancers. There is apparently on his staff an ADC for each army. GHQ are moving on Tuesday to Montreuil sur Mer.

Dined with the 3rd Grenadiers. Oliver Lyttleton, Mark Maitland, Grigg and Thorne also came.

23 March, letter to Mary:

Today I saw Colonel Guy Baring. He said he remembered me in India, at the Durbar for the Amir, but I don't recollect having seen him before. I often see a brother-in-law of Cloche's, by name of Chichester. He tells me Cloche can only write two letters a month.

Cloche had been taken prisoner in January 1915.

25 March, letter to Mary:
Yesterday was John Ponsonby's fiftieth birthday. Curiously enough it was Pat Heyworth's birthday too. The General and I went to the 'Fancies' with the former. I felt rather shy at being alone with two Generals. We then went on to dinner at his billet, an enormous party of twenty. Among the guests were the Corps Commander, Mark Maitland, Heywood and the Brigadier's staff. His is, I think, by far the nicest staff. The Coldstream band played at dinner, Rogan was the Bandmaster. Wonderful food, five courses, and champagne. The table was beautifully arranged; the candles were put in children's toy horns, which acted as candlesticks, and they were put into a bomb case to keep them steady. Sniper Greene, the Mess President, had arranged it all. Afterwards the room was cleared. The most important people played bridge in a partitioned off part of the room, and the rest of us danced. It is rather extraordinary to think we should be doing this hardly more than ten miles from the German trenches. John Ponsonby apologised for not having produced any ladies!

Sloggett was here yesterday. I did not have an opportunity of speaking to him and telling him what I thought of him!

26 March, diary:
Went to church in the Cinema Hall. The Corps Commander read the lesson. Mr McCormick preached a very good sermon.

Left at 1.15 for Ypres, which was being shelled. Looked in to see General Heyworth. Each time one goes to Ypres one realises more the millions of pounds and shells that must have been wasted in its destruction. There is absolutely no house untouched. All who saw it before the bombardment were unanimous in saying what a pretty town it was.

Went around a portion of the line. It was my first time to go into the trenches. Leaving by the ramparts we started being in the open for nearly a quarter of a mile. Passed the École de Bien Faisant, a complete ruin, crossed the Menin Road, and into the communication trench, known as West Lane. It was very quiet on the Front; I think what struck me most was the absolute stillness of everything. It seemed impossible that but a short distance away were thousands of men underground taking part in the greatest of all wars. Not a sign of any animal, nothing living but the birds, and one felt that one was miles away from all human beings. The stillness was only occasionally broken by a shell into Ypres.

When we got to the support trenches a heavy bombardment of high explosive shells started on the frontline trenches, and later a general bombardment. We waited some time and, after a bit, the Germans devoted most of their time to the frontline trenches. We then made our way to the HQ 4th Grenadiers, (under) Lord Henry Seymour. We watched the bombardment for a bit. The Canadian trenches were on our right. We retaliated heavily, and before we left things seemed to be quietening down. I never realised what a tremendous salient Ypres is. The Germans have most of the high ground and are on all sides; it is only about 3,000 yards wide.

I saw Hill 60 which the Germans have had for so long and to which, until comparatively recently, we never admitted.

Made our way back to Potijze. Had a look into an Observation Post on our way back. These Observation Posts are only in what remains of a deserted house; they direct the fire of the artillery, and watch the German roads. The holes used for seeing are probably made by shrapnel, and are no bigger than the lens of a telescope. As there are so many ruined houses it is hard for the Germans to know which we are using as Observation Posts.

This visit would have been poignant for Esmond, for Bob Wendover had been killed at Potijze.

Had tea with the 1st Brigade, General Pereira. On our way back met Lord Esme Gordon Lennox, who told us his brother's and Charlie's graves were together at Zillebeke.

27 March, diary:
Visited a Clearing Station. There is an advanced Clearing Station at Ypres for the more advanced cases. At the beginning of the war the number of ambulances provided was nothing like enough for the demand; consequently, the wounded used to be taken away in the empty supply and ammunition wagons.

This morning we sprung a mine at St Eloi. It was the biggest mine used so far in the war. It was dug 80 feet down, and there were 40 tons of explosives. It was dug so deep as to be under all the mines laid by the Germans. The explosion was terrific. The 5th Corps occupy the crater, and so far, continue to hold the ground won.

28 March, diary:
On return from a ride found that Clutterbuck, who has been rather seedy for some time, was being sent to hospital with pleurisy. So, I have taken over his duties as Camp Commandant.

I like the General more each day and wonder why I disliked him so in India.

An officer has been court-martialled for having a Kodak in his possession. I hope to get mine home soon. The whole of the French army have cameras. Some French officers came here yesterday and took photos of our troops which made me furious.

29 March, diary:
Plumer came here in the afternoon. Afterwards I went to the Chateau de Lovie with the General.

I sleep tonight in the office, as there always has to be one officer here. One is always challenged by the Military Police after dark. "Halt! Who are you?" The farcical thing is that you only have to shout out "Officer", or a man his regiment. No one is examined, and they don't check after 10 p.m.!

The Germans are again launching very heavy attacks on Verdun which up to now, as far as we know, have been repulsed. They say the French have not used any of their spare ammunition.

John Dyer, Scots Guards, from the 2nd Brigade, has been attached to us for the last few days. I hope he stays, for he is one of the nicest people I have met out here.

31 March, diary:
There has been heavy bombardment of the 1st and 2nd line trenches.

Generals Wardrop and Wilson dined.

2 April, diary:
At 8.30 went out with the General and the CRE (Commander Royal Engineers) and looked at the ground proposed for our new HQ. Got back in time for church.

The bombardment of the 30th was the heaviest we have ever experienced outside a battle. Considering the severity of it we were lucky to get off with so few casualties, some 150, though the trenches were badly damaged.

General Heyworth and Pip Warner dined before going up to Ypres to relieve the 1st Brigade.

3 April, diary:
Received a letter from Mark Sprott asking me to join the Greys. I have said no. Rode with the General to Brielen to look at what is known as the High Command, a ridge held by the Germans.

Later that day he wrote to his mother. He was pondering the future openly in his letter:

Letter to Mary:

I don't think I shall stay on here very much longer … as to going into the City, I don't think I want to become like the people who think all day long how they are going to make £5. I think I would rather be without it. I believe I would like soldiering the best, but what regiment I don't know. I would rather like the Scots Guards, because they are such an awful nice lot. If I am going to soldier after the war I ought to transfer at once.

4 April, letter to Mary:

I know you will be surprised at my saying in my letter of yesterday that I wanted to leave, but I am sure I am right, for it cannot be good for anyone to do absolutely nothing. My most strenuous duty is to go out with the General, and meeting foreigners etc, who visit the Division. After the war, everything will be so different that it is hard to say what one would like to do. If it was certain that I would pass into Diplomacy I would choose that, but the odds are against it.

5 April, diary:

I was called at 3.45 a.m. to go to up the line with the General. We left at 4.30. a glorious morning, but rather too clear for us. Ypres looked magnificent in this early morning light. The front was fairly quiet, not much shelling, and only a few rifle shots. This was the first time I had heard rifle fire since I have been out here.

The Germans started shelling the frontline trench, which we wanted to get to, so we had to stop short of it. The number of shell holes in one portion of the ground near the communication trench, known as West Lane, is extraordinary; there must be 500 in one place, all practically touching each other. This is all the result of the bombardment of the 30th.

Got back for breakfast at 8 a.m. At 12, rode with the General to see a parade of the 1st Irish Guards for a Russian General. We arrived at 12.10 and found the Russian already inspecting them. He arrived at 12, but was not due till 12.15. He is Ex-Chief of Staff of the Grand Duke Nicholas, so is a really important man. He had two other Russian officers with him. General Plumer, Prince Alexander of Teck, and Colonel Campbell, acting for General Pereira, now on leave, were also there.

The Russian General was a small man, covered with medals and stars – in fact he had them on both sides of his tunic. Dressed in blue knickerbockers with red lining, and top boots, and khaki tunic, he also has some Orders round his neck. I believe he is now attached to the French GHQ. He was very impressed.

The programme consisted of Inspection, Rifle Drill, Drill and March Past. One might have thought they had been practicing this for a week, but they only came out of the trenches two days ago.

Our manners are appalling. The General and I mounted our horses after the Parade, but the remaining Generals went away, the British all walking together leaving the Russians to themselves.

7 April, diary:
Went up the line near Ypres. We walked as far as Potijze, and went into the left of the right sector, going in by the trench known as Haymarket. Went to the reserve line, where we found Colquhoun and Abercromby, the former looking the most awful ruffian, dirty and, of course, unshaved. We also met Colonel Murray Threipland.

We went on through Duke Street but were unable to get to the very frontline owing to the damage done to the trenches by the recent bombardment. We stopped about 150 yards short. It was very quiet on the front, only some sniping.

8 April, diary:
Heywood told us that at GHQ they issue 3 communiques; one for the BEF – fairly accurate; one for the French – less accurate; and one for the Press – in which it is very difficult to recognise any truth.

9 April, diary:
Edward Tennant, Lord Glenconner's son, arrived today and is going to be attached for 6 weeks. Apparently, his mother is going to have a baby and, while she is doing the patriotic thing, she wants to feel he's in a safer place than the trenches. There is absolutely nothing for him to do. I like him, he seems awfully nice. He wears an eye glass and, when he reads, tortoise-shell rimmed glasses, which I think is a little against him. He is supposed to be very clever, and was known at Chelsea Barracks as the 'Boy Wonder'. He is rather amusing and there is no person in society that he cannot imitate, and no song he cannot sing.

Letter to Mary:
If I decide to soldier after this war, to my mind it would be folly to stay on here and lose months of seniority. I am sorry you want me to make a name for myself; I have no ambition for that. My ambition is to do interesting work, and to do it well, and I think Father's was the same, and he incidentally made a name too. I have not an ambition like F.E. Smith or any of those corrupt politicians.

10 April, diary:
Today the Germans shelled the 20th Division HQ on the Elverdinghe road, causing several casualties; an officer killed and about 16 wounded.

11 April, diary:
The Army and Corps Commanders came today to see the General. The 2nd Army is very short of shells; of course, we have to use more here than on other fronts. What would be considered a quiet day here would be quite the contrary further south.

The difficulty is apparently, not so much in the turning out of shells, but the scarcity of ships to transport them across.

The German artillery is being most active; they bombarded our 2nd line positions on Tuesday, doing much damage in the dug-outs and sent one shell into the mess room and office of the HQ of the 3rd Brigade.

The Germans are launching another tremendous attack at Verdun, believed to be 20,000 men. Their original plan was to attack with such force that it would compel us and the French to attack them to relieve Verdun. They have massed troops on difficult parts of the front, and had hoped by this means to have gained some local success which would have led to greater things. They always have held this line very thickly, and just now we believe it to be very strongly held.

Two days ago, a German Fokker came down in our lines. It was just out of the workshop. The pilot, who was taking it to their Army HQ from the workshop, lost his way in the mist and followed the wrong canal, and came down. Our people were on him before the pilot was able to destroy it.

12 April, diary:
Tennant is leaving us and going to the 2nd Brigade. He gave a turn at the '*Fancies*', a really good show.

13 April, diary:
Rode to Ypres with the General. Very quiet there. We rode as far as Reijenberg Farm and walked the remainder of the way. The General told me that the first three days of the Battle of Verdun were most critical, and that 50% of the French guns were knocked out.

There were several exchanges with his mother in the middle of April where he discussed the subject of moving to another regiment; he apologised for 'grousing' and went into more detail about what he found frustrating about his job, where the novelty had worn off; it showed his capacity for reasoning and for seeing the situation from more than one perspective. He found the combination of the "maximum amount of comfort and the minimum amount of danger" totally uncongenial.

15 April, letter to Mary:
I am very sorry I wrote you that letter yesterday; I was in a very bad temper, it was posted by mistake and I hope that you have burned it by now.

The General is the most independent of Commanders. He prefers, when off duty, to go out alone, and when he goes anywhere important, he naturally takes a senior officer with him. All the others have got their particular work to do, and they are not going to ask, quite rightly, a very young and junior officer, about whom they know nothing, to help them.

On paper, I know my job is the cream of the Army, but in reality, to this Commander, though I like him awfully, it is a wholly unnecessary appointment. Of course, I realise that in a Regiment out here there must be deadly dull moments, but the difference is one is then with fellows of one's own age, instead of either being alone, or with men 15 to 20 years older than oneself. I believe the youngest is 36 and the average age is 41.

16 April, diary:
Went to church. The Bishop of Khartoum preached an excellent sermon. Afterwards he and McCormick lunched.

In the afternoon motored to Ypres with the General. We then went on to Potijze, and then up the left sector as far as Garden Street. Had tea at St Jean with 2nd Scots Guards; Tempest and Coke there.

It was very quiet on the front, but they were shelling Ypres fairly heavily. And there were several German aeroplanes up, flying remarkably low; one, which was up about 1,500 feet, was being fired at by our guns. It suddenly dropped to about 500 feet to avoid the bursting shells. It was the most extraordinary thing to see that none of our aeroplanes was up.

We walked back to Vlamertinghe where we found the car. Dined with General Ponsonby. It is extraordinary how popular he is; anyone will do anything for him.

18 April, diary:
Walked with the General to Corps HQ to see an experiment with a wireless apparatus. There was such a crowd that it was impossible to see or hear much.

The Germans have listening posts and wireless machines capable, I believe, of hearing conversations 400 yards from their wire. On one of the prisoners taken at St Eloi was found a complete list of all our messages sent opposite their front. The thing we went to see was an experiment in the same direction, but capable of doing only 150 yards.

19 April, diary:

There was a terrific bombardment during the late afternoon on the left sector. And at about 7.30 p.m. they attacked in two parties; one of 30 men and the second 100 men. No officers took part. They succeeded in getting into the Wieltze Salient [Wieltje], held by the 3rd Scots Guards and 4th Grenadiers. They were soon turned out by our Heavies, which they say shot with extraordinary accuracy. The Grenadiers took two prisoners. Our casualties were between 50 and 100, and three officers. All wounds were very slight on the whole. They hope the German losses were heavy.

An attack was also made on the 8th Division and, apparently, the Germans have taken a trench. Another attack was made on the Canadians at St Eloi, but they were immediately repulsed.

20 April, diary:

It is strange that the last three times the Germans have given us the heaviest bombardment it has been the night of our Brigade's relief. The relief was carried out alright on the night of 18th and 19th, though not completed till about 3.30 a.m. Everyone seems satisfied with the results of yesterday. As far as can be found out the 6th Division have not driven the Germans out of the lost trench, but will attempt to do so in a day or two.

Tennant has come back to us from the 2nd Brigade which makes things much better.

22 April, diary:

I hear Larry is coming out here in charge of the Scots Guards band. It will make the whole difference to me his being here.

The 6th Division got back their trenches last night, but the Canadians have lost the St Eloi craters. Today is the anniversary of the first big attack with Gas, when the French lost so much ground, including St Julien.

Edward Stanley asked me to dine with him but had to go to Boulogne to get a tooth sorted which had fallen out. I found Cary there and Lascelles. I had not seen the former since Eton, when we were great friends.[6]

Esmond went with Tennant to the cinema to watch a film about Scott's Antarctic expedition. They also went together to the Communion Service on Easter Sunday which was held in the cinema hall "crammed full" with around 800 soldiers. Word was out that all leave had been stopped; he wrote to his mother saying that he didn't know when he might be able to get away. Two days later, he turned 21. Mary gave him some money which he called "an enormous fortune" and which he asked her to reconsider giving: "It is far too good of you and just a hundred times too much." It was a beautiful sunny day and the country was enjoying a particularly hot spell. He had received many birthday wishes; in thanking Eileen for her congratulations, he told her he was now sporting a moustache:

> It is decidedly humorous to think that I have reached this great age. I must carry my years well, for I was taken a short time ago for 18! Since then I have grown a bushy moustache, which gives me a very dignified appearance though it's some-what patchy as yet (in places). I only hope I shall wear as well and have as good a time, in the next 21 years: if so, I shall have no reason for complaint.

> 25 April, diary:
> Dined at B Mess, sat next to a man called Evans, who has an anti-aircraft battery in the Ypres area. He told me that the range of an anti-aircraft gun was 4,000 yards, that the shell took 18 seconds to reach its mark. Consequently, the shooting is pure luck, as a fast aeroplane can do half a mile in that time and considerably change its course. He said that at 2,000 feet it is impossible to see, in spite of the glasses supplied, whether a trench is manned or not. At 7,000 feet it is only possible to see large bodies of troops on the roads, and very difficult to see if they are moving. The majority of accidents and damage are caused by bad landings.

> 27 April, diary:
> The [Fourth] Army commander (Rawlinson) came to lunch and, in the afternoon, I took him to see the 2nd Grenadiers and 3rd Coldstream. He is such a nice old man and not the least alarming.

News from France was temporarily overshadowed by a serious turn of events in Ireland, which Esmond noted in his diary. The Easter Rising in Dublin, begun on 24 April, was exercising many. John French, now Lord French and Commander-in-Chief, Home Forces, sent two infantry brigades across the Irish Sea and put other formations on standby; the rising coincided with a renewed fear of a German invasion.

> 28 April, diary:
> A heavy gas attack was made on Wednesday on the Anzacs [16th (Irish) Division] at Loos. Our casualties were 438, and they say they were repulsed with very heavy casualties.

> 30 April, diary:
> A most disturbed night. The Huns made a gas attack on the 5th Corps, which is on the Canadian right, south of St Eloi. They got into a trench but were immediately

put out again. The noise from the artillery between 1 and 2 a.m. was terrific. I have
never heard anything like it since I have been here. The bells in Poperinghe were
all rung and whistles blown giving the alarm.

I went over to the office at 1.45 a.m. to see if anything was wanted, but all was
quiet on our front. At 3.30 we were bombed, some of the bombs falling uncomfort-
ably close, a lot of broken glass falling on my window sill.

Esmond considered the timing of his conversation with Feilding:

Letter to Mary:
The heat here is extraordinary and if it were not for the dust, it would be perfect.
The General goes on leave tomorrow. I had hoped that I should be going with
him, but find the old dog is going to Paris, so I don't think there is any chance of
my getting away, as my leave is not really due yet. I think I had therefore better, if
possible, give warning before he goes. If I had been going to get leave with him I
should have said nothing until I had seen you, but I may have to wait indefinitely if
I don't speak to him before he goes."

As the General left for Paris, Esmond was granted leave and mustered the courage
to announce his intentions: "I said I wanted to see some action. He was very nice and
understanding about it. I told him I wanted to join the Indian Cavalry, but he strongly
advised my joining the Cavalry here. He said he would write to Sir Philip Chetwode."

1 May, diary:
Crossed over about 11 a.m. Passed the torpedoed *Sussex*, only her masts showing
above the water. Near Folkestone one of our airships flew over quite low; it looked
like a toy. I believe it was submarine hunting. Reached London at 4. Violet was out,
but came in just before 5. On leave till 8th.

Esmond spent the week in London. The days were occupied with stocking up on
essentials, walks with Mary and rides in the Park with Violet, and small family
lunches. Eileen and Francis made an effort to see him; they went to several plays
together and one evening they went to the Scala Cinema, where newsreels brought
home the horrors of war, something which Esmond found uncomfortable and which
Mary later regretted doing.

On the Saturday, Lord French, a neighbour at 94 Lancaster Gate, walked across
the street that divided the terrace, to pay the family a visit. He told Mary quite openly
that he considered Esmond giving up his Staff job to be a great mistake, adding that
it was most important to have efficient, hard-working officers in supporting roles

as the whole success of a campaign often depended on staff work. Mary defended Esmond's decision and said that she sympathised with her son's desire to be with his own contemporaries in a regiment, knowing his father would have held the same view.

When Esmond returned to France, he was met with sad news.

9 May, diary:
I was greeted this morning with the news that poor General Heyworth has been killed. He was going up Muddy Lane this morning with Colonel Glyn in front and Pip Warner behind him. Dodging a shell hole, he was sniped, the bullet entering just below his steel helmet. He will be a great loss to the Division. Everyone is very upset.

10 May, diary:
Went to Ypres with the General. He said he quite understood my wishing to leave and would write to General Campbell, Commanding the 6th Cavalry Brigade and Colonel Vaughan to see if I could get attached to the Royals.

Ypres has been even more damaged since the last time I was there. We went round looking for Machine Gun emplacements and penetrated into the 6th Division area to a place called Fruscate [Frascati], from where we had a splendid view of the German line. Their parapets are infinitely higher than ours, and in much better condition.

In the afternoon, everyone went to General Heyworth's funeral, which took place at Brandhoek.

11 May, diary:
About 11 a.m. the Germans started shelling Poperinghe, one falling fairly close to this billet. As a result, I had to go over to the Office. I had not been there a few minutes before a shell, or a fragment, struck the Town Hall. Though we were on the 2nd floor a bit of the shell came right through and covered us with dust and dirt. Two men were wounded, one in the yard streaming with blood. They put another shell into the billets, and on to the road by the billets of the 1st Coldstream, killing 12 and wounding 15 men.

12 May, diary:
Tennant leaves us tomorrow. It has made the whole difference to me having him here.

13 May, diary:
In the afternoon went to the cinema with Heywood to see Charlie Chaplin. We arrived too late to see his film but saw others. Amongst them we saw Mother with the Queen leaving St Paul's after the unveiling of Florence Nightingale's Memorial.

15 May, diary:
Went to Hazebrouck with the General to see an oculist, as the General's eyes have been bad lately. We arrived too early for the appointment so spent half an hour with the 11th Army workshop. It is an enormous place, run by a man called Newton. He is responsible for many of the improvements and inventions. They had a 6" trench mortar there with which they were going to experiment the next day. There were also shells with wings on them: sometimes the fuse fails to explode. As the shell goes through the air the wind catches the wings and screws on the cap of the shell even tighter…they hope to prevent so many shells not exploding.

17 May, diary:
Yesterday we were shelling some of the towns behind the German lines. One naval gun was to fire at Roulers, this being the first time it had fired since being up here. It fired only twice, both of which failed to explode, so they were useless even for registering.

Some big guns, I think 6", went through last night. They are drawn by sort of steam rollers called Caterpillars, which go 3 mph. Motored to Ypres in the afternoon. During the recent German artillery activity, a great deal more damage has been done to the Cloth Hall and the Cathedral. I saw Pat Bradshaw.

Last night we had a large raid, 48 aeroplanes taking part for reconnoitring purposes.

The Archbishop of Canterbury lunched.[7]

18 May, diary:
Went to the '*Fancies*' with Walter Dalkeith – rather disappointing.

There is a rumour going about that the 36th French Corps, the troops between us and the Belgians, are leaving here on June 1st, and that their line is to be taken over by British troops. The 20th Division starts relieving us today.

20 May, diary:
Went to Ypres in the afternoon with the General; motored as far as Vlamertinghe and walked the rest of the way. Walked through Ypres, its utter destruction seems ever worse. I would have given anything to have taken a photograph of what remains of the Cathedral and Cloth Hall. In spite of the incessant shelling, in front of the Cathedral a young oak still stands, which adds to the splendour of the ruin.

On 21 May, General Feilding and his staff returned to Chateau Esquelbecq. Esmond was waiting to hear about a transfer; he was very keen to get into a cavalry regiment and Feilding had written to General Campbell, as promised. His thoughts, however, were primarily with his family and on what they were doing. Violet was on the brink of announcing her engagement to her long-standing admirer John Astor; it was an exciting moment and there was much to be thankful for. He was just what she needed – steadfast and devoted, honourable and courageous; he was a comforting presence in her life and very much liked by all the family. He had great positive energy and seemed undaunted by the fact that she was a widow with two young children. Violet's twenty-seventh birthday was coming up on 28 May and Esmond was worried that he hadn't found a present to send her. In a letter to Mary on the 22nd, he told her:

> I got a letter from Vi on Monday night. I am very glad she has said "Yes". Please do not forget to answer my questions, as I'm wearying to know, and many more besides.

John had written Esmond a very nice letter from Minto; Esmond admired him for his military dash and the bravery demonstrated by his return to the front after being wounded at Messines in October 1914.

In the meantime, Larry had arrived in France in charge of the band of the 1st Battalion Scots Guards; for about a week he was quartered at the Chateau and so was able to see Esmond.

23 May, diary:
A Company of the Grenadiers, Pilcher's, did an attack, their object being to take two lines of German trenches.

The Division is now in what is known as GHQ Reserve, which means that we have to be ready to move, entrain and everything in nine hours. Last night they telegraphed to ask if we had everything ready in case of an order being sent, in view of the heavy attack of the 1st and 2nd Armies near Loos.

The Germans have apparently taken the frontline trenches, on a distance of 1,500 yards, 200 prisoners and 6 officers.

28 May, diary:
Grigg returned from leave, and says the impression in London is that Asquith must go, and that Lloyd George will succeed him with a cabinet of five. He also says that there is no chance of the Russians being ready before next year.

I am unable to join the Cavalry here as they are full up with large reserves of young officers longing to come out. In the meantime, Lord George has applied for me to return to Haddington.

The General says it is very unlikely that the War Office will forward that application. And if it does, it will probably not be for two or three months as, once in the BEF, one cannot be used to reinforce a unit at home, even if it is your own regiment.

I suppose it would be easy enough to join an infantry battalion here, and I am seriously thinking of trying for the Scots Guards. I could either do my training with them out here, or be transferred by them to their home battalions. I do think in peace time the Guards are the best regiment to be in, very nice people, a great deal of fun and many openings, what with Staff jobs and the Egyptian and Camel Corps.

29 May, diary:
General Haking, Corps Commander 11th Corps, lunched yesterday. The Division was in his Corps before it was sent up here to the 14th.

In the afternoon rode over to see Larry, with the 1st Scots Guards in camp K, just this side of Poperinghe. Whilst I was there they were shelling it very heavily. In the official report, it says they put no less than 22 bombs into the town. Our 12" was going to fire this afternoon in retaliation, so I imagine that it will be an unhealthy spot today.

We watched the shelling for a bit from the camp. I only had a short time with Larry, as I had to be back to censor the letters, and it took me two hours getting there.

Pat Bradshaw told me he took Larry to see my billet, 17 Grande Place, on Saturday, and that since I left they have put a shell right into my room.

3 June, diary:
Have been riding recently with John Dyer, who is exceptionally nice, but he left us to return to his Brigade yesterday.

On Wednesday after lunch the General told me that Darrell had heard in a private letter from de Vesci that I was shortly leaving, which means that GHQ has granted Lord George's application for my return.[8] It was a great shock to me. With the General's help I am trying to join the Scots Guards, who are willing to have me, but I am afraid it is too late. If I joined out here I should probably be sent home for three month's training and then come out again; whilst if I wait till I get to Haddington, the transferring will take much longer, and I probably shan't get out so soon. We expect to go into the line on the 15th, relieving the 6th Division.

5 June, diary:

The Germans have delivered a very nasty attack on the Canadians south of Ypres; they attacked on Friday, after an intense bombardment of five hours. They have taken the whole front system of trenches at a front of 2,000 yards, inflicting very heavy casualties estimated at 3,000, equal to those at Magersfontein in the South African war. The ground lost is high ground, and it is most important that we should take it back as it makes the position of the troops holding the salient alarmingly difficult. In the official communiqué describing the attack it said at every point the enemy was repulsed.

On Wednesday, 31st, an important naval action took place off Jutland. Though at first the accounts officially published were very disquieting, it now appears that the Germans have suffered as heavily as we.

5 June, letter to Mary:

Yesterday, John Ponsonby had a great Fourth of June celebrations. All his Commanding Officers and 2nd in Command are Old Etonians, which is an extraordinary coincidence. I was going too but, at the last moment had to join the General and dine with General Hely d'Oissel of the 36th Corps. I sat next to the French General and Commandant.

Today I am feeling like nothing on earth, as after last night's dinner I have just come in from déjeuner with a French Brigade. As you know they all eat like hippopotamuses and take it as an insult if you do not have every course and drink a different wine with each one. In the middle of lunch the band played "*God Save the King*" and we all stood up holding our champagne glasses. Immediately afterwards the "*Marseillaise*" struck up and we remained in the same position. The French General then made a charming speech with many compliments to the General. The General only said "Je vous remercie Mon Général", but he really might have proposed the General's health and the Verdun troops, for he speaks French well enough!

When we have to say good bye, he always says to a Frenchman "Adieu", whereupon their faces fall yards, and each time comes the same reply "Mais, Mon Général, j'éspère que nous nous reverrons bientôt." But he has never yet realised the faux pas it is.

Lord George's official application for me to return to Haddington arrived today, so I expect to leave any day this week.

7 June, diary:

News arrived that Lord Kitchener and all his Staff were drowned on 5th June south west of the Orkney Islands.

9 June, diary:

The German attack on the Canadians developed on Tuesday. They attacked the 20th Division, taking some frontline trenches and entering Hoogue [Hooge]. Hoogue has always been easy to take, and has often changed hands, but it was made easier by the German capture of the Canadian trenches, which enabled them to look right into West Lane.

On Tuesday rode over to Volckerinckhove with the General to see the 2nd Brigade, and in the morning motored to Dunkirk to get some food for the mess. The town had suffered much more than I expected by the recent air-raids.

The 2nd Brigade have dug an exact facsimile of the Ypres Salient. The Royal Engineers planned it on exactly the same scale as the real thing. The air photographs have enabled them to get the German line accurately.

The 1st Coldstream and 2nd Irish were practising attacks. The plan is that they advance in three waves of a Company front. The first two waves go straight to their objective, the German third line, the third wave to the German second line, and the fourth wave, on the signal being given, to the German frontline.

The German line is one mass of network of trenches, and this scheme of practising an attack will be the greatest help, especially to the officers.

The Russians are attacking, and claim to have taken 900 officers and 45,000 prisoners, but I can hardly believe this.

13 June, diary:

The Cavalry the other day, I am told, had a cross country ride, two Divisions taking part. They were told to get to a place five miles off as soon as possible. 16,000 started at the same time; it was a great success, and only three men were killed.

The fighting round Ypres is still very heavy, and the Canadian losses have been enormous, 7,000 I believe. In the first attack, only 60 men remained of one Company.

Yesterday I went to see the 2nd Brigade attack the salient; it was just the same as the other day except for two extra Companies and Engineers who came up the rear to consolidate. It is not yet settled whether they will advance under an artillery bombardment, or take them by surprise. The latter course is, I think, favoured by the majority.

On my return, Colonel Darrell told me my orders had come, and I leave tomorrow for Haddington. I have been out here just four months.

Dramatis Personae

Abercromby, Lt. RA, *'Bobby'* MC. Eton/Scots Guards. Wounded by a bomb when hunting for military treasure which required a year's recuperation in England. Mentioned in Despatches. 1895-1972.

Prince Alexander of Teck, *'Alge'*. 1874-1957. Eton/7th Queen's Own Hussars. Second Matabele War, Boer War. Mentioned in Despatches three times. Later Major-General the Rt Hon. 1st Earl of Athlone, KG, GCB, GCMG, GCVO, DSO, ADC, PC. His Earldom was created in 1917 when the Royal Family changed their name to Windsor. Governor-General of South Africa 1924-1930. Governor-General of Canada 1940-46. Very popular in these appointments. On Committee to organise 1953 Coronation.

Allston, Lt.-Col. Francis, *'Cook'*, DSO. 1878-1961. Eton/Scots Guards. On Staff at Guards Division HQ. Mentioned in Despatches five times.

Astor, Captain the Hon John. 1886-1971. Eton/1st Life Guards/Legion d'Honneur. Gold Medallist 1908 London Olympics. Severely wounded 1918. MP for Dover, later 1st Lord Astor of Hever.

Beckwith-Smith, Captain Merton, *'Becky'* DSO, MC. 1890-1942. Eton/Coldstream Guards, transferred to Welsh Guards. Wounded. Mentioned in Despatches three times. Carried out first trench raid in the War. Later Major-General. In February 1942, POW on the fall of Singapore. Senior British Officer in Changi before being transferred to Karenko Concentration Camp, Formosa/Taiwan, where he died of diphtheria after being refused medication by the guards.

Bradshaw, Captain WPA *'Pat'*, DSO. 1897-1966. Eton/Scots Guards. Mentioned in Despatches. Later Lieutenant-Colonel. Eton friend of Esmond.

Briand, Aristide. 1862-1932. French Socialist Prime Minister 11 times. Introduced compulsory sickness and old age insurance. In the Salonika crisis of 1914-15 he hoped to bring Greece into the war and make his mistress, Princess George, the Queen of Greece. As Foreign Minister first suggested a 'European Federal Union' that would eventually result in the European Union.

Campbell, Colonel John. VC, CMG, DSO, Legion d'Honneur. Croix de Guerre. 1876-1944. Eton/Coldstream Guards. Boer War. Mentioned in Despatches four times. Commanding the 3rd Coldstream Guards rallied his troops, who had been decimated by machine gun fire, by sounding a hunting horn during an attack at Ginchy in the Battle of Somme in September 1916. They captured the machine guns and killed all the enemy, for which he received the VC. Dubbed the *'Tally-Ho VC'*, he was a very popular commander. Later Brigadier-General. He addressed troops of the 137th Brigade from the Riqueval Bridge over the St. Quentin Canal on 2 October 1918.

Cary, Lt. the Hon. Philip Plantagenet. 1895-1968. Eton/Grenadier Guards. Wounded twice. Later Officer of Arms, Bluemantle Pursuivant 1912-13, York Herald 1923-32.

Cavan, Lt.-Gen. 10th Earl of Cavan, Frederick Rudolph Lambart, later Field Marshal, KP, GCB, GCMG, GCVO, GBE. 1865-1946. Eton/Grenadier Guards. Called '*Fatty*' for no obvious reason as he was slim. 1st GOC of newly appointed Guards Division August 1915. Mentioned in Despatches eight times. GOC British Forces in Italy. Commanded troops at George VI's Coronation.

Chetwode, Lieutenant-General Sir Philip, Bart. 1869-1950. Eton/19th Hussars. Boer War. Wounded. Mentioned in Despatches nine times. Commander in Chief India 1930. Field Marshal 1933. Created Baron Chetwode 1945. GCB, OM, GCSI, KCMG, DSO.

Chichester, Major the Hon Arthur, DSO, MC, Croce de Guerra. Irish Guards. Deputy Assistant Adjutant General. 1889-1972.

Clemenceau, Georges. '*The Tiger*'. 1841-1929. Fought 12 duels. French Independent Radical Prime Minister 1906-09 and 1917-20. Popular with troops as he often visited the Front. His strong speeches left a vivid impression on Churchill, who studied his technique closely and copied it in the Second World War.

'Cloche', Captain Clive Bell. 1871-1956. Eton/Scots Guards. Joined Scots Guards in 1890. ADC to Governor General of Canada 1900-1904. Much loved by the Minto family. Retired army 1908. MP for Honiton 1910-1931. Re-joined army 1914. POW January 1915 at Cuinchy. Interned PofW in Switzerland December 1917-April 1918. Created Baronet 1923.

Coke, Captain the Honourable Richard '*Dick*'. Eton/Scots Guards. Boer War. Commanded the 2nd Battalion in 1916 in Captain Paynter's absence. Wounded twice.

Colquhoun, Capt. Sir Iain '*Luss*' Colquhoun of Luss, Bt, KT, DSO and Bar. 1887-1948. Fettes/Scots Guards. Army Lightweight Boxing Champion 1913. A very popular and brave officer. Court Martialled as a Company Commander in December 1915 for "approving a truce with the enemy" to allow each side to bury their dead on Christmas Day. Found guilty and reprimanded, but this sentence was rejected by Haig, and he immediately returned to full regimental duties a hero to his men. During the Battle of the Somme he clubbed six Germans to death with an entrenching tool with a steel nut at the end. In November 1917 bought a lion cub, which didn't like the cold and quickly died.

Dalkeith, Lt. the Earl of. Walter. 1894-1973. Eton/Oxford/Grenadier Guards. A neighbour of Esmond's parents in the Borders. MP for Roxburghshire and Selkirkshire 1923-1935. Later 8th Duke of Buccleuch and Queensberry, KT, GCVO, TD, PC.

Darrell, Colonel William, DSO. 1878-1934. Eton/Coldstream Guards. Boer War. Assistant Adjutant and Quartermaster General at HQ Guards Division. Mentioned in Despatches five times. Later Brigadier CB, CMG, DSO.

de Crespigny, Claude. 1878-1941. Grenadier Guards, CB, CMG, DSO. Later Brig General Sir Claude. Known as '*Crawley*' to distinguish him from his elder brother '*Creepy*' in the 2nd Life Guards. His light hearted, rebellious and fearless spirit found expression in various ways, especially in the kind of jokes which gave great pleasure to his battalion. He was one of those Commanding Officers who believe in being in the thick of the fighting; a colourful and inspired leader, he used to lead his men over the top with a 'loaded stick' as a weapon. In Flanders, he charged a German machine-gunner and, with one mighty swing of his stick, he broke the enemy's neck, and the regiment went on. Ended the war as a Brigadier-General commanding the 1st Guards Brigade.

Whilst in the Ypres Salient he collected all the first-class tickets that he could from the ruined railway stations. These were printed 'Bruges to Ypres', 'Brussels to Ypres' and so on. He crossed out 'Bruges' or 'Brussels' and substituted 'War Office', 'GHQ, BEF', etc. He then sent the amended tickets to various staff officers who, in his view, should come out to Ypres and take part in the fighting.

After the war, Crawley was invited to dinner at White's by a brother officer. Someone bet him £10 that he could not walk on his hands from the dining room floor, down the stairs and into the hall below. Crawley accepted the challenge. The upper stairs formed a continuous bend and halfway down there was a landing. When he reached the landing, Crawley toppled over and his heels cracked a very old long glass mirror. The Club took a very serious view of the incident and he had to pay £400 for the broken mirror. He took the mirror to a glazier who was astonished by its quality and offered him £1,400 for it, which Crawley accepted.

The former Prime Minister, Harold Macmillan, wrote of him: "He was a magnificent regimental officer unequalled by any that I have known … Sometimes I felt I had earned his approbation, not from any words he spoke, but a particularly pleasant grin. Strangely enough, such was this man's attraction that if, at any time after the war, he had asked me to undertake some service – however disagreeable or however interfering with my own plans – I should unhesitatingly have accepted. He was a true leader of men."

de Langle de Cary, Fernand. French General. 1849-1927. Had seen service in Franco-Prussian War 1870-71. Overall Commander of French troops in Verdun in 1916. Removed by Joffre in January 1917 as he was blamed for the unpreparedness of Fortress Verdun prior to the German offensive.

de Satgé, Philippe Cosme Henri. Modern Languages tutor at Eton 1903-1931. He became a British citizen in 1925. Several masters joined up on the outbreak of war, some finding themselves under the command of boys they had taught.

Dyer, Capt. Sir John Swinnerton Dyer, Bt, MC. 1891 to KIA 31 July 1917. Eton/Scots Guards. Wounded. Mentioned in Despatches. Very popular.

Evans, Brigadier-General LP, VC, CMG, DSO and Bar. Eton/Black Watch. Wounded. Mentioned in Despatches three times.

FitzGerald, Lieutenant-Colonel Lord Desmond. MC. 1888-1916. Eton/Irish Guards. Mentioned in Despatches. A close friend of the Prince of Wales. Killed in a bombing accident 3 March 1916.

Gathorne-Hardy, Major-General the Hon JF, CB, CMG, DSO. 1874-1949. Eton/Grenadier Guards. Boer War. When commanding at Aldershot he was known as '*Stop me & buy one*' as he resembled a local ice cream salesman. Mentioned in Despatches 10 times. Later General Sir (John) Francis GCB, GCVO, CMG, DSO.

Gibbs, Captain Arthur, '*Leggs*' MC. 1894-1945. Eton/Oxford/Welsh Guards. Wounded.

Gibbs, Captain J Evelyn, '*Evie*' MC. 1879-1932. Eton/Coldstream Guards. Boer War. ADC to Esmond's father when Viceroy of India. Seriously poisoned in Government House, Calcutta, after drinking contaminated milk. Won Army Cup Steeplechase in India. Captured 3 November 1914. Later Colonel.

Glyn, Brevet Colonel Arthur. 1870-1922. Eton/Grenadier Guards. Mentioned in Despatches twice. Temporarily in command 1st Bn. Accompanied Brigadier-General Heyworth to the frontline when he was killed by a sniper.

Gordon Lennox, Brigadier-General Lord Esme CMG, DSO, MVO. 1875-1949. Eton/Scots Guards. Wounded twice. Mentioned in Despatches four times.

Gort, John '*Tiger*', 6th Viscount, VC, GCB, DSO & 2 Bars, MVO, MC. 1886-1946. Harrow/Grenadier Guards. Commanded BEF to France 1939. Governor of Malta 1942-44. Field Marshal.

Green, Lt. Cecil. 1892-1924. Eton/Coldstream Guards. Wounded twice.

Greene, Capt. Sir Walter, Bt. '*Sniper*'. 1879-1947. Eton/3rd County of London Yeomanry (Sharpshooter). Sharpshooters were raised in the Boer War to compete with the Boers, with men selected for their skill as horsemen and marksmen. In the First World War, they were converted to machine gunners with officers attached to different units who benefitted from their skills. Wounded. Mentioned in Despatches. Later Lieutenant-Colonel, MP, DSO, TD.

Greville, Captain Charles CH, DSO. Eton/Grenadier Guards. Wounded twice, including in the attack on Boesinghe on 31 July 1917. Mentioned in Despatches three times. ADC Governor of Gibraltar.

Haking, Lt.-General Sir Richard. Hampshire Regt. 1862-1945. Burma, Boer War. Commander X1 Corps. Commander British troops in Egypt 1923. Full General 1925 GBE, KCB, KCMG.

Hamilton, Lt. Col. Lord Gilbert Claud *'Claudie'*. CMG, DSO. 1889-1975. Wellington/Grenadier Guards. One of 4 surviving officers who brought the remnants of the 1st Grenadiers out of the 1st Battle of Ypres. Personal ADC to the Prince of Wales.

Hanbury, Lt. Nigel, OBE. 1879-1952. Eton/Coldstream Guards. Wounded in bombing accident that killed Lord Desmond Fitzgerald. Mentioned in Despatches twice.

Hely d'Oissel, Alexis. 1859-1937. French General. Commanded 8th Corps.

Heywood, Lt.-Col. CP *'Griffin'*, CMG, DSO. 1880-1936. Eton/Coldstream Guards. Staff Guards Division. Later Brig. General Commanding 3rd Guards Brigade. Mentioned in Despatches six times. Severely wounded 1918.

Heyworth, Brigadier-General Frederick *'Pa'*. 1863-1916. Eton/Scots Guards, CB, DSO. Mentioned in Despatches three times. Commanded 3rd Guards Brigade. KIA Ypres 9 May 1916.

Hunter-Weston, Lieutenant-General Sir Aylmer, KCB, DSO. 1864-1940. Wellington/RE. Nicknamed *'Hunter-Bunter'* and described by Haig as a "rank amateur" due to previous Gallipoli experience. MP for Bute and Northern Ayrshire. An eccentric man whose *Who's Who* entry filled an entire column. He died after a fall from a turret at his ancestral home.

Jeffreys, Major-General Darrell, CB, CMG. 1878-1960. Eton/Grenadier Guards. Known as *'Ma'*, when he joined the regiment, after Ma Jeffreys a famous Madame who kept a well-known *maison de rendezvous*. Later General Sir George Jeffreys MP for Petersfield 1941-51. KCB, KCVO, CMG. 1st Lord Jeffreys. Wounded. Mentioned in despatches eight times. Mahdist War. Boer War. For a brief spell in 1917, he kept a pet lion in France which he inherited from General Sir Tom Bridges. Bridges had won *'Poilu'* in a raffle in Paris earlier in the year. He took it back to HQ in a picnic hamper, much to the surprise of his regiment. An officer was tasked with scouting the battle torn country for dead horses to feed the lion. "The Germans usually obliged by killing at least one horse in the vicinity, but there was sometimes a shortage. General Bridges lost his leg on 20 September. When told it would be buried he suggested that it should be given to the lion as he had been short of meat!" (*A Guard's General – The Memoirs of Sir Allan Adair*, Edited by Oliver Lindsay, Hamish Hamilton 1986).

Joffre, Joseph. *'Papa Joffre'*. 1852-1931. Popular French Marshal. His victory at the Marne in 1914 saved France. Commander-in-Chief of French forces on Western Front from the start of the First World War to the end of 1916, when he was replaced disastrously by Robert Nivelle. Joffre had a furious temper. After an argument with Haig in August 1916 he had to be calmed down with "liberal doses of 1840 brandy".

Lane Fox, Rev. John, MC. Roman Catholic Chaplain attached to Irish Guards. Mentioned in Despatches.

Lascelles, Lt. Col. Viscount. Later 6th Earl of Harewood, Henry George. 1882-1947. Eton/Grenadier Guards/DSO and Bar. Wounded three times; Mentioned in despatches twice. Ended the war commanding 3rd Battalion. Married the Princess Royal, daughter of King George V and Queen Mary in Westminster Abbey.

Law, Hugh Alexander. 1872-1943. Rugby/Oxford. Irish Nationalist MP for Donegal West. A supporter of the pro-war policy of John Redmond during the War. His son served in the Irish Guards.

Lloyd George, David MP. 1863-1945. Minister of Munitions May 1915 – July 1916. Many Generals could barely conceal their contempt for his military opinions. Secretary of State for War June – December 1916. Prime Minister December 1916 – 1922. Later Rt Hon. 1st Earl Lloyd-George of Dwyfor, OM, PC.

Lyttelton, Lt. Oliver. DSO, MC. 1893-1972. Eton/Grenadier Guards. Mentioned in Despatches three times. Brigade Major, 4th Guards Brigade. Severely gassed April 1918. MP for Aldershot 1940-1955. President of the Board of Trade 1940-1941. Minister Resident in Cairo 1941-1942. Minister of Production 1942-1945. Colonial Secretary 1951-1954. Later Rt Hon. 1st Viscount Chandos, KG, DSO, MC, PC.

McCalmont, Brigadier-General R.C.A., DSO. Eton/Irish Guards. Mentioned in Despatches twice.

Maitland, Lt. Col. Mark. 1882-1972. Eton/Grenadier Guards. CVO/DSO. Boer War. Nigeria. President of Court Martial in December 1915 which tried Captain Miles Barne and Captain Sir Iain Colquhoun for the 1915 Christmas Truce.

Maxwell, Major Henry Maxwell-Stuart. 1887-1917. Coldstream Guards. KIA October 1917. One of four brothers killed in the war.

McCormick, The Rev. WPG *'Pat'*, DSO. 1877-1940. Senior Chaplain to the Guards Division. Before the war, he worked in a gold mine in South Africa. In 1927 became Vicar of St Martin-in-the Fields. In 1937, he was the first clergyman to appear on TV with his Christmas message.

Murray Threipland, Lieutenant-Colonel William. 1886-1942. Grenadier Guards & appointed founding CO of Welsh Guards in February 1915. Sudan, Boer War. Colonel, DSO, JP, DL.

Nugent, Captain TEG, MC. Eton/Irish Guards. A contemporary of Esmond at Eton. Wounded twice, including in the bombing accident which killed Lord Desmond Fitzgerald. Mentioned in Despatches. Equerry to HRH the Duke of York. Brigade Major, Brigade of Guards 1929.

Pereira, General Cecil *'Pinto'*. 1869-1942. Oratory, Edgbaston/Coldstream Guards. Commanded 1st Guards Brigade 1916. Became Major-General Sir Cecil, KCB, CMG.

Pétain, Philippe. 1856-1951. Marshal of France. Commander-in-Chief French Army 1917-1920. He showed outstanding military leadership during the War. At the opening of the Battle of Verdun, he was fetched in the night by a staff officer who knew exactly where he would be enjoying the company of his mistress, the aptly named Eugenie Hardon. Chief of the French State 1940-1944. After the war, he was tried and convicted for treason. He was sentenced to death, but the sentence was commuted to life in prison.

Pilcher, Major WS, DSO. 1888-1970. Eton/Grenadier Guards. Second in Command 4th Battalion. DSO for helping two of his soldiers save the lives of four men of his Company. The Sergeant Major and eight soldiers had been buried by shells. In daylight and under heavy enemy rifle and machine gun fire he personally helped to dig the men out. Wounded. Mentioned in Despatches three times.

Plumer, General Sir Herbert. 1857-1932. *'Plum'*. Eton/York and Lancaster Regiment. Mahdist War. Second Matabele War. Boer War. Mentioned in Despatches eight times. Commanded Second Army, responsible for the Ypres Salient. Oversaw the great victory at Messines in June 1917. Later Field Marshal, Viscount, GCB, GCMG, GCVO, GBE. After the War, he became Governor of Malta and High Commissioner in Palestine.

Ponsonby, General Sir John 1866-1952. Eton/Coldstream Guards. Commanded 2nd Guards Brigade. Later Major-General Sir John, KCB, CMG, DSO, commanding 40th Division. Wounded. Mentioned in Despatches six times. A famous character, he was the central figure of innumerable stories and incidents; he had a highly-developed sense of humour and of the ridiculous. Universally loved by everyone and well thought of by the troops. He adopted a stray kitten and named it *Pop-it*. He was very fond of Esmond and attended his funeral.

Rawlinson, General Sir Henry. 1864-1925. Eton/Coldstream Guards. Later General Lord Rawlinson of Trent, *'Rawly'*. GCB, GCSI, GCVO, KCMG. Mentioned in Despatches nine times. Commander of 4th Army. Had a pet boar also called *Rawly*. After the War, he was appointed Commander-in-Chief, India where he died.

Rogan, Major Mackenzie. 1855-1932. The Coldstream Guards Bandmaster. Became Lieutenant-Colonel CVO and Senior Director of Music, HM Brigade of Guards. When serving in India Rogan had played for the Viceroy.

Ruthven, Lt.-Col. the Honourable Alexander Hore-Ruthven, '*Sandy*'. 1872-1955. Eton/ Welsh Guards (on formation). Sudan (VC). Gallipoli. Wounded. Mentioned in Despatches four times. GSO1 of the Guards Division. Governor South Australia 1928-1934. Governor of New South Wales 1935-1936. Governor-General of Australia 1936-1944. Deputy Constable of Windsor Castle 1944. Later the Right Honourable Brigadier-General, 1st Earl of Gowrie VC, GCMG, CB, DSO and Bar, PC.

Seymour, Brigadier-General Lord Henry '*Copper*', DSO, and Bar. 1878-1939. Grenadier Guards. Commanded 4th Grenadiers and then 3rd Guards Brigade. He was considered an outstanding commander. A self-exile, on account of gambling debts, he was in Africa at the beginning of the war. Although badly wounded in service, he evaded a medical board to get to France with the Grenadiers. Known as '*Copper*', on account of his red hair.

One day two parties of the Guards Division met head-on in a dark and narrow communication trench. The following exchange took place between the conducting NCOs:

> *Make way!*
> *Make way!*
> *Make way for Captain Sir Walter Barttelot, 2nd Battalion Coldstream Guards.*
>   *Make way!*
> *Make way for Major Lord Henry Seymour, 1st Battalion Grenadier Guards.*
>   *That beats you on all counts. Make way!*

Shaw-Stewart, Captain Guy, MC. 1892-1976. Eton/Coldstream Guards. Wounded twice. Younger brother of Patrick Shaw-Stewart KIA 1917.

Smith, F.E. 1st Earl of Birkenhead. 1872-1930. A Conservative politician and barrister; he had meteoric career during the First World War. Attorney General 1915 and Lord Chancellor in 1919, he was one of Churchill's best friends.

Smith-Dorrien, General Sir Horace, GCB, DSO. 1858-1930. Derby Regiment. Anglo-Zulu War (he was one of the few survivors of the Battle of Isandlwana), Battle of Omdurman, Tirah Campaign, Sudan, Boer War. Commanded Second Army at 2nd Battle of Ypres but unfairly forced to resign by French for requesting permission to retreat from the Ypres Salient to a more defensive position. In 1918 became Governor of Gibraltar.

Stanley, Capt. Lord *'Eddy'* MC, PC. 1894-1938. Eton/Oxford/Grenadier Guards. Wounded. Later Secretary of State for Dominion Affairs, May-Oct 1938. Died aged 44 and did not live to succeed his father, the Earl of Derby.

Stopford, Lieutenant-General Sir Frederick, KCB, KCMG, KCVO. 1854-1929. Eton/Grenadier Guards. Anglo-Ashanti War, Boer War. As Commander IX Corps, he was blamed for the failure to attack following the landing on Suvla Bay in 1915. He had chosen to command the landing from an off-shore ship, but slept as the landing was in progress, and was quickly replaced.

Sutherland, Duchess of, Millicent *'Meddlesome Milly'*, 1867-1955. Hostess, social reformer, author. Married three times, her first husband being 4th Duke, whom she married on her 17th birthday. Established and financed No. 9 Red Cross hospital in northern France. Wrote autobiography *'That Fool of a Woman'* in 1924.

Tempest, General Roger *'Stormy Weather'*. 1876-1948. Stonyhurst/Scots Guards. Brigade Major on formation of 3rd Guards Brigade in August 1915. Commanding Officer 2nd Battalion Scots Guards February 1916. Very exacting taskmaster and his successor as CO, Norman Orr Ewing, was a good deal more popular.

Tennant, Lt. the Hon. Edward *'Bim'*. 1897-1916. Winchester/Grenadier Guards. KIA 22 September and buried next to Raymond Asquith at Guillemont Communal Cemetery. He was a poet and wrote a number of letters to his mother, Pamela Lady Glenconner, who published a biography after the war, *Edward Wyndham Tennant, A Memoir (1919)*. The baby daughter she was carrying in April 1916, referred to in Esmond's letter, died soon after birth.

Thorne, Brigadier-General Andrew, *'Bulgy'*. 1885-1970. CMG, DSO and 2 Bars. Eton/Grenadier Guards/DSO and 2 Bars/Mentioned in Despatches seven times. Later General Sir Andrew. An exceptionally fit man: as Commanding Officer his training was so strenuous that everyone longed to go back to the trenches. Military Attaché in Berlin 1932-35.

Vaughan, Lt. Colonel Arthur, DSO, OBE. 1863-1919. 1st Royal Dragoons.

Wales, Prince of, *'David'*. 1894-1972. Dartmouth/Grenadier Guards. Staff appointment HQ Guards Division 1915-16, he welcomed Esmond as someone of his own age. On his return to England he gave Esmond his horses and saddlery. He succeeded his father in January 1936, and abdicated in December 1936. Determined to see active service in the trenches, he was thwarted by the King and Kitchener. He needed much exercise and thought nothing of walking six miles before breakfast. *'The Prince eats little and walks much: we eat much and walk little,'* wrote Oliver Lyttelton, a brother officer. He would lend his Daimler to any brother officer who asked. Took Mary flying in his plane after the War, he admired her and often sought her company when she was with his mother at Court.

Wardrop, Brigadier-General Alexander. 1872-1961. Commander Royal Artillery, Guards Division 1916-18. Later General Sir Alexander GCB, CMG.

Warner, Major Edward *'Pip'*, DSO, MC. Eton/Oxford/Scots Guards. Coxed the Oxford VIII in 1904 Boat Race. Mentioned in Despatches seven times. Witnessed Christmas 1914 Truce. As Adjutant, he acted as Prosecuting Officer in the 1916 Court Martial of Private Reid who was found guilty of desertion and sentenced to death, the only guardsman to be executed in the War. Appointed Staff Captain on formation of 3rd Guards Brigade in August 1915 and Brigade Major in February 1916. Was accompanying General Heyworth when he was shot.

Wilson, General Sir Henry, GCB, DSO. 1864-1922. *'The Intriguer'*. Marlborough. Royal Irish Regiment. Burma (wounded above left eye which left him disfigured and he was also known as *'Ugly Wilson'*), Boer War. Commander 4th Corps. Chief of Imperial General Staff 1918. He became a Field Marshal in 1919. Briefly MP 1922. Murdered by IRA outside his front door in London in June 1922.

6

Joins the Scots Guards

If you are going to fight you might at least have the thing done properly. You know that your men will turn up on parade and you know throughout these incidents, it's ten to one that, owing to the system, and the pride they have and what they have been taught, it will work … All the successes I've had afterwards in life can be put down almost entirely to the good luck to find myself connected with the Grenadier Guards and the Brigade of Guards generally.

Harold Macmillan[1]

I have seen many institutions in my life, universities, colleges, Government offices, joint stock companies, colonial administrations, Cabinets, but the best human organisation, the most efficient and the most closely knit of which I know is the Brigade of Guards.

Lord Chandos, Memoirs

It was Friday 16 June 1916 and, whilst preparations were being made across the Channel for a great offensive on the Somme, Esmond had woken up at Minto, in a house full of women and children, and in the most tranquil of settings that could not have been further from the horror of a battlefield: the garden, a blaze of colour with its flowers in full bloom, and the light of the midsummer evenings dimming slowly against the backdrop of the Border hills.

That first weekend back was a cause for celebration and an outing was organised to Carter Bar, a high point on the boundary between Scotland and England, where the views over the Cheviots are spectacular. Esmond drove the Sunbeam there with Mary, Aunt Louisa, Violet and her two children, and Ruby's two daughters, Rosemary and Letty. After a picnic tea, he took the little ones, all aged 8 and under, to the top of the moor where he entertained them and made them laugh. The following evening, he let Rosemary dress up in his uniform and pretend to be a soldier. The other two days were spent taking the children out riding on Pat, his old pony; he would let them have a gentle canter, running along beside them to make them feel safe. Memories of these times would stay with the children long after the war. The announcement of Violet's engagement to John appeared in *The Times* on 19 June, the day after Esmond's return to Haddington.

Away from the front, Esmond took a pause from his journal. He was in a state of limbo, waiting to leave the Lothians and hoping to get orders to join the Scots Guards, his father's first regiment. His experience with Feilding had convinced him that joining the Guards would be the best thing he could do – he had seen at first hand the unshakeable *esprit de corps* and iron discipline that made these regiments such an extraordinary force, ready and able to take on the toughest Prussian fighters.[2]

At a sporting event at Hedderwick in the middle of July, where the Lothians had been in camp the previous year, the absence of horses rendered it somewhat absurd. He met an old friend Helen Maxwell and they exchanged news. Attention was focused on the opening of the Somme campaign which had claimed so many casualties.

> 16 July, letter to Mary:
> Claud Lambton arrived last night to be our Adjutant; he seems exceptionally nice. Billy Lambton has telegraphed asking him to go to him as his ADC, so naturally he is trying to get out of this. I see the Deccan Horse have been in action. I suppose they were sacrificed to see if it was possible to use Cavalry. Billy Lambton's Division at Thiepval lost 6,000 men in the first two days.[3]

He received a letter from his old school-friend James Stuart, in the Royal Scots, telling him that he was now Second in Command. It was a sobering piece of news and an even more sobering reflection on the state of his regiment, given that James was only nineteen.

Esmond spent the Bank Holiday weekend at Minto and it was there on 7 August, that he finally received his orders to join G Company, 2nd Battalion Scots Guards.[4] As he prepared to leave for London, he dropped his mother a line telling her that he thought the place was looking "too lovely and it seems wrong no one should be here to see it."

In joining the Army from a Yeomanry corps, Esmond had to accept a demotion and he was gazetted on 9 August, as Second Lieutenant, Scots Guards. When drilling began at Wellington Barracks, he was told by the Sergeant to forget that he didn't have a horse.

The same week Larry returned from France and, for a brief time, Mary had both her boys near her in London, in addition to two of her daughters: Eileen and Francis had just had their first baby, Pamela, and Violet was awaiting John's safe return from France for their wedding. When not at the Barracks, Esmond spent as much time as he could with the family; one Saturday he, Mary and Larry, went for an outing to Maidenhead and took an electric canoe upriver to Cliveden to see Nancy Astor. After a week with the King and Queen at Windsor, where she heard all about the sovereign's recent visit to the front, Mary gathered the family together for an informal pre-wedding dinner at home. The following afternoon, 28 August, Violet and John were married at Christ Church, Lancaster Gate; it was a quiet affair for close relatives and the groom's fellow Life Guards officers. Lord Lansdowne, Charlie's father, made an appearance; on what must have been an unspeakably painful day for him, he steeled himself to demonstrate to Violet that he approved of her new-found happiness and security.

The documentary *The Battle of the Somme*, a blend of real footage and reconstructed drama, was on general release and Mary and Esmond went to see it: the cinemas were crowded with people curious to see what is was like for their men in France. An estimated twenty million went to see the film in the first six weeks of its opening, just over half the country's population.

The next day, Mary went home to Scotland. The London skies were playing reluctant hosts to several Zeppelins and there was a great feeling of unease on the home shores. One was brought down by a plane at Enfield, scattering flaming debris over a large area. From the middle of September, after a Lewis Gun course in Chelsea, Esmond spent three weeks at Tadworth. Whilst he was on a firing range at Rainham, he witnessed a massive explosion at the nearby Chemical Works, where they were manufacturing a TNT substitute called Dinitrophenal; seven people were killed and over 80 people injured. The press played down the extent of the disaster.

Esmond was hoping to return for a weekend to his beloved Minto, but couldn't get away. He wrote to Mary on 21 September:

> Are not our casualties awful? Welsh, 10 officers; Irish 17; Scots 20; Coldstream 37; Grenadiers 40. We have 13 officers going out on Saturday, including the Colonel, to the 2nd Battalion, and it is rumoured that the Adjutant, Coke, goes as well. People say the Division was not supported on its Flanks, but I don't think anyone really knows what happened.

On the Old Etonian grapevine and through reports in the newspapers came news of further losses on the Somme affecting Esmond personally. Eleven old boys in Macnaghten's had been killed that summer, four in his year alone, including Michael Lawrence, who fell just over a year after his elder brother Oliver; they were the only sons of Herbert Lawrence, who would become Douglas Haig's Chief of General Staff at the beginning of 1918. Another casualty was Billy Congreve of the

Rifle Brigade, who died at Longueval on 20 July; he was one of two VC winners from Macnaghten's.

> 3 October, letter to Mary:
> We came up from Tadworth today. This is just a line to tell you that I was warned this morning that I should be the next officer for the front; as the Division is now behind, it may be two months before I go out. I shall probably receive a week's notice.

On arrival in London, Esmond went to stay with Violet to keep her company now that John had returned to the front; he helped her move from Hyde Park Terrace into the upper storey of 18 Carlton House Terrace, her father-in-law's home.

Knowing that she might only have a week with Esmond, Mary returned south at once and the family regrouped at Lancaster Gate. The week was spent collecting kit, ensuring Esmond had plenty of warm clothing for the months ahead, and going on a few trips to the theatre. There was also another visit to Bassano and, on Sunday morning, 8 October, the customary early service at Christ Church. Following on from this, Esmond and his mother drove to Carlton House Terrace, collected Violet and continued to St Martin in the Fields where they listened to the Vicar, Dick Sheppard, preaching "an admirable sermon."

> 11 October, Mary Minto's journal:
> Eileen and Francis lunched and dined in order to have a family gathering. Esmond in great spirits. Dancing to the gramophone. He is really glad to be going to the front. He told me again how thankful he is to be able to go and do his bit, so many are physically unfit, and he thinks it must be so hard on them. He has begged me not to worry.

On this occasion, Eileen gave Esmond a little medal which he promised to have fastened to the chain of his identity disc; on it was written "Que Dieu Vous Garde."

Memory will live forever: The Guards Brigade in 1915

They call them the feather-bed soldiers, and by many an ugly word,
But I who have seen them in action can laugh at the taunt absurd.
I've followed their fights and their marches, through the whole of the present war,
And to find a braver Brigade of men, by the Gods you'll travel far.
I recall the great retirement, and the frightful carnage there,
When every man had his work cut out, and nobly did his share.

The Guards were there from the morning till the last red gleam of the sun,
Through the shot and shell, with the thirst of Hell, the most glorious deeds were
    done.
And then again at Ypres, by the early morning light
The way they countered the German attack, was indeed, a glorious sight.
With courage bold (like the men of old) and a ringing British cheer,
They drove the Huns at the bayonet point, like a herd of frightened deer.
Next came the long terrible winter, and I saw them entrench each night,
Straining their eyes o'er the shimmering ground, of hard frost, in the pale moonlight,
Whilst fierce cold winds were howling, midst sleet and torrential rain,
And there never was heard, a grumbling word, though their limbs were racked
    with pain.
Till the weather broke, and to Neuve Chapelle the gallant Guards did go,
And there done a wonderful feat of arms, as the scroll of fame will show,
They never knew fear as they charged at the foe, each man was a hero, real brave,
But before the position was taken, more than half found a soldier's grave.
Yet again, (at bloody Festubert) 'gainst teeming odds they fought,
And gained a brilliant victory though t'was dearly bought.
Givenchy next, then on to Loos, these warriors brave advanced,
To seek honours afresh at "Hill 70", as soon as they got the chance.
And so to the end of the chapter, the Guards Brigade will go on,
Wherever the fight is thickest to avenge the dear comrades gone.
But a truce to idle boasting, for history's page will tell –
What their actions were, in the days gone bye, and t'will say that the Guards did well.
And memory will live forever, vivid, fresh and sweet,
And to it we'll drink, in silent praise, wherever the Guards shall meet,
The toast shall be "To our Gallant dead," may the shadows never fall
On that heroic band, serene and grand, who died at their country's call.

Author unknown

The Guards came through, Arthur Conan Doyle. *The Times*, 23 June 1917

At Loos (Sept/Oct 1915) the whole of the Brigade of Guards went forward in full
view of the Germans on the high ground and were heavily shelled for two miles on
the approach. The Guards historian wrote: "Perfect order was maintained. Nothing
more splendid has ever been recorded in the annals of the Guards than the manner
in which every battalion in the Brigade faced this trying ordeal." (Since August
1915 all Guards regiments had been re-formed into a single 'Guards Division').

Men of the 21st
Up by the Chalk Pit Wood,
Weak with our wounds and our thirst,
Wanting our sleep and our food,
After a day and a night –
God, shall we ever forget!
Beaten and broke in the fight,
But sticking it – sticking it yet.
Trying to hold the line,
Fainting and spent and done,
Always the yell of the Hun!
Northumberland, Lancaster, York,
Durham and Somerset,
Fighting alone, worn to the bone,
But sticking it – sticking it yet.

Never a message of hope!
Never a word of cheer!
Fronting Hill 70's shell-swept slope,
With the dull dead plain in our rear.
Always the whine of the shell,
Always the roar of its burst,
Always the tortures of hell,
As waiting and wincing we cursed
Our luck and the guns and the Boche,
When our Corporal shouted "Stand to!"
And I heard someone cry,
"Clear the front for the Guards!"
And the Guards came through.

Our throats they were parched and hot,
But, Lord, if you'd heard the cheers!
Irish and Welsh and Scot,
Coldstream and Grenadiers.
Two brigades, if you please,
Dressing as straight as a hem,
We – we were down on our knees,
Praying for us and for them!
Praying with tear-wet cheek,

Praying with outstretched hand,
Lord, I could speak for a week,
But how could you understand!
How should your cheeks be wet,
Such feelin's don't come to you.
But when can me or my mates forget,
When the Guards came through!

"Five yards left extend!"
It passed from rank to rank.
Line after line with never a bend,
And a touch of the London swank.
A trifle of swank and dash,
Cool as a home parade,
Twinkle and glitter and flash,
Flinching never a shade,
With the shrapnel right in their face
Doing their Hyde Park stunt,
Keeping their swing at an easy pace,
Arms at the trail, eyes front!
Man, it was great to see!
Man, it was fine to do!
It's a cot and a hospital ward for me,
But I'll tell 'em in Blighty, wherever I be,
How the Guards came through.

Dramatis Personae

Congreve, Major William, *'Billy'*, VC, DSO, Legion d'Honneur, MC. 1891 – KIA July 1916, Longueval. Eton/Rifle Brigade. He had only been married for seven weeks before he was killed. In a letter of condolence, he was described as 'glorious'. Nine months after their wedding, his wife gave birth to a baby daughter, whom she called Mary Gloria.

Lambton, Major-General the Hon. Sir William, *'Billy'*, KCB, CMG, CVO, DSO. 1863-1936. Eton/Coldstream Guards. Mahdist War, Battle of Atbara, Battle of Omdurman, Boer War. Mentioned in Despatches three times. Commanded 4th Division in the First World War.

Lambton, Captain Claud, DSO. 1888-1976. Eton/Lanarkshire Yeomanry. ADC to his uncle Billy Lambton. Mentioned in Despatches. Wounded.

Sheppard, Rev Dick. 1880-1937. Anglican clergyman, Vicar of St. Martin-in-the-Fields. His sermons gained him national fame when he became the first clergyman to broadcast services on the BBC. The war had a profound effect on him and he became a committed pacifist. He wrote to *The Times* in 1925 to protest against a proposed Charity Ball at the Albert Hall on Armistice Day; in its place was organised a Festival of Remembrance, which continues to this day.

Stuart, The Hon James, MC and Bar. 1897-1971. Eton/Royal Scots. A good Eton friend of Esmond. Later Captain the Right Hon. 1st Viscount Stuart of Findhorn, CH, MVO, MC, PC. Married sister of Lady Dorothy Macmillan. MP for Moray and Nairn 1923-1959. Chief Whip 1941-1945. Secretary of State for Scotland 1951-1957.

7

The Diggers

What a privilege it is to be able to come out at last and take one's share, infinitesimally small though it may be, in this tremendous struggle.

Esmond

12 October, Mary Minto's Journal:
Esmond, my beloved boy, left at 10.15. I watched him from the window drive away in the Bijou. The Guards Division are at Le Havre reforming, as they have had terrific losses.

Three short lines were all Mary could manage to write in her journal that day. It was yet another parting, which would imprint itself on her memory: a smiling Esmond in his little car pulling off and disappearing from sight on Bayswater Road; the leaves on the trees opposite, in Kensington Gardens, a swathe of copper and gold; and her own ineradicable sense of sadness and dread.

The previous day she had written him a letter; safely tucked into his breast pocket, it was to be opened once the journey to France had begun:

11 October, Mary's letter:
My Own Blessed Darling, My heart is so full of all the things I wanted to say to you, and yet I seem unable to put them into words. I want above all things to be brave for you for your sake. You know what it means to me your going into danger. You have always been like a ray of sunshine to me and I love you with my whole heart. It is because I love you so that I wouldn't wish you not to go. I am so pleased to think you are in Father's old regiment, going out to do your share in the struggle for a just and righteous cause.

Esmond joined his fellow officer, Mahomed, at Wellington Barracks and, together in charge of a draft of 150 men, they set forth for Southampton.

13 October, diary:
We reached Southampton about 2 p.m. but did not sail till 9 p.m. We were put on an absolute cockleshell of a boat, the *Mona's Queen* by name, a paddle steamer which, in pre-war days, was used for excursions between Holyhead and the Isle of Man. The crossing took nine hours, fairly smooth, though I managed to be sick, and we disembarked at Le Havre at 7 a.m.[1]

He found himself in a bunk next to Lord Vivian, brother-in-law of the Commander-in-Chief. He was quite a character: having been very badly wounded in the Boer War, he was now ADC to King Albert of the Belgians; extraordinarily, he recognised Esmond from Henley.

Esmond's first stop was the Guards Base Depot at Harfleur where he waited for orders to join his company. He found an amiable group of Grenadier officers whom he recognised at once and whose presence he found reassuring: Arthur Penn, Basil Blackwood and John Craigie. The other officers more or less permanently based at the depot were 'Jumbo' Royds, Lethbridge, Boyd-Rochfort and Ipswich. He was struck by the gardens which the soldiers had created around Harfleur to add a bit of cheer and give it some semblance of normality. It was home to some 7,000 troops.

15 October, diary, Harfleur:
I have been posted to the 2nd Battalion and Mahomed to the 1st. He goes up tonight, but I have not heard when I am to go up.

Apart from the excitement of a change to the King's Regulations concerning facial hair, with moustaches no longer being mandatory on officers, Esmond's initial days in France were fairly mundane.

19 October, letter to Mary, Harfleur:
This place is one mass of camps. All the gardens to each camp are quite extraordinary: they all have their Divisional or Regimental colours.

We start our day at 7 a.m. with a rifle inspection and then leave at 7.45 for the training camp, where we stay until 3.30 or 4, but we wretched officers have to rush back between 12.30 and 2 and after luncheon have the most awful hill to walk up. The Training Camp is very dull: the only interesting thing we have done is to go through a gas chamber with a mask and through another room full of lachrymatory shells without glasses. The latter hurts like the dickens but in the former I felt nothing, though most people had a parched feeling in their throats. I should rather like some books, as there is a fair amount of time for reading in the evenings.

26 October, diary, Harfleur:
Every day is spent in much the same way: on fatigue, which means unloading ships, or loading motor lorries at the various dumps with 'empties'. Or the whole day is spent at the Central Training Camp. The latter is incredibly dull as we, unlike officers of the line regiments, are considered sufficiently well trained not to have to go through the same course as the men and do nothing but supervise.

28 October, diary:
Today we took part in the most extraordinary show, the commemoration of the Battle of the Yser. The Belgians had a colour presented to one of the Regiments. We had to provide a Guard of Honour. We waited at the station hours for its arrival, and finally it arrived, not from the train as we expected, but from the cloak-room where it had spent the night!! There were some French troops there, and their band, and about six Belgian soldiers. We then had to march behind the French and the Belgians for about two miles to the Belgian HQ at the most impossible pace. Of course, the show meant that we had to carry swords, so we had to go round the country to beg, borrow or steal. I ended with an Artillery sword, which weighed about as much as their guns. At the Head Quarters we were all called up to the Belgian Colonel, to get, what we thought, at least the Leopold Order or a drink, but all he said was 'Thank you and your beautiful soldiers for what you have done'!! Last Monday we were again acting as a Guard of Honour, to a General who was leaving. One hardly expects to have to do these things out here.

28 October, letter to Mary:
I was warned that I would be going to the Entrenching Battalion, tomorrow, which I believe is the worst job out, mainly road mending. However, it's no use grousing before one gets there, and even if it's as bad as people make out, one must try and make the best of it. A Grenadier commands the 'Diggers'.

Entrenching Battalions, where officers typically would spend a short time before going to their units, were formed to relieve the frontline troops of digging reserve trench lines during their rest. They made emplacements for field guns, howitzers and machine guns and they repaired roads. It was punishing but valuable work and accustomed newcomers to the incessant shell-fire. It was an established custom in the Guards that officers should take off their coats and work with the men.

Esmond left on 29 October in charge of 253 men with the support of two more junior officers from the Coldstream Guards. They stopped at Romanes Camp, where soldiers were assigned destinations and duties and there Esmond had to make sure that his men were heading for the right places. Eventually, after two days of marching through heavy rain, getting soaked to the skin, they arrived at another camp just south of Fricourt, a "long way behind the line" as he reassured his mother.

> 1 November, diary, Camp near Albert:
> We had really rather a terrible journey from the Base. Self and two Coldstream officers, of whom I was the senior, in charge of 253 men. We paraded at 6 on Sunday evening in the most awful deluge, and marched to the station four or five miles away. We changed on Monday morning and marched to the nearest Rest Camp, still in pouring rain, and left again at 2pm, pretty thoroughly wet. We arrived here shortly after 8pm and Tuesday evening, after a six-mile march, in the muddiest of muddy roads.
>
> There are four other officers here, all of the Brigade, and very nice. Ellice commands, poor man, he lost his son a short time ago. We are about six miles at the nearest point from any excitement.

Marching through the town of Albert they had found it in a state of devastation; the golden Virgin on top of the Cathedral, which had been shelled in 1915, was still hanging precariously at right angles to the spire. Esmond commented on the rolling Picardy countryside: "It must have been once rather a lovely country, but it certainly cannot boast of that now."

He wrote to Mary, on 4 November, asking her to send some Keating's flea powder, as he had been "absolutely devoured. I suppose rats bring them, as I have an unlimited number in my tent." He also requested copies of *The Eton College Chronicle* which he was receiving in London, together with *The Times* complaining that only "rotten papers such as the *Daily Mail, Express* and *Mirror*" were available in the Camp. He had spent the whole day in the French area supervising fatigues and had heard a rumour from a French officer, which he didn't believe, that the Russians were prepared to sue for peace. The previous day, his men had worked mending roads alongside German prisoners of war "all as happy as the day was long." The rain had not stopped and the mud seemed to have got worse – horses had drowned in it.

The post was very irregular and on 7 November Esmond made sure to allow plenty of time for his birthday wishes to reach his mother:

> Very many happy returns of the day. I shall think of you so much on the 13th. I am afraid I have not even a tiny present to offer you. The last letter I got from you was October 28th. I have not heard for a fortnight. I suppose the posts are being held up somewhere. You cannot think how one longs for news out here. When one only grovels in the mud one only has those at home to think about and the most insignificant little happenings there are of the utmost interest to us here. A most

incessant downpour today and cold wind. Paraded at 7.30 a.m., out till 3.45 p.m., wet through. The wretched men had nothing to change into. I would give anything to be sent to the Battalion, as if I must mend and drain roads somewhere, I would far rather do it with them.

He liked his CO, Major Ellice, even though he seemed very absent-minded and impervious to the cold. Esmond stopped writing his diary whilst he was with the Diggers and any spare time at the end of these exhausting days was dedicated to letters.

13 November, letter to Mary:
Just in from road mending on the Citadel road. I then had my hair cut, a ceremony which rather resembled Bairnsfather's drawings. Before I knew where I was he had run the hogging machine up one side of my head, the thing once done I had to let him do the other side, and now it looks as if I have a cockatoo sticking up on top.[2]

15 November, letter to Mary, Camp near Albert:
Yesterday I spent the whole day at Mametz. Breakfasted at 5.30 am, left here at 6, and got back just before 4 p.m. There were no signs even of the remains of a house. All I could find in the village was a Machine Gun emplacement, absolutely as the Germans had left it and undestroyed; though our big guns had had direct hits on it, they had had no effect, as all its walls were about six or seven feet thick, made of cement.

   Living in tents one becomes rather like an animal, and one gets more hardened to the cold than I expected, though I must own my hands and feet are bad. I have a bath only once a week, and it is extraordinary how much more one feels the cold for two days after it.

   Ellice, or the 'Old Man' as we call him, is fairly in his element today. He loves discomfort, so is really happy with his teeth chattering and shivering all over. Yesterday he made me take my coat off, but of course after he left I put it on again. He has just come in, wearing his thinnest tunic on this, the coldest of winter days. Mud up to his thighs, icicles very thick on his moustache and tears streaming from his eyes.

Esmond was only just recovering from bronchitis which had developed from a chill caught whilst marching in his wet uniform between Harfleur and Fricourt. It was perishingly cold and he was getting very little sleep.

19 November, letter to Mary, Camp near Albert:
The last week has been colder than anything I have ever felt anywhere before. Getting up at 4.30 a.m. and being out till 4 p.m. and then, when one does get back, there are no prospects of getting warm. It doesn't matter how many clothes we put on – and most of us sleep with gloves on.

There has been no church again today: the Old Man has had no service since I have been here. I really believe the men rather mind.

The rats last night ate one of my shirts.

Yesterday I shared my luncheon with an Australian officer. He told me that the Australians over here voted to a man against conscription. He was in the 5th Australian Division, and said they were a most discontented lot. Many had left Australia in 1914, had been through, like himself, the whole of Gallipoli, and had been refused even eight days leave to England. He said that by far the majority of the Division had had no leave since enlisting two years ago."

20 November, letter to Mary:
On Monday I suddenly started the most awful headache, a thing I never had before, and on Wednesday my eyes got bad. I consequently went to the Medical Officer. Our own man, who is a rotter, was away on leave, which I thought must be an act of Providence, so I went to his substitute who comes here every night at 6 p.m. He gave me something to bathe my eyes with and three pills for the headache, which he made me take before him, with orders to take two more before going to bed. I heard him mutter something about Aspirin, which they were supposed to be. Luckily, I only took one more. From that moment, I was most frightfully ill. I went on Thursday evening and told the doctor he had made me worse. He gave me more medicine, and on Friday I felt worse than ever. I felt ghastly on Saturday, and with a herculean effort, got up for my fatigue at 4.45 in a blizzard, and got back at 5.30 feeling the most awful rag. He took my temperature which was 95.8. Sunday I had a slack day, and by the evening felt quite a different person. But I went to see the doctor in the evening. He greeted me with these words: 'I hope you have not taken any more of these white pills, as I find they are defective. I should never have believed it if some of the men had not been bad too.'

24 November, Camp near Albert, letter to Mary:
I hear that General Ponsonby has gone home for good, and that Evie Gibbs's brother now commands the 2nd Brigade.

There are many things I thought I might do, but I must own I never expected to be made responsible for mending a whole road. It is rather a farce, as I don't suppose anyone knows less about road mending than I do. But officers from the

Labour Battalion from neighbouring roads come and discuss with me the best way of laying a culvert which, till three days ago, I had never even heard of.

The road I work on has about as much traffic on it as Piccadilly in June, with an Oxford Circus at the end of it. I had the whole of one side up, ready to mend the holes with stones, when the Old Man (poor old devil, he is on the verge of a break-down: the death of his son is telling on him more every day) arrived and muddled everything and I had to lay the stones myself.

The traffic comes in terrific bursts for about 30 minutes, and then nothing for 10 minutes. So, with one side of the road up, I have to be a policeman and regulate the traffic. An Indian regiment came by. I stopped them to let some ambulances pass. But afterwards no sign I could make would induce them to move, so I shouted out "Qui hi" with tremendous success, which drew grins and salutes from all of them! I rather enjoyed holding up some Brigade 'Red Caps' who always think it is necessary to blow their horns.[3]

26 November, diary, Camp near Albert:
What a life! It has not stopped raining since 5 o'clock yesterday morning, with the consequence that, where we are not up to our knees in mud, we are up to our waists in water! Everyone came into the mess with the same question: 'Is it worth it?' the noise of the rain on the tent last night was extraordinary, and one kept waking and holding one's breath, wondering where it was going to come through. It came at 6 am, a most persistent drip on my head, which I could not dodge.

2 December, letter to Mary:
You have been so splendid in the way you have always sent everything out so quickly and the numbers of letters you have sent me. There are so few mails I generally get two or three letters together and would far rather you wrote fewer in your leisure than so many hurried ones between your meetings. These rigmaroles I send you are always so inexpressibly dull and absolutely devoid of news. In future I am going to write only once a week. With the exception of two days off, the whole week has been spent on the usual fatigues and I have now reached that state of decay when I have actually quite enjoyed life, though one thinks of practically nothing but food and drink.

I have made tremendous friends with the Australians. I have never seen any of their officers, only the NCOs and men. Whenever they see me on the road they always get a fire ready in their tiny hut for me to cook my turtle soup tablet, which is extraordinarily nice of them. Individually no one could be nicer, and I tell them they are collectively perfectly unbearable! They love to find someone who will listen to their yarns and I seem to know backwards Perth, Adelaide and Melbourne. They are splendid men if treated properly; of course, absolutely ignorant of the meaning of the word discipline.

One of them went on leave the other day. He had never been in England before and insisted on getting a ticket to Dundee. We could not find out why he had selected Dundee. After he left one of his friends told us the reason was that Dundee was the farthest point they would issue a warrant to, and that he was going to work his way south at the expense of the Government!

Latterly we have generally gone to the hut of a Royal Engineers officer, by name Sandiman, for lunch. We have used his hut practically as our own, but have fed him in return. The prize meal was last week when Jack Buchanan, Pixley and Eastwood were up there – turtle soup, Dutch paté de fois gras and paté of pheasant; strawberries and cream; chocolate, and biscuits and wine. In spite of the dullness of the work, we four have had great fun up here; all of them with an intense sense of humour. The Grenadiers have made just the whole difference to life here. I like all of them enormously.

Mary had sent Esmond a food hamper which included the strawberries and cream for his feast. He requested that she sent him a pocket diary: "One quite small, with the dates and days printed, just to make a note of the amusing incidents which are always happening even out here." His watch was stopping, probably on account of the cold, so he asked her if she could get his gold wrist watch at home repaired and sent over to France.

He sent her two parcels: one with his battered and mud-spattered tunic; and one with a souvenir from Mametz Cemetery, a broken metal figure of Christ, found while looking for spare stones for the road.

An enjoyable day's leave in Amiens came just before Esmond heard he was to join his Battalion; he then resumed his diary.

10 December, diary:
Went into Amiens yesterday with Eastwood; it took us three hours, getting lifts on four lorries and one car. Lunched at the Hotel du Rhin, where we met de la Chesnaye with a lady other than his wife! We were led to a table where were seated a French officer and a lady. We naturally assumed they were together, but they proved not to be. Eventually we were left alone with the lady. And naturally we entered into conversation with her, which was the cause of much laughter after-wards. We were told we must be waited on by a fairy called Yvonne. She, unfortu-nately, was not there, but Josephine, a vision in blue, came to the rescue.

We then went on to the Rumplemayer of Amiens, where we were fortunate enough to secure the services of Georgette as waitress, garbed in grey with silk stockings. Amiens seems to be over-flowing with lovely ladies. We had the best day I have spent out here and got very hearty and a little tight![4]

We had to rush back at 5 p.m., as we were anxious as to how we should get home. We got lifts in two cars and three lorries. We passed lots of prisoners working on the roads. I was struck by the discipline of the Hun. It's apparently not the custom of the German private soldier to salute officers, but only for NCOs to do so. We were riding for some time in a coal lorry, and it would have been quite easy for them not to have seen us. But we never passed one single batch of prisoners without the NCO coming to attention and saluting.

We got back in just over three hours, to find that I was under orders at last to leave the Entrenching Battalion and go to the 2nd Battalion, which meant more champagne and merriment.

Esmond was on a 'high'; forgetting the exertions of the previous six weeks, he expressed excitement in a letter to his mother:

9 December, Camp near Albert, letter to Mary:
I am lucky to be going, as I have been here six weeks which, in spite of the dullness of the work, has been great fun. No one has got more enjoyment out of life with so little material provided for amusement here than I have. What fun one does have in the world!

I don't know where the Battalion is but, as the Division is in the line, I suppose we shall be going into the trenches sooner or later. I do ask you not to worry about me – it makes it so hard for us out here if we feel that those whom we love are worrying about us, and I do love the whole family so very much. I do hope I shall do all right and prove myself worthy of the affection of one of the happiest families in the world. Anyway, I will do my best.

What a privilege it is to be able to come out at last and take one's share, infinitesimally small though it may be, in this tremendous struggle. I go at a very lucky time when the country is being organised by a man who is a patriot at heart, so it makes it far easier when one knows that back home all that can be done to ensure victory is being done.[5]

Please do not worry about me I am more than a fatalist than ever, and everything is always done for the best, though we may not understand at the time the reason why certain things happen. It is so hard to write, the room crammed full of fellows, and the gramophone playing rag-time. But I thought I would just send you this line before leaving here to try and tell you how much I love you all.

12 December, diary:
My luggage went this morning; it looked an enormous amount, but I don't see what I could do without. The pack and revolver take up so much room; I hope it will pass the Regimental authorities. I think my new servant, Milne is going to be a success."

The night before, he wrote a letter to his Aunt, Louisa Antrim, enclosing a message for his mother, his 'Last Letter' to be opened in the event of his death. He asked her to keep it safe and not to tell anyone about it. In Louisa's reply to this letter, she promised that it would remain their secret and that she was glad that he trusted her with such a message. Furthermore, she was praying most earnestly that God would watch over him and protect him and enable her to return it to him at the end of the war.

Dramatis Personae

Antrim, The Countess of Louisa. 1855-1949. Lady Minto's elder sister. Lady in Waiting to Queen Victoria and Queen Alexandra. She married the eccentric Earl of Antrim, known as *The Buzzard*.

Blackwood, 2nd. Lt. the Lord Basil. 1870-1917. KIA on a night raid across the Yser Canal 4 July 1917. Harrow/Oxford/Grenadier Guards. Illustrated many of Hilaire Belloc's books. Joined up aged 44 readily serving under men half his age.

Boyd-Rochfort, Major Cecil. 1887-1983. Eton/Scots Guards. Croix de Guerre/Wounded five times. Later Sir Cecil, CVO. Flat racing Champion Trainer five times. Trained for George VI and then the Queen. Won many Classics including the Epsom Derby.

Buchanan, Lt. John *'Jack'*. 1887-1969. Charterhouse/Grenadier Guards/DSO/MC. 1st class cricketer.

Craigie, Captain John. MC. 1890-1975. Eton/Grenadier Guards. Wounded four times. Mentioned in Despatches.

Eastwood, 2nd Lt. John. 1887-1952. Eton/Grenadier Guards. OBE. Later MP for Kettering. Lost two brothers in the War.

Ellice, Major, Edward, *'Kerby'*. Grenadier Guards/DSO. Competent amateur water-colour painter. Commanded Entrenching Battalion. Kindly but with a reputation for organising useless fatigues. His son 2nd Lt. AR Ellice, Grenadier Guards KIA 29 September 1916. Carroll Carstairs described Ellice in his book *A Generation Missing*, a personal tribute to the Grenadier Guards, published in 1930: "He was the perfect Foot Guards officer, with that sublime ability to exercise authority and inspire obedience by day, combined with a supreme capacity to unbend when off duty. He made himself one of us and joined in our jokes and laughter and lingered with us, listening to our songs. He was a child at heart and so could look upon us as children, whose time for playing was short, and the death of his only son had sweetened, not embittered him."

Ipswich, Lt. Viscount WHA. Harrow/Cambridge/Coldstream Guards/RAF. 1884 – Killed in a flying accident 23 April 1918.

Mahomed, Lt. Claude *'The Prophet'*. Scots Guards. KIA 31 July 1917 Pilckem.

Lethbridge, Captain Sir Wroth Bt. 1863-1950. Eton/Grenadier Guards.

Milne, Private William. Scots Guards. Esmond's batman. That Esmond's notebooks survived is thanks to Milne. KIA 29 July 1918.

Penn, Captain Arthur. MC. 1886-1960. Eton/Cambridge/Grenadier Guards. Wounded. Croix de Guerre. Mentioned in Despatches. Best Man at marriage of Harold Macmillan to Lady Dorothy Cavendish in 1920. Later Sir Arthur Penn GCVO. Private Secretary to Queen Mother as Queen & Treasurer to the present Queen.

Pixley, Captain Jack. Eton/Grenadier Guards. Sister Olive wrote a book about contacting him in after-life. 1888 – KIA 12 October 1917 Houthulst Forest.

Royds, Major Albert *'Jumbo'*, OBE. 1876-1952. Eton/Scots Guards. Mentioned in Despatches twice. Commanded the Guards Divisional Base Depot at Harfleur.

Vivian, Lord George. 1878-1940. Eton/17th Lancers. Boer War. DSO, TD, Mentioned in Despatches twice. ADC to King of the Belgians in the War. George Vivian's sister, Dorothy, married Douglas Haig.

8

Platoon Commander

He learned that it was no fool's or sluggard's paradise into which he had wandered by chance, but a battlefield ordained from of old, where there are no spectators…and the stakes are life and death.

Thomas Hughes, *Tom Brown at Oxford*

13 December 1916, diary, Maltzhorn Farm:

Buchanan, Curwen and I picked up an ambulance at Fricourt which took us to Trones Wood, dropping Buchanan at Mametz Siding. Inside was an Indian Medical Warrant Officer getting a lift too. I of course spoke to him and told him I had been in India. He then burdened me with questions, so I had to tell him my father was Viceroy. He at once jumped up from the seat and placed himself opposite to me and treated me with the most astonishing respect.

I reported at 11.30 a.m. to the Battalion at Maltzhorn Farm. They had just come in from the trenches and everyone was very "beat", most of them still in bed, after a terrible time in the mud. I am posted to G Company, Knollys is my Company Commander, he seems very nice. Victor Perowne, who was at Wellington Barracks with me, and who I knew at Eton, is also in the Company. We mess with Left Flank consisting of Ally Boyd, Gilpin and Priaulx.

All the officers, with the exception of the CO, 2i/c and Adjutant, are in one hut together, between 16 and 17 in all, rather like a dormitory at one's private school! One half of the hut is divided off for meals, where there are two tables for the four Companies, so there is not much room, but I don't think it will be too uncomfortable.

Esmond joined the 2nd Battalion Scots Guards and was given his own Platoon, No 12, G Company. He wrote to his mother saying how happy he was and asking her to send him a small writing pad which he could carry into the trenches in his pocket.

14 December, diary, Maltzhorn Farm to Bronfay by Trones Wood:
We left Maltzhorn this morning entraining at Trones Wood for Bronfay Farm. Frankie Lloyd and Archie Douglas, who are out here, accompanied by Geoffrey Feilding came to see us off.

Frankie Lloyd described the rest camp at Maltzhorn as: "a miserable place, built on nothing but mud… the desolation of the whole country is as I have never seen. There is nothing but absolute mud, so deep that you cannot walk about – the only way being over duck-boards, of which they have many thousands. No buildings to be seen; trees all cut down by shells; no woods, no houses, no villages, no anything. The site of Guillemont is merely a site, nothing there at all".

15 December, diary, Bronfay:
Last night we had a Sing-Song, the HQ coming to dine with us.
    I saw Arthur Penn on Tuesday; he said the mud was perfectly appalling, and that it had taken 48 hours to dig some men out.

16 December, diary, Bronfay to Maltzhorn Farm
Left Bronfay at 10.30 by Companies to march to Maltzhorn Farm. Putrid weather and snow falling. Reached Maltzhorn between 12 and 1.
    The 1st Battalion went to Bronfay today. They have had a bad three days in the line; 31 cases of Trench Feet, 25 of which were stretcher cases. One man died in the night of exposure.

17 December, diary, Maltzhorn Farm
I share a partition of the hut with Knollys. We go into the line tomorrow for two days. Very strict orders have been issued as regards the Bosche trying to fraternise with us at Christmas. The CO tells us that they have tried already to be friendly with the 4th Division, commanded by Billy Lambton. Our orders are to shoot any Bosche who may try to come over, which I think is ridiculous. They come over unarmed. Why not take them prisoners?

18 December, diary, into the line by Guillemont and Combles:
Paraded at Maltzhorn at 2.30 and marched up into the line. We got up to Company HQ about 6.30 p.m. Edmunds went straight into the frontline, and I stayed at Company HQ with Knollys. We relieved the Welsh Guards, and the relief was completed by 7.30.
    After dinner went up to the frontline with Knollys; the communication trenches absolutely impassable from all the rain! All movements, including

reliefs, could only be done at night over the top. The weather was fine and freezing. The trenches were in better condition than expected, but there was in them still a great deal of mud. I was wearing gum boots, and very early in the evening got stuck in the mud. A Corporal tried to pull me out, but without success, with the result that I had to leave the boots there! I had to walk all down the trenches with no boots. I luckily brought a spare pair of boots with me so, on getting back to the Dug-out, put them on again as Knollys thought I should get trench feet. We then went back to Company HQ till Tuesday (19th) at dusk when I relieved Edmunds. It is an extraordinary life this – living just like a rabbit in a deep burrow.

19 December, diary, in the line:
Two men killed in the morning from shell fire. Our own artillery very active, some of our shells falling very short between our wire and the trench. The trenches dried up remarkably well, and now one can get along the whole of the Company front without going along on top, though in places it is still very muddy.

We are not connected on our right, nor on our left. About 100 yards distant in the first case and 30 yards in the second. So communication has to be kept up at night over the top.

The Bosche use a great number of star shells, as snipers are most active. Their line is about 400 yards away, but between us and Left Flank they have a sap about 60 yards distant where they have a sniper.

The Dug-out in the frontline is about 8 feet by 4 feet. I had, besides myself, two signallers and the telephone.

The Division is holding a front of about 400 yards from Sailly-Saillisel in the direction of Morval-Les Boeufs. It is hilly country, and from our trenches we looked right on to the Transloy Road.

There were several Hun aeroplanes flying very low up and down our line, and at the same time a Squadron of 16 of ours who took absolutely no notice of the Hun planes.

Esmond received his weekly bulletin from Mr Macnaghten, including the note: "I hear of you as the 'most cheerful person in the Regiment' which I don't doubt. I know you always wanted to fight, 'just to see if you would be frightened'. I am very sure you love it." Each week, throughout the war, Macnaghten sent letters to his old boys at the front giving news of the House and School and enclosing copies of the *Chronicle*. He would enlist the help of twenty junior pupils to produce these round robins, dictated by him and topped and tailed with a short message that would be personal to each recipient.[1] Edward Lyttelton's replacement as Head Master at

Eton, Cyril Alington, had penned the evocative poem, *School at War*, whilst still at Shrewsbury. It summed up the feelings of boys for their older friends at the front:

We don't forget – while in this dark December
We sit in schoolrooms that you know so well,
And hear the sounds that you so well remember,
The clock, the hurrying feet, the Chapel bell;
Others are sitting in the seats you sat in,
There's nothing else seems altered here – and yet
Through all of it, the same old Greek and Latin,
Be sure we don't forget.

20 December – in the line:
We were relieved at 6.30 p.m. by the 1st Battalion, Henry Dundas in charge of the two platoons that relieved me. I think him very reckless, both as regards himself and his men. And I cannot think why the Hun does not more often discover when our reliefs are on, since everything is done over the top. Just as we were leaving, after the relief was complete, they did start shelling, and I think they had smelt a rat that something was on.

At Combles a soup kitchen has been opened, which makes just the whole difference to the men. Combles, unlike Guillemont, has some semblance of once having been a village. You could go through Guillemont, and most of the other villages, without knowing there was ever a house in them. We marched from Combles – the men wonderfully cheerful – to Trones Wood Station, where there was more soup. The men were entrained here in a few trucks, and we officers in one of those covered-in wagons which one sees all over France marked *Hommes 40; Chevaux (en long) 8*. The officers of the 2nd Coldstream were also there, so we were very crowded.

21 December, diary, Bronfay:
We were entrained at 10 p.m. but, owing to bad arrangements, they kept us at the station for two hours, and we could have marched it in less. The train left till half after midnight and we got to Bronfay about 2 a.m. on Thursday 21st.

The Gilded Staff, who I am beginning to loathe, are odd people. We don't stay at one camp more than a single night before we go back to the line again. There is nothing so tiring for the men as to pack up each morning and march to a different camp. For the men it means hardly any rest on going out of the trenches. For us officers it is different, for we have our servants.

Before going to the line I rub my feet with whale oil. It is wonderful stuff to keep the circulation going. The only disadvantage is it rather stinks putting it on.

22 December, diary, Bronfay to Maltzhorn Farm:
Left Bronfay at 2.30 p.m. for Maltzhorn Farm, where we spent the night.

23 December, diary, Bronfay:
A tremendous amount of rain has fallen and we all rather dread the condition in which we must find the line tomorrow; something appalling I suppose!

The Battalion left Maltzhorn at 2 p.m. for Haie Wood, Bouleaux Wood and Combles where they are stopping the night before going into the line tomorrow.

Knollys thought that Perowne and I had better relieve each other in the front-line at half time. So I went back to the waggon lines at Bronfay and return to the frontline on Christmas night to relieve Perowne. Only Gilpin is here at Bronfay. Francis Ward, Ivan Cobbold and Powell came in to dinner. Fuzzie Baillie arrived half way through dinner from a dull instruction course. We had a very amusing evening with plenty of champagne. We have, I think, a most awfully happy lot of fellows and I am in a very nice half of the Battalion.

25 December, diary, into the Line:
In the afternoon rode to Haie Wood and walked on from there to relieve Perowne in the frontline. I met Perowne at Battalion HQ and he left early as he was feeling unwell. Had dinner at Company HQ and went on up to the frontline afterwards. We had a party out wiring whom I went out to see; the rest were occupied in the trench.

British and German troops had fraternized freely with the enemy on the first and, to a lesser extent, the second Christmas Day of the war. This year, there were no demonstrations of friendliness on either side.

After weeks of heavy rain, turning to sleet and snow in early December, Christmas 1916 was unusually warm. A biting wind, which had blown for days on end, finally abated and, in the sunshine, it felt like Spring. Shell-craters, previously filled with thick, icy mud rendered the landscape "comic in its extravaganza of quagmire", as described by *The Telegraph* correspondent Philip Gibbs. Lorries carrying extra Christmas rations in long supply columns, drenched soldiers and civilians alike in foul smelling water.

Esmond received a number of presents, a Christmas box from Minto village containing cake and shortbread, four cooked pheasants (after he had hinted that they might be quite welcome) and, by far the most appreciated, a rabbit-fur lining for his coat from Ruby. He arranged for his batman, Milne, to be sent a woollen waistcoat and some gloves. Mary sent Esmond a dark blue pocket notebook and a canvas diary, together with some Hardtmuth soft leaded pencils.

26 December, diary, in the line:

The Corps had arranged for the "Heavies" to have a shoot today. This necessitated our re-arranging the distribution of our men. Ally Boyd evacuated his line except for the strong points and brought his men over to us, and we sent a platoon to F Company to make room. This was done as a precaution as our artillery invariably shell our own lines! Ally Boyd then took charge of the frontline, and at 6.30 a.m. I returned to Company HQ.

Our bombardment started at 12 noon and lasted till 4 p.m. The Huns retaliated a bit, more on our support line than anywhere else, and we had 3 killed and 1 wounded here. One shell blowing in the funk hole next to our Dug-out, missing it by about 6 feet. It of course put out all our candles and covered us with muck.

At dusk the Left Flank Company went back to its own line and we held our section the same as before.

One Hun came in and surrendered himself to Right Flank.

The mud was very bad.

27 December, diary, Bronfay:

At midnight, we were relieved by the 1st Battalion, Ivan Cobbold in charge of the two platoons. Then a long march to Trones Wood via Combles, which we reached at 4 a.m.

I have never been so dirty in my life, mud everywhere, even in one's hair. My coat was so heavy with all the mud on it that I had to throw it on a limber at Haie Wood. The train did not leave Trones Wood till about 5.30 and we arrived at Bronfay Camp around 6 a.m.[2]

Breakfasted and to bed at 7.15 a.m. The men were all pretty beat. Got up at 1.30 p.m.

The men had their Christmas dinner tonight. Not much to show for it; plum pudding, pineapples, whiskey and rum besides their ordinary rations. We had a Battalion officer's dinner and the usual Sing-Song afterwards.

28 December, diary, Bouleaux Wood:

Left Bronfay about 5 p.m. for Bouleaux Wood, which we reached about 10 p.m. After Leuze Wood we had to go across country through the most awful mud. Company HQ are about 1½ miles away, and Borrett and I have to go over there for all meals. We got back from dinner about 1 a.m.

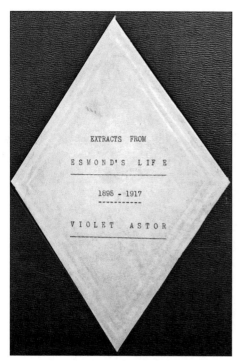

Violet's copy of
'Extracts from Esmond's Life'.

Mary Minto and her grandson Gavin Astor.

Violet Astor.

John Astor.

Esmond aged two.

Admiral of the Fleet the Hon Sir Charles
Elliot, founder of Hong Kong.

Minto House.

Esmond on stage in Ottawa wearing his father's medals and feathered hat.

The 'Family of Bears', Violet, Larry, Ruby and Eileen with Esmond in front, Ottawa, February 1899.

A Canadian $4 bill bearing the picture of Lord and Lady Minto.

HMS *Crescent* anchored in the St Lawrence, September 1899.

Ruby, Larry, Violet, Esmond and Eileen. On board HMS *Crescent*, Quebec.

Esmond escaping to join the sailors on parade and being retrieved by the ADCs. Quebec 1899.

The 'Commodore'. Esmond on boat, Charlotte Sound, Vancouver, July 1900.

The Viceroy – The 4th Earl of Minto by
Philip de Lazlo.

The Vicereine.

The Viceroy with the Viceroy's Bodyguard.

Viceroy's Procession.

The Household at Government House, Calcutta.

Government House, Calcutta.

State Procession with the Viceroy and Vicereine.

Lady Minto joins Esmond on an elephant.

Esmond in a carriage with his mother, November 1906.

Esmond arrives at Bhatinda and is met
by Violet, November 1906.

Lord Kitchener with the Amir of Afghanistan,
January 1907.

The Amir of Afghanistan with Lady Minto.

The Amir playing croquet.

Group photograph with the Duke of Connaught (son of Queen Victoria), March 1907.
Esmond sitting next to his mother, Major Feilding in back row far right.

Lord and Lady Minto with the Begum of Bhopal, her daughter-in-law and her grandsons.
The Begum kissed Esmond through her veil.

Esmond riding Creepy and Violet riding Crawly at Barrackpore.

Esmond at Henley, 1911. Eton won the Ladies Plate in record time.

Esmond shaking hands with the
King at Henley, 1911.

Esmond as a Page at the Coronation of
King George V, 1911.

Esmond as cox of the *Britannia*, 1911.

Esmond with Mr Macnaghten, 1913.

Esmond coxing the 10-oar
Monarch, 1913.

Esmond in 'Pop',
1913.

Esmond and his troop at Haddington.

Esmond leading his troop.

Esmond with Helen
Maxwell, Hedderwick,
July 1916.

At The Haining.

Chateau Esquelbecq.

The Prince of Wales with Lord Claudie Hamilton. (Archives Grenadier Guards)

FM Sir Douglas Haig with his ADC, Major Thompson and 17th Lancers escort with Nova Scotia Highlanders.

Esmond photographed by
Bassano, 7 October 1916.

The Church at Albert. Esmond marched past on 31 October 1916.

Nissan huts at Bronfay Farm, December 1916.
(Courtesy of the Regimental Trustees Scots Guards)

Mud on the Somme, December 1916. (Courtesy of the Regimental Trustees Scots Guards)

The main street of Combles. Esmond marched through these destroyed villages on
18 and 19 December 1916.

The main street of Guillemont.

Scots Guards soldier wading through the Somme mud, December 1916.
(Courtesy of the Regimental Trustees Scots Guards)

Victor Perowne and Esmond, 'The Long and the Short', outside Maltzhorn Farm
before going into the line, 23 December 1916.

Ferryman, Victor Harbord, Pretyman, Priaulx.

Full strength of officers at Billon Camp. Esmond is third from the left, smiling at the camera.
Note the Irish Terrier in front to his left.

Scots Guards near Billon Camp.

Cathédrale d'AMIENS
Les Stalles protégées par des sacs à terre

Amiens Cathedral. Visited by Esmond 28 February 1917.
Note the sand bag protection that Esmond mentioned.

Pretyman and Esmond
at Ville sous Corbie,
near Amiens,
February 1917.

2nd Bn, Scots
Guards laying
sleepers on
Péronne-Roisel
railway line,
25 March 1917.
(Courtesy of
the Regimental
Trustees Scots
Guards)

2nd Battalion
building the
Adjutant's
hut. Cartigny,
April 1917.
(Courtesy of
the Regimental
Trustees Scots
Guards)

Ally Boyd and Joseph Chamberlayne on Péronne Road, 1 April 1917.

Ross photographing rugger team, 24 April 1917.

Milne and Pretyman, 24 April 1917.

Esmond's platoon, No 12, awaiting foot inspection, May 1917.

Michael, 2nd Battalion's car. (Courtesy of the Regimental Trustees Scots Guards)

Sergeants Agres and Lindores (on right). Lindores carried Esmond's body after he was hit. He wrote: "We have lost our idol…" in his letter to Mary.

Sergeant Lindores, Esmond's Platoon Sergeant (in middle).

Ferryman, Chamberlayne, Milne and the Doctor.

Priaulx with the barber.

Priaulx in his bath.　　　　　　Jessie, Major Stirling's dog.

Esmond and officers in front of mess tent. Lts Perowne, Knollys, Priaulx, Gilpin, Esmond, (in shirt sleeves) Milne and Pretyman, Cartigny. (Courtesy of the Regimental Trustees Scots Guards)

The Adjutant,
Captain Tommy
MacDougal,
Cartigny.
(Courtesy of
the Regimental
Trustees Scots
Guards)

Mess dog at
Cartigny. Kit
Cator and Billy
Wynne Finch.

Mess dog at
Cartigny.

Esmond's Company
Commander, Knollys
(on right) and senior
NCOs.

Pretyman,
Peter Gilpin
and Tommy
MacDougal.

Officer's kits.

Esmond's tent
struck.

G Company
lines.

Esmond's
kit packed.

Bella and Bertha with Chamberlayne, Perowne and Private John Slidders 'Sludders'.

G Company marching off from Cartigny to Nurlu, 2 May 1917.

Arriving at Nurlu Camp.

Officers resting.

Scots Guards making the aerodrome at Nurlu.

RE 8 reconnaissance aircraft being serviced.

Esmond going on patrol with Warburton.

Tug of War.

Watching sports, 13 May 1917. Note officer nearest to camera wearing a private purchase Havelock attachment on his Service Dress cap for sun and fly protection.

General Feilding
with other Generals
gathering for
the sports day,
May 1917.

Doctors and nurses and in front
Milne and Priaulx.

Esmond at Hever
Castle, during his last
leave, 20 May 1917.

Esmond with Violet in her car, outside 95 Lancaster Gate, with Larry standing beside them. The next morning Violet drove him to the station for the last time, 27 May 1917.

The family with whom Esmond was billeted at Brandinghen, June 1917.

Outside mess in Cherry Orchard, Woesten, 25 June 1917.

Victor Perowne and his father. "I don't know when I have been so struck by anyone as I was by Victor's friend Elliot." (Perowne's father who met Esmond once.)

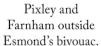

Pixley and Farnham outside Esmond's bivouac.

Pixley and Cecil Keith, Esmond (with binoculars) and Milne.

Yser Canal. Esmond's raid on 24 July meant crossing this canal.
(Courtesy of the Regimental Trustees Scots Guards)

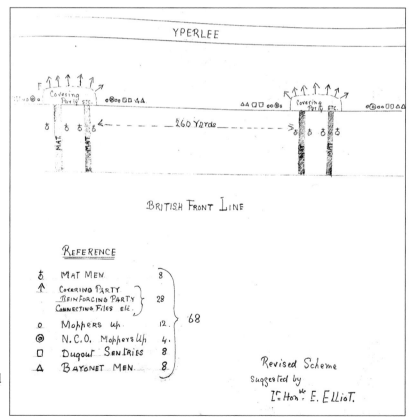

Esmond's revised scheme for the raid.

Malcolm, Esmond and Milne. Coppernollehoek Woods, 28 July 1917.

'Stuck fast in the Mud' by Captain Alexander Jamieson, depicting the plight of a soldier in the 10th Battalion York and Lancaster Regt, who was stuck in a flooded shell hole. It took four nights to get him free, his comrade standing by him, day and night under fire, feeding him by means of a long stick. They both survived.

Lieutenant Colonel Orr Ewing and orderlies back from visiting the line after Battle of Pilckem Ridge. (Courtesy of the Regimental Trustees Scots Guards)

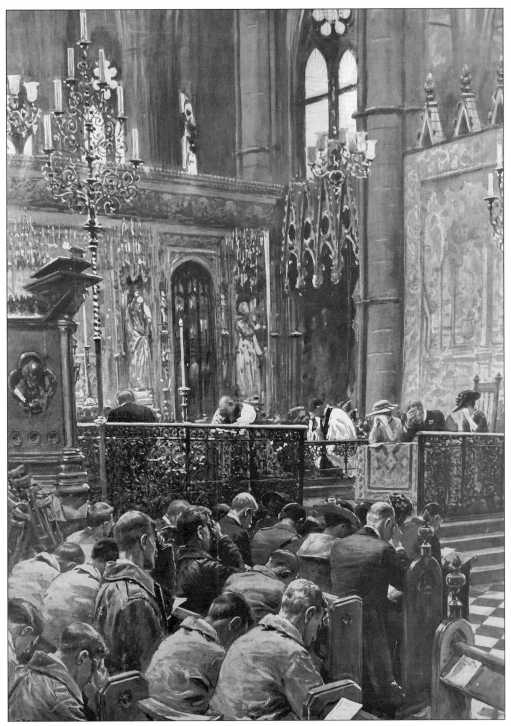

Westminster Abbey. Mary sat next to the King, 5 August 1917.

Field Marshal Lord Plumer addressing Eton boys in School Yard, 20 May 1919.
(Courtesy of Eton College)

Old Etonian Generals visit Eton, 20 May 1919. Among them, and featuring in Esmond's
diaries, were Generals Sir John Ponsonby, Sir Cecil Romer, Sir William Pulteney, Sir William
Lambton, Sir Henry Rawlinson, FM Lord Cavan and FM Lord Plumer. Lord Plumer sits on
the right hand of the Head Master, Cyril Alington. (Courtesy of Eton College)

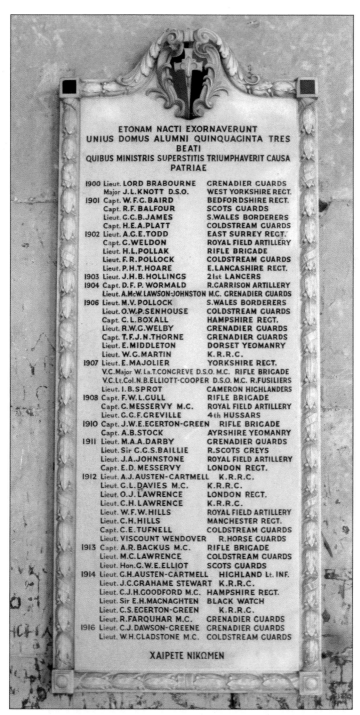

Macnaghten's House War Memorial, Eton. The Greek inscription at the bottom, 'Hail we are Victorious', became the House 'motto'. (Courtesy of Eton College)

Minto War
Memorial face
modelled on
Esmond.

Unveiling of Minto
War Memorial
by FM Earl Haig
(saluting), 18
September 1921.

Mary by Esmond's grave, 12 May 1922. The wooden cross that marked Esmond's grave now hangs on the wall by the family pew in Minto Church.

Mary in front of the blockhouse from where Esmond was commanding his Company when he was killed, 20 May 1925.

Esmond was commanding his Company from the blockhouse on the right.

The Padre, Macrae,
who officiated at
Esmond's funeral.

Mary in front of
Esmond's grave with
the new IGWC
headstone, 1925.

Mary with Violet,
9 June 1932

Mary (on right), with the Queen and Princess Mary on board HMY *Victoria and Albert*,
10 July 1920. (Courtesy of the Royal Archives)

Mary with the King and Queen in a war cemetery in Italy, 13 May 1923.
(Courtesy of the Royal Archives)

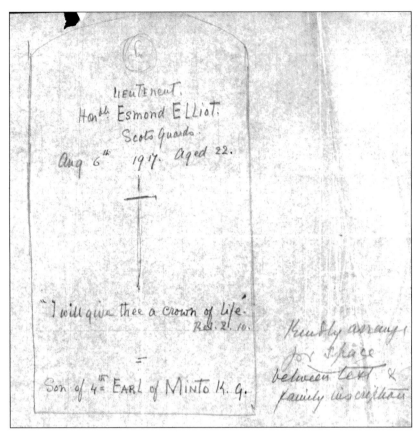

Mary Minto's design for the Imperial
War Graves Commission headstone.
(CWGC)

Painting of Esmond by
W. Wirgman. Presented to Hawick
Cottage Hospital by his mother,
25 April 1931. The painting was
destroyed in a fire.

ITINERARY FOR THE VISIT OF THE DOWAGER COUNTESS OF MINTO

AND LADY VIOLET ASTOR.

THURSDAY
16th. June,
1936.

11.00 a.m. Leave LONDON.

2.10 p.m. Arrive CALAIS

3.36 p.m. Arrive HAZEBROUCK, and met by Commission Car.

via STEENVOORDE

FRONTIER - STEENVOORDE-ABEELE

Abeele Aerodrome Military Cemetery
4.15 p.m. Lijssenthoek Military Cemetery (VISIT)

POPERINGHE
PROVEN

VISIT Grave of Lieut. the Hon. Esmond ELLIOT,
2nd. Bn. Scots Guards, III. D. 2
MENDINGHEM BRITISH CEMETERY

5.15 p.m. POPERINGHE - Tea at Skindles Hotel

Red Farm Cemetery
Hop Store Cemetery

VLAMERTINGHE

YPRES

9.00 p.m. Ceremony of Sounding "Last Post" at Menin Gate
Memorial.

Sleep Hotel Skindles, Ypres

FRIDAY
17th. June,
1936

9.30 a.m. Leave YPRES via Menin Gate Memorial

Potijze Chateau Cemeteries
Aeroplane Cemetery
French Military Cemetery of Saint Charles.

ZONNEBEKE

Tyne Cot Cemetery and Memorial to the Missing

New Zealand Memorial, Gravenstafel.
Canadian Memorial, St. Julien
Cement House Cemetery, Langemarck
Artillery Wood Cemetery, Boesinghe
Bard Cottage Cemetery
Essex Farm Cemetery
Duhallow A.D.S. Cemetery

12.00 Noon LUNCH - Hotel Skindles, Ypres

1.30 p.m. Leave Ypres

POPERINGHE
CASSEL
ST. OMER

CALAIS

3.40 p.m. Boat leaves for Dover

6.55 p.m. Arrive London (Victoria)

Itinerary of
Mary and Violet,
July 1936.
(Courtesy of the
Commonwealth
War Graves
Commission)

'Can you identify this soldier?' From the *Border Telegraph*, 13 Aug 1974. The sculptor, Thomas Clapperton's daughter recognised the bust and helped Robert Rider to identify Esmond.

Can you identify this soldier?

Lord Astor laying a wreath by Esmond's grave when a Defence Minister, 2014.
(Photo: Glyn Prysor, CWGC)

29 December, diary, Bouleaux Wood:

At 3 a.m. I got orders to go on fatigue at 6 a.m. It was pouring and we waded through the mud to Haie Wood where we had to carry trench boards. Got back again about 9.30 a.m.

We really are in the most extraordinary place. Borrett and I are in the same Dug-out as No 12 Platoon with a blanket to separate us. And in our little partition we had our two servants. The smell in there is awful!

Bouleaux Wood is one of the few woods out here that shows signs of once having been a wood. All the ground is riddled with shell holes. A hundred yards away a wrecked Tank and an unburied corpse. I have never seen so many guns in such a small area; along one sunken road they are as close as possible, and two deep.

30 December, diary, into the line:

Went into the line this evening, relieved the Welsh. Arthur Gibbs in frontline. The thing that surprised me most was relieving them over the top of the trench, particularly as the Huns could not be accused of being too friendly and there was always a certain amount of shelling. It was bright moonlight and, in addition to the hundreds of star shells the Hun is always sending up, it seemed impossible that we should be able to get in without being seen. Whenever a Star shell goes up the chief thing is to keep still. But the whole country seems to be alive with men crouching when the flares go up, so that I cannot imagine why we are not seen more often. I believe that, unless they get you absolutely in the right angle and if you keep perfectly still, provided you are over 200 yards away, it is difficult to see a man.

Trenches in a disgraceful condition because the people before us had done no work. Water up to the men's knees; my Dug-out with 1½ feet of water in what is supposed to be the officer's Dug-out.

31 December, diary, in the line:

The men worked very hard all night and we managed to get the trench boards down and a certain amount of mud and water out. Our artillery had a shoot, which drew some retaliation.

The Bosche line in front of the Company is about 500 yards away with a sap from which the lights are sent up about 150-200 yards. The Huns send up so many flares that we usually put up only a few lights during the night.

1 January 1917, diary, in the line:

Except for a short but sharp outburst of artillery on both sides, no incident happened at midnight. The Hun's artillery started at 11 p.m., their time being one hour ahead of us. They sent a few whiz-bangs over today but we had no casualties.

At 6.30 p.m. we were relieved by the 1st Battalion, Ellis relieving me. My cape was caked with mud and was too heavy to carry out so I left it in the trench. Got to Trones Wood at 10 p.m., but the train didn't leave till 12.30. Officers and men all in open trucks, and it was pretty cold.

2 January, diary, Bronfay Farm:
Into Bronfay Farm about 1.30 a.m. Up at 6 a.m. on fatigue, carrying what becomes the necessities of life in the trenches. The other two Subalterns in the Company have gone sick. There is no chance of my doing the same. For, much as I loathe the trenches, I find that they agree with me! For, each time, I have gone in with a streaming cold and have come out cured

3 January, diary, Mesicourt:
Left Bronfay at 9.30 a.m. and marched to Mesicourt L'Abbe, which we reached about 2 p.m. Rumour that we are to go back immediately to the line.

We are in billets in farm houses; Priaulx, Pretyman, Borrett and self in one small room. Our mess is a nice room, unfortunately about a quarter of a mile away.

4 January, diary, Mesicourt:
Cleaning up trying to get some of the mud and dirt off our clothes; men had baths & I had one in my billet. The waistcoat for my servant arrived yesterday; he is very pleased with it.

5 January, diary, Mesicourt:
Inspection of Company by the CO. Knollys left last night for England, his sister being seriously ill. Pretyman has come from the Left Flank to command us (G Company).

The Parson, Rev. Alexander Macrae, arrived from England. Dined at Battalion HQ with the CO and Jack Stirling.

Jack Stirling was often accompanied by his terrier, Jessie. Most battalions in the line would have trench dogs as companions, mostly abandoned by their fleeing French or Belgian civilian owners. Apart from keeping the men's spirits up, they were useful for catching rats in the trenches. After the war, many officers, including John Astor, brought their dogs back with them. The following poem appeared in *Punch* in December 1918:[3]

Elegy on the Death of Bingo Our Trench Dog

Weep, weep, ye dwellers in the delved earth,
Ah, weep, ye watchers by the dismal shore
Of no man's land, for Bingo is no more;
He is no more, and well ye knew his worth,
For whom on bully-beefless days were kept
Rare bones by each according to his means,
And, while the Quartermaster-Sergeant slept,
The elusive pork was rescued from the beans.
He is no more and, impudently brave,
The loathly rats sit grinning on his grave.

Him mourn the grimy cooks and bombers ten,
The sentinels in lonely posts forlorn,
The fierce patrols with hands and tunics torn,
The furtive band of sanitary men.
The murmuring sound of grief along the length
Of traversed trench the startled Hun could hear;
The Captain, as he struck him off the strength,
Let fall a sad and solitary tear;
'Tis even said a batman passing by
Had seen the Sergeant-Major wipe his eye.

The fearful fervour of the feline chase
He never knew, poor dog, he never knew;
Content with optimistic zeal to woo
Reluctant rodents in this murky place,
He never played with children on clean grass,
Nor dozed at ease beside the glowing embers,
Nor watched with hopeful eye the tea-cakes pass,
Nor smelt the heather-smell of Scotch Septembers,
For he was born amid a world at war
Although unrecking what we struggled for.

Yet who shall say that Bingo was unblest
Though all his Spratless life was passed beneath
The roar of mortars and the whistling breath

Of grim nocturnal heavies going West?
Unmoved he heard the evening hymn of hate,
Unmoved would gaze into his master's eyes,
For all the sorrows men for men create
In search of happiness wise dogs despise,
Finding ecstatic joy in every rag
And every smile of friendship worth a wag.

6 January, diary, Mesicourt:
Route March. Passed Billy and Claude Lambton. The latter, who shouted at me, rather disturbed my salute which I was preparing to give his General.

The Huns are apparently going to attack through Switzerland. And the French are trying to prepare an offensive in Champagne before the Hun-Swiss enterprise. Hence the cause of us being suddenly called back to the line to take over more from the French. According to present arrangements the Division goes in between the 9th and 11th, one Brigade at Pierre St Vaast Wood. Our Brigade, the 3rd Brigade, is to leave on 10th when we go to Pierre St Vaast Wood, where we train for eight days. Then go up and carry for eight days, and in for sixteen. This, of course, will probably all be changed again.

7 January, diary, Mesicourt:
Went to church in the morning for the first time since my first Sunday out here; a very Presbyterian service, but such a nice old minister.

I saw Geoffrey Feilding motoring through here yesterday, he recognised me and waved.

Men's New Year dinner and concert afterwards, with rum punch to drink; then to dine with the 4th Grenadiers for a 'Temperance' dinner. Only their HQ and Company Commanders there, and several Welsh. The evening ended with practically everything being broken!

9 January, diary, Mesicourt:
Rode to Ville to the Divisional Baths with Priaulx, Ferryman and Williams. This was my first bath since December 10th in Amiens! A most amusing ride, as neither Ferryman nor Williams can ride at all, and both were run away with!

10 January, diary, Mesicourt to Bois Billon:
Left Mesicourt at 10.30 a.m. and marched to Bois Billon arriving about 4 p.m. There is only accommodation for two Battalions, but for some unknown reason they have put us with the 1st and 4th Grenadiers and the Welsh. The consequence

is that we are all, including the CO and HQ, feeding and sleeping in the same hut. The hut is very cold. The Camp is just opposite Bronfay Farm.

The weather then turned exceptionally cold with plummeting temperatures breaking all previous years' records. The waterlogged craters froze and duck boards laid down over the mud became like polished slides: "so that men go slipping and stumbling along communications trenches and fall against snowdrifts all crusted with tiny crystals. The men are 'sticking' the cold as they 'stuck' the wet – as they endure everything in this war, with a stiff upper lip and no moan". *The Telegraph's* Philip Gibbs ended this report on the desired upbeat note: "In spite of the hard weather the health of the Armies is amazingly good. The men are hard – hard as steel."

11 January, diary, Bois Billon:
Cold and some snow. Cleaning up Camp and making officer's Hut comfortable. HQ now have a Hut to themselves. The Welsh have left so there is much more room.
    The CO has lent me one of his spare horses, the one I rode on Tuesday, to ride whenever I like.

When not in the line, Esmond would try and ride most days.

12 January, diary, Bois Billon:
For the sake of a ride, I rode over to Corps HQ to get the money to pay the men, instead of sending the Transport Officer.
    Left at 12.30 in *'Michael'*, the Battalion car, with Victor Harbord and Priaulx for Amiens. Lunched at Corbie on the way and arrived at Amiens about 3.30 p.m. Had to spend most of the afternoon shopping for the Mess. I bought a very good mackintosh for 35 francs, the same as issued to the French Army, absolutely water-proof, and as light as a feather. Had a bath at the Belfort, dined at the Savoy, and home at 12.30 a.m.

13 January, diary, Bois Billon:
On fatigue, making a convoy road through the Camp. Geoffrey Feilding came round in the morning.
    Very cold with deep snow.

14 January, diary, Bois Billon:
Church in the morning.
    On picquet. In the afternoon we all went ratting; had a first rate time; bag totalled about 20.

16 January, diary, Bois Billon:
We were lectured in the morning by the Brigadier, Charles Corkran. He told us that he had read a German official document in which it said that it took five or six direct hits from our 9" to "do in" well-built Dug-outs. He also said that it was of the utmost importance, from every point of view, for us all to be as cheerful as possible, and that we were in future to be much more careful in what we said in the presence of strangers.

17 January, diary, Bois Billon:
Training in the morning. In the afternoon Left Hand Battalion took on Right Hand Battalion at a snowball match; the men loved it.

18 January, diary, Priez Farm:
Moved here today. Was sent on ahead to take over from 4th Grenadiers. What a nice lot they are. Keith, Jack Pixley, Alec Hardinge, Rupert Farquhar, Paton and Needham, who is temporarily CO.

The Dug-outs are about three quarters of a mile south east of Combles, 3,000 yards behind the Pierre St Vaast line, the new bit we have taken over. There are numberless guns within a quarter of a mile of us; without exaggeration, quite 60 counting the heavies, and probably more.

19 January, diary, Priez Farm:
Fatigues all day. Still very cold, and ground covered with snow. Perowne and Pretyman sleep on stretchers, but self on a Duck Board on the ground.

Our own guns make a good deal of noise firing, and shake our Dug-out each shot.

We worked hard and have rigged up some sort of beds, a table and a bench to sit on and cleaned out and improved our Dug-out enormously.

Met Griffin Heywood, the GSO1 to the Division. He was very nice.

Fuzzy Baillie has gone to hospital with what is expected to be dysentery. The French found this place very bad for dysentery.

HQ is practically the only real Dug-out, as all the others are Huts or funk holes above ground. It is the deepest I have seen – 38 steps below ground.

20 January, diary, Priez Farm:
The Huns have shown signs of being friendly. Both sides have been walking about on the top lately with impunity. Copper Seymour, the Brigadier, allowed this to go on till we got our line fairly good. But on Thursday night (18th Jan) he sent Brodie with Abercromby of the 1st Battalion and an officer of the Irish (Guards) over to

their wire with a written statement that any Hun showing himself after 7 a.m. would be shot. The former delivered their message to an officer who said that, although we might fire, they would not fire back! The Irishman, when he asked for an officer, was told there were none there, so gave his message to the Private soldier, who gave him a tremendous salute!

21 January, diary, Priez Farm:
Fatigues all day. the Huns shelled the batteries round the Dug-outs. Two German aeroplanes overhead reconnoitring.

22 January, diary, Billon Camp:
Returned here today. Was sent on ahead to take over from the 1st Grenadiers. After I left Priez they started shelling our Dug-outs; four casualties.
    Alan Swinton, Arthur Howard and Chamberlayne have joined.
    Very cold night.

23 January, diary, Billon Camp:
Bitterly cold! The uncorked Perrier froze despite fires in the Hut! But this weather has the advantage of making one feel astonishingly well and full of life.
    Knollys returned yesterday but has retired with flu, so temporarily commanding Company.
    Tonight, three enormous parcels arrived from Paris, sent by John and Violet. The most wonderful consignment of food. A bottle of 1830 champagne, excellent pate and cold birds – each mouthful tasted as if it cost a sovereign. The others have insisted upon asking the temporary CO, Kit Cator (the real CO is acting Brigadier) to dinner to drink the brandy.

24 January, diary, Billon Camp
Most icily cold! Went to hear the Welsh Band this afternoon. Dined with Bubbles, Alan Swinton and '*Damp*' Turnbull of the Royal Engineers at Brigade HQ.

25 January, diary, Billon Camp:
Training; bombing; still very cold. Water frozen, so only clean clothes available, without baths. The frozen Perrier burst the bottles during the night.

27 January, diary, Maurepas:
Left Billon at 8 a.m. in the most intense cold and reached Maurepas about 10.30. in our Hut are Gilpin, Perowne, Chamberlayne, Milne and self. A very draughty Hut.

28 January, diary, Maurepas
Church at 9.30 a.m. The second Episcopalian service I have been to since leaving England. Holy Communion at 12.

Tommy MacDougal has arrived as Adjutant.

29 January, diary, into the line in front of St Pierre Vaast Wood:
At 8.15 p.m. left Maurepas to go into the Line. Milne and I taking the Company up. Marched by Combles and Fregicourt and relief was complete by 10.30 p.m. Very quiet; saw only one Bosche shell going up.

30 January, diary, in the line:
The Company is holding a one Company front in front of St Pierre Vaast Wood, with one Company in support. And two, Left Flank and us in Reserve to do fatigues.

Exceptionally quiet day, and still freezing. No real Dug-outs in the Reserve Line except Company HQ. Only shelters for the men.

31 January, diary, in the line:
Clear and cold. Our HQ, when completed, will be the new Battalion HQ. It is about 30 feet down, and we are enlarging it at present.

The wire is pretty good on all the three lines, front, support and reserve. The frontline is entirely held by posts. The Bosche is not at all aggressive and they let us walk about more or less.

1 February, diary, in the line:
Today Arthur Howard was slightly wounded in the leg and face. Another very quiet day; the shelling has been conspicuous by its absence. The Company has been in reserve the whole time. We spent the day mostly playing poker. Great rumours of the Huns offering goodish peace terms; everything except Lorraine.

2 February, diary, in the line:
A very quiet day. Relieved about 11 p.m. by the Welsh, Lisburne's Platoon. Milne has a bad throat, so he went on early and I brought the Company out alone.

On returning to Maurepas, Esmond wrote in his diary: "It's such a treat to be in a country again where there is some grass and every tree not blown to pieces by shell fire." The bitter cold added to the misery of an outbreak of 'flu at the camp; six officers had to be hospitalised, including Knollys and Perowne; Gilpin and Chamberlayne were soon to follow. On a visit there, General Feilding was alarmed to see so many in such a pitiful state. Esmond was tasked with measuring temperatures and he wondered how long it would be before he got sick. In a chatty letter home, he touched on a range of subjects, including the German government's decision in favour of unrestricted submarine warfare, which two months later would bring the United States into the war.

4 February, diary, Maurepas
Went to Presbyterian Service. Lunched with Ross at the Transport.

Geoffrey Feilding came round here; nearly everyone was in bed, which looked bad, but they all feel so seedy. Perowne has gone to hospital. The fact that Geoffrey brought a parcel out for me greatly excited the Quartermaster Sergeant. As we came out of the line he met me some hour after midnight on the road and, with a terrific salute, said: 'The General has sent down a parcel by special messenger for you, Sir.' I did not show particular surprise so he then came up again and said "I hope I made myself clear, Sir, it was the Divisional General who sent the parcel down." I still did not show much astonishment, which apparently hurt him very much, for he came up a third time with a terrific salute and said "Pardon me, Sir, but I hope you understand the parcel was sent by Major-General Feilding, CB, DSO." So as not to hurt his feelings, I said "What can it be?" and tried to appear interested. The result of it is I think I have gone up much in his estimation.

6 February, letter to Mary, Maurepas:
We go up to the line this afternoon again and I hope we may have as quiet a time as last trip. It's pretty cold today, with icy wind, but it will do us no harm and personally this weather suits me.

We are all waiting to know what America is going to do. I hope she won't come in really, as, if she does, she will say that she won the war. I suppose her fleet would be useful, as before the war it was the third largest. Germany can never surely have sent a note like that without meaning her to declare war, and if she does, I suppose Hun-land will chuck it at once, declaring the whole world to be against her. I feel that peace will be so soon that it will come before I get leave.

We are no longer getting potatoes, but are to be given figs or chestnuts instead. I wonder if you are getting potatoes? I daresay, when one gets used to them, figs or chestnuts will be just as good.

6 February, diary, in the line St Pierre Vaast Wood
Left Maurepas this afternoon to go into the line in St Pierre Vaast Wood trenches; Knollys and I taking the Company in.

Intensely cold; bitter wind; little shooting from both sides. Left Flank are in the frontline, we in support, and Right Flank and F in the reserve.

We are living in the same Dug-out as Battalion HQ just off the Péronne-Bapaume road. Tommy MacDougal and the artillery Observation Officer sleep in our partition.

Relief was complete by 6.30 p.m. The men have no Dug-outs in the support line, only shelters.

7 February, diary, in the line:
Quiet day. Tomorrow the Division on our left is going over the top, and the French too have a show further south. The Yorks do the attack on a front of about 500 yards at Saillisel just to straighten out the salient. It is thought that the Hun may counter-attack here. If the Yorks are successful we have been ordered to hold the line absolutely at all costs.

In the evening had two parties out repairing the wire in front of this line. But, as we only had one pair of wire cutters, not much headway could be made.

The water the men were issued with in many cases froze in the petrol tins, and with their small fires they were unable to thaw it. So I brought it down to thaw at Company HQ, where it is very warm.

8 February, diary, in the line:
Zero hour was 7.30 a.m. at which time it seemed that every gun opened fire on the German line, putting a barrage from Saillisel to beyond Rancourt. At that time the 17th Division, that is the Division on our immediate left, were to attack the high ground in front of Saillisel. We were all naturally out at 7.30 a.m. as the Authorities thought the Hun might try and counter attack on our front or across it from St Pierre, where he could best mass his men. Our Company was in support that day, a line of posts again, and the worst shelled of the line.

One of our aeroplanes, flying low, went up and down the line giving signals to our artillery. About 20 minutes after zero hour the Germans began retaliating heavily on Battalion HQ and the support. It was the most glorious morning; an ideal morning for an attack, for there was a low mist. About 8 a.m. the Hun started shelling pretty heavily, which he kept up the whole day, particularly on the Orchard, and on our right, centre and on the left of our support.

They got several direct hits on our Dug-out, one killing the sentry, Trotter of 9 Platoon and blowing the entrance in. About 9.30 a.m. several wounded in No 12 Platoon and Sergeant Morden was killed. Such a nice man who came out from England with us. They had two direct hits on No 12 Platoon in Sinister Post killing Sergeants Gordon and Robertson and burying Sergeant Graham and others, who we got out, and wounding seven. We moved them down to No 8 Post in the Orchard, where they were shelling pretty heavily too but no direct hits on them.

Later in the day we heard that all our objectives had been taken, in addition to 70 prisoners.

We were to relieve Left Flank in the frontline at 7 p.m. and I went up to Heilly Post then. But, owing to the shelling and barrage the Hun put up being so bad, the relief was not complete till after midnight when it was completed without any casualties.

9 February, diary, St Pierre Vaast Line Heilly Post
A good deal of shelling; only one man wounded. Yesterday the Huns counter-attacked the 17th Division, who had gained their objectives, at 5.30 p.m. and again at 10 p.m. and the barrage came down as far as our front. But he got in nowhere. During this time the shelling from both sides was pretty intense.

This line is held entirely by posts; the furthest apart being about 50 yards. The Hun line varies from about 300 to 100 yards.

At night so far there has been no sniping or rifle fire, so both sides walk about on top with impunity. One of our posts reported that one of the Hun sentries, who was relieved every hour, was suffering from a bad cough! There is no communication trench so an aggressive spirit should not be encouraged among the men until this is completed.

10 February 10, diary, St Pierre Vaast Line to Maurepas:
A fair amount of shelling today. Relieved by 3rd Coldstream and got out with no casualties.

The St Pierre Vaast Line is the most extraordinary line…held by posts and no communication trench, but duck boards the whole way up, and from post to post.

The Bosche line, which is also posts, is about 30 yards on the right, and slightly further on the left, 150-200 yards. There is no communication trench on either side, and the lines being so close, it is obvious that each of us can see what the other is doing. The Hun infantry is perfectly friendly and naturally neither of us shoots, as each of us could make the other's position untenable. Though he puts up Verey lights, one of which fell not 10 feet from me, he never sniped us once. The first night I went round the posts and told no one to fire unless it was a raid or an attack; but there being snow on the ground at the time, and bright moonlight, it would have been difficult for any man to have crept up unseen.

One cannot walk about in the day time as the enemy's Ops see one, and they immediately whiz-bang you.

Our artillery shells incessantly, and it is surprising he does not retaliate more than he does. Heilly Post, the frontline Company's Dug-out, is a good Dug-out about 30 feet deep, but they shell it a good deal and have got the range pretty accurately. They constantly get direct hits, one day putting the candles out three times, and another time 10 times!

A letter from home was full of news of the State Opening of Parliament, with all its pomp and splendour undimmed by the war. Mary was in the Procession as Mistress of the Robes to the Queen. Esmond came out of the line on the 11th and was in comfortable billets in a house in Ville sous Corbie which he described to his mother.

11 February, letter to Mary, Ville Sous Corbie:
"After a great deal of arguing with an old French woman I have, I think, made myself pretty comfortable. To get the room I wanted cost me 10 francs and a threat to kiss her. Her face of horror and the terror that the last suggestion might really be fulfilled did the trick, for she offered me her own bed mingled with cries of "*la la, le petit taquin*", the meaning of which I have not yet discovered. Ross has lent me a stove and lamp.[4]

12 February, diary, Ville Sous Corbie:
Spent the day at drill. In the afternoon went over to the Divisional Baths and had a bath; the first since we left Mesicourt! (January 10th) Then had tea with Pearson, who gave me a fur jacket.

15 February, diary, Ville Sous Corbie:
A whole day at bombing (on 4 day Bombing Course), throwing dummies and Mills adapters, rather boring and at times dangerous. Yesterday a man gave us a lecture on Artillery. He said that, from July 1st till the end of November, 16,000,000 shells were fired on the Somme front.
  The thaw has started and I expect the line we were in will be awful.
  Just heard that Rupert Farquhar was in the leave train accident. He says 27 killed, two of whom were officers, and about 50 badly wounded.

This collision, involving a supply and a leave train, combined with the closure of Boulogne, following a shipping accident, resulted in leave being suspended. Esmond didn't seem to mind. "Unlike most people, I am not longing for it to such a degree. I suppose it is owing to the fact that I have been with the Battalion such a short time and am only just beginning to know the men, such splendid men too." Some of the men in his Company had not been home for sixteen months, he told his mother.

16 February, diary, Ville Sous Corbie:
Bombing. Found we were using two live bombs by mistake instead of dummies. This might have caused a nasty accident.

The Bosche bombed the Plateau last night and got the ammunition Dump. It was still burning at 3 p.m., though it had been bombed at 2 am!

19 February, diary, Ville Sous Corbie:
Training in the morning; artillery formations. In the evening, I was told I should have to attend a Lewis Gun course at Meaulte tomorrow for six days.[5]

21 February, diary, Ville Sous Corbie:
Lewis Gun course; very boring, and I think a badly run school. Bicycled over and back to the Battalion in the evening.

After dinner we went over to Ross's billet where we had lessons in the Reel. Ross in great form and told us many amusing stories of things happening when he enlisted in the Regiment.

22 February, diary, Ville Sous Corbie:
Lewis Gun course all day.

No hope of getting home. No boats have been crossing owing to fogs & submarines. 750 Officers, who were sent down to Folkestone, had to return to London as the traffic congestion was so great. I was offered Paris leave, but gave it up to someone who has been out longer than me. I shall probably be offered the next leave going. But, as most of the theatres are shut, I am not certain that it would be worthwhile going, so I shall probably give it up again.

Ally Boyd had a dinner this evening; a tremendous rag! Paton, Calverley Bewicke, the CO, Cator and some of the Right Flank. Everyone rolling tight! Windows, doors, furniture all broken!

23 February, diary, Ville Sous Corbie:
Our Landlady complained to the French authorities about last night. She was however pacified by bribes.

Lessons in Reel dancing with Ross after dinner. Ross in great form.

The Brigade was inspected today by Lyautey, French Minister of War.

24 February, diary, Ville sous Corbie:
There have been no mails till tonight for four or five days. Today I received my first letter for over a week.

Nasty reports of the Saillisel line, where we are to go.

25 February, diary, Ville sous Corbie:
Lewis Gun in the morning. In the afternoon, we all went for a ride. Great fun; galloped as far as Sailly le Sec. Rode home with Tommy MacDougal; saw a fox which we galloped after for about a mile, the first I have seen out here.

Great news! The Huns are retiring all along the Vth Army front and we now have Serre and Warlencourt. It is believed they are withdrawing to the Cambrai line. They apparently started on the 21st, according to the statements of prisoners, but we only found it out yesterday. On the 21st, owing to the misty weather, our aeroplanes were not able to go up; on the 25th they went up and reported that, on XIV Corps front, the roads were one mass of transport retreating. And we know that the Vth Army are in Serre, Pys and Pigeon House, La Barque and Ligny, about 3 kilometres from Bapaume.

Bapaume has, I believe, been blown sky high, and I expect every road, bridge and village is mined.

On the Fifth Army front I don't think they have actually withdrawn yet from the frontline, only their back areas. But I hope we shall start a "biff" at once before they are ready for it.

It was the beginning of Operation Alberich, the German strategic withdrawal to prepared defences, the Hindenburg Line, designed to forestall an allied offensive. The line was shortened to reduce the number of troops needed to hold it. As the Germans withdrew they devastated the countryside; villages were burnt, wells poisoned, bridges blown up and trees felled across the roads to render them impassable. Mines along roads and railways further hampered the British advance. Booby traps, including those set under helmets, favoured by souvenir hunters, and delayed action explosives killed many unsuspecting soldiers and civilians.

26 February, letter to Mary, Ville Sous Corbie
I was offered Paris leave but gave it up to someone who has been out longer than I.

Will you send me my sketching materials, and of course brushes too. I hope you understand.

This was their agreed code for his Kodak vest pocket camera.

27 February, diary, Amiens, on leave:
The Battalion left at 8 a.m. for Priez Farm. Self, Ally Boyd and Milne have been given leave to go to Amiens. Stopping at the Grand Hotel du Rhin. We came in an Australian ambulance, in which there were three wounded fellows. One not at all bad, one gassed, and another poor fellow groaning and writhing in what I

thought was pain. As the Orderly was in the front on the box, which I think was quite wrong, we had to keep putting the blankets on him. But finally it was getting so bad we made the Orderly come and look after him. We then found he was a very bad case of shell-shock, and he had no wound at all. Poor devil, he was a most pitiable sight.

28 February, diary, Amiens, on leave:
Did not get up till after 11. It is such a treat to be able to live once more, more or less like a gentleman: a bath before getting up, and a proper bed and sheets, the first time since October 12th! Fooled about the town and got photographed.

The Cathedral here is a most extraordinary sight. Every wall of it sand-bagged up inside; there must be nearly, if not more than 200,000 sand bags there!

The shops are all coining money, and the prices are perfectly enormous: 7 francs for tea. But now that we have taken the town over I hope we shall put some check on it. But when one is here for such a short time, it is not worthwhile haggling over prices, and the French people realise this.

Pilcher dined with us and after dinner we drove round the town.

We have occupied Le Baynes and Ligny, but Pilcher says he hears our casualties have been high, and that three more Ambulance trains have been applied for.

According to present arrangements we go into the line on March 9th after a push has been made at Saillisel.

1 March, diary, Amiens, on leave:
The German withdrawal is still proceeding. Our authorities are much impressed by their retreat; everything has been destroyed, no billets or anything left.

Met Jack Buchanan and went round the town with him.

Esmond returned to Maurepas the following day. Amiens had been the 'greatest fun', but it had proved quite an expensive leave. The bill for the hotel, where they had had their meals, had come to between £5 and £6 a day, roughly £350 in today's money. He wrote to his mother saying: "I met a fellow yesterday just back from leave. He says that except for those people who have suffered by the war, no one cares two straws about it, that many are positively enjoying it, as they are making so much money. It is not an encouraging state of affairs."

5 March, diary, Maurepas:
The CO lent me his horse and I rode with Ally Boyd, Caryl Hargreaves and Knollys round by Nurlu. Caryl showed us the line as it was before July 1st 1916.

We are told we shall have to move to Fregicourt and Haie Wood.

Yesterday we saw an aeroplane come down in flames; the petrol tank caught fire. It seemed absolutely impossible that either the pilot or observer could get down unharmed. Neither was hurt. The observer placed the fire extinguisher on to the fire and kept it behind the pilot all the time till they got down. But precious little of the aeroplane seemed to be left when they got out.

6 March, diary, Haie Wood:
Knollys went to Amiens for the day and I brought the Company here, with Chamberlayne. We are in Dug-outs on the Haie Wood Road, just by the cemetery at Combles. The men in very good Dug-outs with wire beds; Knollys and Chamberlayne in a Dug-out with beds; myself in another Dug-out on a stretcher.

Left Flank are about one mile further along the road.

7 March, diary, Haie Wood:
Bitterly cold wind; on fatigue the whole morning on Haie Wood Road. Freezing hard at night. The Welsh, whom we relieved, have had a good many casualties from the Minenwerfers.

8 March, diary, Haie Wood, into the line at Sailly-Saillisel:
Marched up at 6 p.m. from Haie Wood by Platoons at 50-yard interval. The Welsh, whom we were relieving, provided us with guides, three of whom lost their way! Eventually Reid, 2nd Company Orderly, found us and took us into the line at Sailly-Saillisel. It was pretty quiet going up. The relief is done over the top except for the last 70 yards up a very shell-beaten communication trench.

The Welsh, who had, during the four days 82 casualties, were very 'windy' and went out pretty quickly, the officer even refusing to show me round!

Knollys and Chamberlayne are in Paltz trench held by three posts; and I have Nos 11 and 12 Platoons in Potsdam and the communication trench to Paltz. I am responsible for the Lewis Gun and Bombing section in the communication trench and two other Bombing posts in Potsdam.

Shortly after the Welsh had gone out the Germans started shelling pretty heavily, and a Minenwerfer, known as 'Minnie', gave us a good deal of trouble. These come over like slow rockets and the last bit is heard. It has the most tremendous explosion, and is far the most frightening thing I have seen or heard.

In the day time, we withdrew the men from the communication trench owing to the shelling. There is absolutely no shelter of any sort in Potsdam; there are however shafts in Paltz where the men can get a bit of shelter.

Freezing tonight, which is infinitely preferable to the mud.

This is an extraordinary looking country – every foot a shell hole, and very few trees standing.

9 March, diary, Sailly-Saillisel Line:
They were shelling us a good deal at 2 a.m. and by then we had a good many casualties. Going up to see Knollys in Paltz about 2.30 a.m. Reid, my Orderly, was hit by a Minenwerfer in the wrist and leg.

About 3 a.m. I went down to Ally Boyd's Dug-out where I was to stop the day owing to there being no Dug-out in Potsdam. Ally's HQ is about 50 yards from Potsdam. A very good Dug-out, but we were shelled practically the whole day.

The thaw has started and the line is getting very, very muddy.

10 March, diary, Sailly-Saillisel line:
They shelled us in Left Flank Company Dug-out a good deal today. At 9 a.m. the shelling, rifle grenades and Minenwerfers began again. We were shelled all day and, owing to a bad Artillery Liaison Officer, could get no artillery retaliation. No one, who has not been through it, can imagine the agony of sitting in a trench being shelled and waiting for our retaliation which never comes. But the men were perfectly magnificent. During the shelling I began talking to one of the men and found he came from Hawick! He knew all the paths in the Minto Crags where he has often been for walks on Sundays! The world is small!

In the evening, we were relieved by F Company after suffering 22 casualties, 6 or 7 being killed and 4 cases of shell-shock. The Battalion as a whole had 45 casualties. The mud up the line is beyond words bad, and F Company had to come in over the top. Before we could get out the Germans started shelling us and we had two casualties before going out.

Knollys hurt his foot so I was responsible for bringing the Company out. When F Company were all in, I sent my men out and took Wright, the F Company Commander, round the line, keeping Corporal Greenslade as my Orderly.

As we were leaving we came upon a man groaning near Left Flank HQ. I bent over him to see if there was anything I could do to relieve his pain. He immediately recognised my voice and said:

"Oh, Mr Elliot, I'm blinded." It was Corporal McQueen hit in the head and suffering a great deal. He begged for water, but I only had brandy to give him. The Germans plumped a shell pretty near us. We got him into a Dug-out and washed and bandaged him, and I sent Corporal Greenslade for a stretcher.

Esmond remained alone with Sergeant McQueen under heavy shell fire for a very considerable time before the stretcher bearers arrived, one shell bursting within three yards and covering them both with debris.

> 11 March, diary, in support at The Hebule:
> Today our artillery was much more active and there were one or two quite sharp bombardments. The whole country is riddled with shell holes. And the mud caused by the shells makes it look like an enormous grouse moor. The Hun still puts a good many shells into Morval which we watched for some time.

> 12 March, diary, in support at The Hebule:
> A good deal of shelling. We were relieved by the 3rd Coldstream. The Doctor, Clark, who had only just come to us, was killed coming out of the line, a gas shell. The Coldstream had an officer killed just after the relief.
>   Had tea with Jack Buchanan and to bed very early, very tired.

Esmond brought the Company back to Billon alone as Knollys and Chamberlayne were preparing to go on leave to Paris. They were all having to reduce their kits, Company Commanders being allowed 100 lbs and Platoon Commanders 70 lbs.

> 15 March, diary, Billon:
> The Huns have withdrawn on the front where we were holding the line. Very few casualties advancing.
>   In the evening HQ dined and we were all made to box. Victor Harbord knocked me all over the place.

It was the occasion of another post-frontline duty Battalion dinner, at which the tension was eased by copious quantities of alcohol: "the CO absolutely blind. In fact, everyone was tight. As a result, Lucian Knollys has gone to hospital with a fractured ankle."

On 15 March, Mary received a letter from Feilding which she recorded in her journal:

> The Guards have been in a tight place and have had many casualties. He says 'Esmond is a great success and a real chip off the old block. I saw his CO yesterday, and he tells me that Esmond is quite one of the best boys in the Battalion, and as brave as a lion. He had been in rather a disagreeable part of the trench, and had done really well, bossing up his men, and doing all that he should have done, and they are all delighted with him.'

18 March, diary, Billon:
Lunched with Castlerosse. Afterwards he and I, the CO and Kit Cator rode and
saw the country given up by the Huns last week. We went to within 3 miles of
Péronne which we took yesterday

19 March, diary, Billon:
The Huns are retreating fast and we have got Bapaume, Péronne and Le Transloy.
The Corps Cavalry has gone there. I hope John Astor will be all right, and that the
1st Life Guards won't be used.

20 March, diary, Maurepas:
Marched here this morning. In the afternoon, Caryl Hargreaves, Victor Perowne
and I walked to Péronne, about 7 miles away. We went by Clery, one of the
small villages on the Somme taken last autumn. It was, of course, destroyed, but
unlike Mametz, Montauban etc, where all the heavy fighting has been, it was not
completely obliterated. The most glorious country from Clery onwards.

The road from Clery for about 2 miles is very bad. After about half a mile we
came to our frontline trench of two days before. We passed 'no man's land', one
mass of shell holes each side of it! The German line was well wired and they had a
good trench.

On the main Péronne road there is the strongest Machine Gun Emplacement I
have seen; a miniature cemented fort commanding the whole country and, behind
this, three rows of very strong and thick wire.

Péronne was still burning when we got there, for they have destroyed the whole
town, not one house undamaged. The Cathedral looked as if they had mined one of
the supporting pillars. In the middle of the Square the Huns have left the following
notice:

NICHT ÄRGERN
NUR WUNDERN[6]

They have also made a big dummy French soldier, which I expect is some trap, for
all the places are full of them. It seems that they also blew in most of the front of
the houses. Péronne is a second Ypres.

The German withdrawal on this front started two days after we were relieved,
that is the 14th, and on about 18th the Corps Cavalry was sent through and then
the town was entered by the 8th Division.

The Germans employed high explosives, solidified paraffin and the contents of latrines, to destroy and sully the once lovely town of Péronne, out of sheer rage at being unable to hold what they had taken. Among the debris, Esmond found a fragment of an altarpiece – it had been attacked with axes before the Cathedral itself was mined. He was astonished and saddened by what he saw: "I wish I could tell you all we saw, for it was so intensely interesting," he wrote to his mother on 21 March, "and I only hope our time will come to chase the devils."

21 March, diary, Priez Farm:
We marched here today. The place has been greatly improved since I was here and there is now lots of room for everyone. Unlike before, there is no sound of a gun, the Artillery being busy moving up those batteries which are still round here.

22 March, diary, Priez Farm:
We crossed our trenches into 'no man's land' at Heilly Post, where we ourselves had been a short time before. The Hun's trenches are unbelievably battered, hardly a foot unshelled and the whole of St Pierre Vaast Wood – a large wood – has been laid flat by our shell fire. The most beautiful shooting by our artillery, and how anyone lived through it, I cannot think. No wonder they have gone back.
   I only saw one trap left by the Hun.

23 March, diary, Priez Farm:
We are at present at Priez Farm and yesterday we did a road fatigue at Government Farm.
   The line is held in the following manner; one Battalion in our original front-line; one Company at Government Farm; and three Companies on out-post duty beyond, with a Squadron of Cavalry.
   We crossed into no man's land over the same trenches we ourselves held about a month ago. The Hun line has been knocked about to smithereens.

24 March, diary, Bronfay Farm:
In the morning walked around Rancourt, where there has been a good deal of heavy fighting with the French. The village is entirely obliterated, and it will take some work to repair the Bapaume road through the village.

The Army's rear guard were now faced with clearing up the devastated areas and restoring communications as a matter of urgency, so that men, horses, guns and supplies could keep moving; most infantry and cavalry units were involved in this operation.

25 March, diary, Bronfay:
Summer Time started today.[7] The Battalion left this afternoon for Clery on an eight days' fatigue to make the Railway from Maricourt to Péronne. They are in tents and, as there is little room, only three officers a Company were taken up, self and Chamberlayne staying behind from G Company. I hate not going up with our men, but will go up on 29th to relieve one of the others for the remainder of the fatigue.

26 March, Mary Minto's journal:
Met Major Romer, Scots Guards. He told me Colonel Orr Ewing was home on leave and had told him Esmond was splendid. He was in a trench when three of his men standing beside him were killed; he hadn't moved a muscle. The Colonel couldn't praise him enough and said that Esmond was such a valuable officer that they wanted to keep him in the Regiment, and he hoped he would make soldiering his career.

27 March, diary, Bronfay:
On Sunday (25th) the Town Hall at Bapaume – a Divisional HQ – was blown up. A seven days' fuse was found. And today a big Dug-out, where Brigade HQ was established, went up. The Hun has mined the whole town.

30 March , diary, Clery:
On fatigue by Clery Village. In the evening walked round by Clery Wood. An awful lot of dead Germans still lying about there. They must have caught it very heavily.

31 March, diary, Clery:
On fatigue from 7.30 a.m. till 5 p.m. laying track for the Railway to Péronne. As the country is one mass of shell holes the work takes a long time. Puce weather, wind and heavy showers of rain and hail.

1 April, diary, Clery:
Fatigue in the early morning. In the afternoon, Ally Boyd, Pretyman and I rode beyond Péronne as far as Aziecourt. The lines of trenches dug on every hill, the intense wire, and deep Dug-outs are amazing. Every hill has a fort. They have destroyed every single thing. I saw no shell holes in Aziecourt and think the town must have been burnt. All Dug-outs are burnt and telegraph poles cut through.

The Times described the wanton destruction of the French countryside by the enemy:

> In village after village they have burnt whole rows of houses for no reason but pure spite. In house after house they have pillaged every room that they had not set on fire and taken all the contents. In the fields between Noyon and Chauny…there are or, or were, a considerable number of fruit trees. Every one of them within a certain distance of the road has been killed. They have either been sawn through a couple of feet from the ground, or else a gash three or four inches deep has been hacked in a circle round the trunk.

In early April, Esmond was sent to Le Touquet for a second Lewis Gun course. He drove to Amiens in 'Michael' and took the train from there.

> 4 April, letter to Mary, Le Touquet:
> This is the most glorious country, and it seems hard to realise there is any fighting going on comparatively near. We are in tents practically on the shore. I believe the 1st Life Guards are only about 10 miles from here but I don't suppose there will be any chance of my being able to see if John Astor is there.

> 4 April, diary, Le Touquet:
> The Camp is by the Golf Links between the sea and the forest, wonderful air. There are 125 officers and we are in tents. I have managed to get put on the five days' course rather than the fourteen days one. Walked this evening to Paris Plage; a lovely walk on the sands. One of our Airships was manoeuvring about quite low.

> 5 April, diary, Le Touquet:
> Lewis Gun from 8.45–12.45 and 2-4.
> Dined with Lady Bridget Coke who has been working at the YMCA. She goes to England tomorrow. Yesterday's Airship was piloted by Lady Bridget's brother who was trying to land here to see her.
> All the Cavalry have gone up to Arras for the 'biff' there on Sunday; they hope to get through on the fourth day.

> 6 April, diary, Le Touquet:
> Lewis Gun all day. Lunched with the Commandant and Staff. The Adjutant, Lewis, who invited me, is a great friend of the Duchess of Westminster, who lives here.
> America has declared war on Hunland at last!

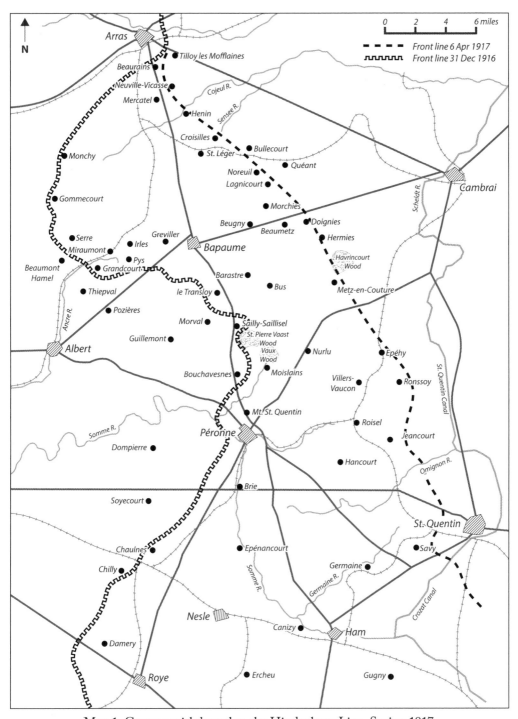

Map 1 German withdrawal to the Hindenburg Line, Spring 1917.

Making headline news was America's declaration of war against Germany; some were of the opinion that this would bring about the end of hostilities. Esmond's walks on the beach – a change of scene from the shell-battered landscape he had become accustomed to – a few good dinners in restaurants and meeting a variety of different people from all regiments and nationalities, had had an uplifting effect.

> 8 April, Easter Sunday, diary, Le Touquet:
> Another glorious day. Church in the morning; afterwards working out a tactical scheme. A triplane flew over yesterday, the first I have seen. Sat in the woods and read in the afternoon.
>
> At 4.30 Lewis, the Adjutant, took me to tea with the Duchess of Westminster. She has a little villa next to where Lady Bridget was.
>
> At dinner in Camp I got a note from the Duchess asking me to return there to dine and go on to the cinema, which I did. We had a very amusing evening. She very kindly sent her motor to collect me.

The Second Battle of Arras was about to begin and Esmond's course was drawing to a close. The weather was wintry, with snow and gales, but there were good reports on 10 April: 11,000 prisoners and a hundred guns had been taken at Vimy Ridge, with the Canadian Corps playing a pivotal role.

While Esmond's course continued, his battalion, with pipers playing, marched from Clery to Péronne and then to what had been the pleasant town of Cartigny, now in ruins since the Germans retreated to the Hindenburg Line.

> 13 April, diary, Le Touquet:
> Rumours that the Cavalry have had a bad time round Mouchon, particularly the 10th and the Blues. No word on the 1st and 2nd Life Guards. In addition to our wounded, there are 900 Huns in the various hospitals round here.

> 14 April, diary, Le Touquet:
> Examined; hope to have got through all right. Dined with the Staff, and then on to the Concert. A very good show. The Duchess of Westminster and Lewis sang two duets. She looked very pretty, and sang well. But it seemed very undignified for her to act as she was the only woman there.

> 15 April, diary, Le Touquet:
> A short walk with Bonham Carter, such a nice man. He looks 100, but I believe he is nearer 40 than 50. He has been a Commissioner in Bengal for heaven knows how long, was refused a commission on account of his age, is in the Grenadiers, and is

here sleeping on the floor in a tent, as an Ensign in the Household Battalion, 18 months' junior to me! It is splendid a man like that joining!

17 April, diary, Le Touquet:
Last day of the Course; I am really sorry to be going. It has been awfully interesting being here with so many of the New Army officers so long. I think every profession is represented; Lawyers, Commissioners, Motor people, Bank Clerks, Dentists and even a Grocer's assistant. One Canadian officer told me he was "tickled to death by the trains on that little island of yours".

18 April, diary, to Cartigny via Etaples:
We left Le Touquet at 3.30 a.m. and the train put us down at 4.30 p.m. at a station 15 miles from here, with no means of getting to the Battalion. Had tea with Henry Dundas of the 1st Battalion and then came up here to the Battalion at Cartigny, about four miles beyond Péronne. I got an ambulance, and by means of bribes, was brought the whole way.

Cartigny was to be a delightful interlude. There was plenty of riding on offer, including horse races in which all the officers took part. Work on the railway to Péronne continued and the wreck of the camp was transformed: wood, brick, stone and iron from the ruins were used to build an Orderly Room, HQ and Messes.

20 April, diary, Cartigny:
Drill and revolver shooting all morning. The CO let me put his charger over a jump here.
   This morning Rawlinson came here alone. He was exactly what an Army Commander should be, cheery and nice to all.

22 April, diary, Cartigny:
Tremendous mine craters at the St Quentin cross roads. All the villages around here are destroyed by fire, as there are no shell holes in them. Quite nice country, but an awful lot of wire about.
   Church in the evening.

The weather had turned much warmer. One day, in blinding sunshine, an entire Indian cavalry regiment galloped through the camp, while an aeroplane flew overhead. Esmond thought it was "rather a splendid sight".
   On 23 April, he was gazetted Full Lieutenant. Two days later, on his twenty-second birthday, he wrote to his mother:

Thank you for the very nice diary case which arrived this morning. Violet has sent me two such excellent hampers. I am afraid I am becoming such a 'Gourmand' that I now appreciate my food if anything even more than some of my friends. A most excellent bottle of cherry brandy came besides and we are all drinking our fair share with little loss of time. According to present plans, we are to stay here a little longer. Such glorious weather, and I have been busy with my sketching.

25 April, diary, Cartigny:
My birthday. Got birthday letters from Mother and Violet.

   We train in the morning, starting at 7 a.m. The afternoons are spent in football matches or sports which one tries to get up. In the evening went out hare hunting, eight or ten of us riding; I rode a Pack Pony, the most awful brute, but great fun.

26 April, diary, Cartigny:
Training. The men worked most of the afternoon on their gardens which are beginning to look most awfully nice. The camp was only a field, but now each tent has its own gardens and Yews and Cypress trees have been transplanted out of the village.

Private Armstrong, who had been a gardener on the estate of Lord Bute in Scotland, had the idea to make gardens amidst the ruins of Cartigny. Soon every soldier was co-operating and prizes were given for the best gardens.

29 April, diary, Cartigny:
The hottest day we've had. Last night in the direction of Cambrai there was a huge fire, one of the biggest I have seen.

   The gardens were judged today; for some unaccountable reason they put "G" last! But the men have made this a really awfully nice Camp.

Judging the efforts were Lord Henry Seymour, recently appointed as Brigade Commander, and Lieutenant-Colonel Viscount Gort, commanding the 4th Grenadiers.

The 2nd Battalion moved to Nurlu on 2 May, where they were to level the ground for an aerodrome.

2 May, diary, Nurlu:
Left Cartigny at 1 p.m. We had to strike our camp before leaving, and all that remains there now are the gardens. We reached Nurlu about 5 p.m. after a very hot and dusty marched through Buire and Templeux la Fosse; most interesting country. Passed several tons of carefully concealed wire.

3 May, diary, Nurlu:

The village, a largish place, is again totally destroyed. The Church is supposed to be mined, and is therefore out of bounds. A Dug-up with six officers in went up a few days ago.

The Air people told us yesterday that their Squadron, No. 9, was only flying in a Machine which, in the House of Commons, had been officially stated was no longer in use!

4 May, diary, Nurlu:

Fatigue in the morning; levelling the Aerodrome. A flight arrived this morning consisting of seven machines. Most of the officers lunched with us.

Romilly, who has got the 1st Battalion, came over here today; he sent for me and was very nice. A piping hot day.

5 May, diary, Nurlu:

Another steaming hot day. went up in an Aeroplane BL 2C with an awfully nice fellow called Warburton. We flew as far as Péronne twice. Wonderful view of the country. We went up to 3,000 feet and were in the air about 30 minutes. The greatest fun but rather bumpy owing to the hot air coming up.

Some of the RFC (Royal Flying Corps) came down after dinner and we had a very rowdy evening.

Flying at the front was a particularly dangerous occupation and new pilots lasted, on average, no more than seventeen days. During April 1917, the RFC lost a third of its number.

8 May, diary, Cartigny:

Pouring rain all day.

Knollys left for Flixecourt and I have taken over the Company. Went to see Ross's new lantern slides.

9 May, diary, Cartigny:

Planning a Scheme of Attack on a German strong point. Rather a failure! Geoffrey Feilding there. In the afternoon rode with Peter Gilpin to see ground where scheme was today.

Rumours that we are going into the line again soon.

Many of the men, including Esmond, needed to be inoculated against Tetanus. Those who didn't, practised bayonet training and took part in a tug-of-war. It was during this lull at Cartigny, that Esmond found the time to take photos, in an attempt to record this extraordinary existence, of which no two days were ever the same.

13 May, diary, Cartigny:
Battalion Sports. A great success with running races, jumping, boxing and wrestling and bathing in the nearby river. Pulteney, John Ponsonby, Copper Seymour, Geoffrey Feilding and their Staffs; 1st and 4th Grenadiers; the Welsh and representatives of all (the Guards) Regiments nearby came. The Grenadiers Band played.

15 May, diary, Cartigny:
A scheme today in which we attacked the village of Beaumetz. The Battalion moves to Corbie on the 18th where the Division concentrates, and then we expect to go north for a 'biff'.

My application for special leave was granted today from 18th to 28th. Very excited!

It was nearly Whitsun and Esmond would be back in England with Mary, for the anniversary of her engagement to Rolly, a date always remembered by the Mintos, and with Violet, for her birthday.

Dramatis Personae

Alington, The Reverend Cyril. 1872-1955. Came to Eton from Shrewsbury. He was educated at Marlborough and Trinity College Oxford and he was elected a Fellow of All Souls. Much liked by the boys. Became Dean of Durham and served as Chaplain to King George V. He officiated at the marriage of Gavin Astor and Irene Haig.

Baillie, Captain the Hon Victor Cochrane-Baillie, *'Fuzzy'*, MC. 1896-195. Eton/Oxford/ Scots Guards. Wounded twice. Mentioned in Despatches. Later Lord Lamington.

Bewicke, Lt. Calverley, OBE, MC. 1883-1963. Harrow/Scots Guards. Had been in the Scots Guards for two years a decade earlier. An excellent horseman. Mentioned in Despatches.

Borrett, Lt. PR. 1889-1963. Eton/Cambridge/Scots Guards. Wounded.

Boyd, Lt. Alastair *'Ally'*. Scots Guards. Commander Left Flank. 1890-1956. As a Lieutenant commanded the 2nd Battalion for a short time as so many senior officers were wounded or killed.

Brodie, Lt. Duncan, *'Deacon'* (given this name by Henry Dundas after an 18th century Edinburgh cat burglar). MC. Born 1887. Eton/Scots Guards. Wounded twice. French and German speaker. Sent by Lord Henry Seymour on 18th January 1917 to warn the Germans that the unofficial truce would end.

Bagot Chester, Major Greville, *'Bubbles'*. Scots Guards. Responsible for billeting for the Guards Division. KIA 28 November 1917 aged 52 at Flesquieres.

Castlerosse, Capt. Viscount. Later Earl of Kenmare. 1891-1943. Irish Guards. First member of British aristocracy to write a gossip column for a newspaper, entitled *Londoner's Log* in *The Sunday Express* owned by his friend Lord Beaverbrook. Notorious as a playboy.

Cator, Captain CAM, *'Kit'*, MC. 1877-1932. Eton/Scots Guards. Wounded three times. In early 1917 he brought the Cator family butler, Ernest Bowles, aged 42, out to be his batman and run the Company officer's mess. Sadly, Bowles was killed almost immediately after arrival. Kit was seriously wounded in 1917 and returned home.

Chamberlayne, Lt. Crinius *'Joe'*. Educated abroad/Oxford/Scots Guards. Fluent French and German speaker. Wounded on 31 July 1917 and spent a year in England recovering.

Clark, Captain William. Royal Army Medical Corps. King's College Hospital. Medical Officer for 2nd Battalion Scots Guards from the beginning of March 1917. Killed almost immediately on arrival 12 March 1917.

Cobbold, Lt. John, but known as *'Ivan'*, a nickname given him by his nurse. 1897-1944. Eton/Scots Guards. Founder of Ipswich Town Football Club. Killed by a V1 flying bomb in Guards Chapel on 18 June 1944. At the time, he was a Lieutenant Colonel commanding the Scots Guards.

Corkran, Brigadier-General Charles, *'Corky'*, CMG. 1872-1939. Eton/Grenadier Guards. Nile Expedition. Boer War. Wounded. Mentioned in Despatches six times. Brigade Commander, 3rd Guards Brigade. Later Major-General Sir Charles, KCVO CB CMG and became the Major-General at Horse Guards. Sergeant-at-Arms in House of Commons.

Douglas, Captain Archie OBE. 1896-1981. Eton/Rifle Brigade and Staff. Wounded. Mentioned in Despatches. Eton contemporary of Esmond.

Ellis, Lt. Donald, *'Wiejo'*. 1891-1940. Cambridge/Scots Guards. Italian Croce di Guerra.

Farquhar, Lt. Rupert, MC (on the Somme). 1897-1917. Eton (Esmond's House)/Grenadier Guards. Mentioned in Despatches. KIA 17 September 1917 Ypres.

Ferryman, Captain William. Edinburgh Academy/Glasgow University/Scots Guards. Boer War. 1876 – KIA as Acting Quartermaster 12 October 1918 by a gas shell. St Hilaire.

Gilpin, Captain Peter Purcell-Gilpin, MC and Bar. Scots Guards. Born in 1885.

Harbord, Lt. the Hon. Victor. 1897-1943. Eton/Oxford/Scots Guards. Page of Honour at 1910 Coronation. Wounded twice. Later Lord Suffield.

Hardinge, Lt. the Hon, MC. 1894-1960. Grenadier Guards. Son of Viceroy/later Lord Hardinge of Penshurst GCB, GCVO, MC, PC. Private Secretary to HM King Edward VIII (during the Abdication crisis) and George VI.

Hargreaves, Captain Caryl. 1887-1957. Eton/Oxford/Scots Guards. Wounded. Mentioned in Despatches three times.

Heywood, Brigadier-General Cecil 'Griffin', CB, CMG, DSO. 1880-1936. Eton/Coldstream Guards. Boer War. Sudan. Very able and bright. Mentioned in Despatches six times. Later Major-General commanding 3rd Division.

Howard, Captain the Hon Arthur. 1896-1971. Eton/Scots Guards. Wounded four times. Croix de Guerre.

Keith, Captain Cecil. Grenadier Guards, MC (on the Somme, aged 19). 1896-1973. In the Second World War, he was a Brigadier planning for Operation Overlord.

Knollys, Major Erskine, MC. Scots Guards. 1884-1952. Esmond's Company Commander. Mentioned in Despatches.

Lloyd, Lieutenant-General Sir Francis, 'Frankie', GCVO KCB DSO MVO. 1853-1926. As GOC, London District during the First World War, Lord Kitchener gave him the task of creating the Welsh Guards. He recorded this exchange with 'K':

Kitchener (very abruptly): *You have got to raise a regiment of Welsh Guards.*
Lloyd: *Sir, there are a great many difficulties in the way which I should like to point out.*
Kitchener (very rudely): *If you do not like to do it someone else will.*
Lloyd: *Sir, when do you want them?*
Kitchener: *Immediately.*
Lloyd: *Very well, Sir, they shall go on Guard on St David's Day.*
Three weeks later, largely composed of former Grenadiers, they did just that.

Lyautey, Hubert. 1854-1934. Marshal of France. Briefly French Minister of War for three months in early 1917.

Macrae, The Reverend Alexander. Padre to 2nd Battalion Scots Guards 1916/1917. Born 1863. Officiated at Esmond's funeral.

MacDougal, Capt. Ernest '*Tommy*'. 1894-1950. Charterhouse/Cambridge/Scots Guards. Adjutant.

Milne, Lt. John. 1888 – KIA 11 October 1917 near Elverdinghe. Scots Guards

Needham, Captain the Hon. FE. 1886-1955. MVO. Eton/Grenadier Guards. Wounded. Took over command of 4th Battalion at Boesinghe on 1 July 1917 when Lord Gort was sent to hospital.

Orr Ewing, Lieutenant-Colonel Sir Norman (The CO) Bt. 1880-1960. Eton/Scots Guards. Became Brigadier-General CB, DSO. Wounded twice. Mentioned in Despatches five times. An excellent and popular Commanding Officer.

Paton, Capt. George. 1895-1917. Clifton College. Grenadier Guards. MC at Boesinghe and VC at Gonnelieu, where he was mortally wounded.

Perowne, Lt. Victor. 1897-1951. Eton/Cambridge/Scots Guards. Seriously gassed in July 1917 and did not recover from this in the War. Left the Army in October 1918. Great friend of Esmond and, after his death, wrote two poems in his memory. Later Sir Victor KCMG, FSA/diplomat. Died in Rome as the British Representative to the Holy See.

Pierce, Lt. Nathaniel. 1897-1917. Grenadier Guards. KIA 25 November 1917. Bourlon Wood.

Powell, Lt. RV, MC. 1884-1930. Eton/Scots Guards. Wounded twice.

Priaulx, Lt. Frank, MC. 1879-1939. Scots Guards.

Pretyman, Lt. Frank. 1891-1917. Marlborough/Scots Guards. Originally qualified as a mining engineer and wounded with a tunnelling company in September 1915. A great friend of Esmond and a close friend of Lady Cynthia Curzon, daughter of Lord Curzon, former Viceroy of India. KIA 4 July 1917 at Boesinghe.

Pulteney, Lt. Gen. Sir William, KCB, KCMG, KCVO, DSO. '*Putty*'. 1861-1941. Eton/Scots Guards. Anglo-Egyptian War. Boer War. Commanded III Corps August 1914 – February 1918. Mentioned in Despatches five times. Black Rod in House of Lords 1920-1941.

Romer, Major Malcolm, '*Flossie*'. 1882-1962. Eton/Scots Guards. Later Lt.-Colonel M, OBE. Commanded 1st Battalion from early August 1917. Suffered from rheumatic fever. Mentioned in Despatches.

Romilly, Major Bernard, '*Romeo*' 1878-1940. Charterhouse/Scots Guards. Boer War (DSO). Had been seconded to the Egyptian Army. Mentioned in Despatches for his bravery in January 1915 at Cuinchy. Badly wounded March 1915. Commanded 1st Battalion for short time but his wounds on 30 July 1917 were too serious to enable him to continue. Governor of Galilee 1919-20. Named his son, born 9 months after Esmond's death, after him. This Esmond, *'Churchill's red nephew'*, became a communist and married Jessica Mitford.

Ross, Major Tom, *'Tam'*. Born 1871. Quartermaster. Scots Guards. Responsible for finding two cows, abandoned in the fighting, to provide fresh milk for the Battalion. They were named Bella and Bertha and remained with the Battalion for the rest of the war, being looked after by Private John Slidders, *'Sludders'*. After the War, they were taken to England and travelled as 'Officers Chargers'. Ross was a keen amateur photographer. Mentioned in Despatches.

Stirling, Major Jack, DSO, MC. Born 1881. Eton/Scots Guards. Mentioned in Despatches three times. Commanded 2nd Battalion during the Somme as so many senior officers were killed or seriously wounded. Esmond's Company Commander.

Swinton, Captain Alan, MC. 1896-1972. University College School/Scots Guards. Witnessed the 1914 Christmas Truce. Mentioned in Despatches.

Trotter, Private Alexander. Scots Guards. 1895 – KIA 8/2/1917. St Pierre Vaast Wood.

Turnbull, Captain William, *'Damp'*. George Watson's School/Royal Engineers. Signals Officer. Ponsonby appointed him to the non-existent post of Deputy Assistant Mess President, hence *'Damp'*.

Warburton, 2nd Lt. George. Royal Flying Corps. 1889- 1917 (flying accident).

Ward, Captain Francis, MC, Croix de Guerre. Scots Guards. 1889-1950. Mentioned in Despatches.

Westminster, Duchess of, Constance Edwina Cornwallis-West, 'Shelagh'. 1875-1970. 2nd Duchess of Westminster. Daughter of Mary 'Patsy' Cornwallis-West, a mistress of Edward VII. She divorced the Duke in July 1919 and less than six months later married Captain John Fitzpatrick Lewis, her private secretary, whom she met while he was being treated at her hospital in Le Touquet. This was a British Red Cross Base Hospital, further back from the front line than the Casualty Clearing Stations; it was converted from being the Casino in 1914. In the early days of the war the Duchess and her friends would dress in full evening regalia, including diamond tiaras, to greet the incoming wounded, whatever the time of day or night. For her work, she was awarded the CBE.

Wright, Lt. HT. 1879-1943. Cambridge/Scots Guards.

Additional Notes

'Michael'
Sometime in 1914 a Life Guards officer brought over his own car which was subsequently seized by the military police at Boulogne. There it had to stay, as there was no transport available to send it back. In August 1915, a Scots Guards officer 'acquired' it and brought it to the 2nd Battalion, where it was christened 'Michael'.

It enjoyed a most useful, if unauthorised career. It resembled and was disguised as an ambulance. On one occasion, taking officers to the leave boat, it was pursued by a RAMC colonel in a staff car, incensed that an ambulance was going so fast. The solution was to replace the number plates with those of an Army Headquarters car known to be undergoing long term repairs. Later a calf of one of the Battalion cows, either Bella or Bertha, was bartered on the military black market for a new set of tyres for 'Michael' and two hundred gallons of petrol.

9

Last Leave

Blessed are they who have the gift of making friends, for it is one of God's best gifts.
Thomas Hughes, *Tom Brown at Oxford*

Esmond left after lunch on 16 May and rode as far as Mons-en-Chaussée, eventually reaching Amiens by getting lifts in a lorry, a motorcycle sidecar and a car. Leaving the cathedral town at midnight, he reached Boulogne at 5.30 am; by teatime, he was back at home in London. His mother was writing to him that day from Sussex, to tell him that she had just received his pictures from the Kodak Company, when the telephone rang and she found herself talking to him for the first time since he left for France in October: "I could hardly believe I was listening to Esmond's voice, the joy seemed too great." She lost no time and returned to Lancaster Gate: "He is looking gloriously well, and not much older, although his moustache is more visible, but he has filled out and seems to have got quite broad. He and I dined with Ruby, an impromptu repast, but I was too excited hearing all the news to be hungry. It is wonderful getting him home."

The following ten days were a whirl of activity, seeing family and friends, riding in Hyde Park on John Astor's polo ponies, and taking in theatre matinees. There was not much time to write a diary; only a few names and impressions were jotted down. Out of all the different species of trees in the Park, their crowns now bursting with life, it was the hawthorns in Rotten Row that Esmond chose to recall. Mary described the week with her boy.

Friday, 18 May:
John Astor has been back on leave but returns to France today. Went with Esmond to Hyde Park Corner to meet John and Vi who were riding. Esmond and I lunched with Eileen and Francis. Had an appointment close by the dressmaker. Esmond came with me and while I was fitted he kept up a ceaseless flow of conversation in the broadest Scotch, criticising my appearance in this latest creation. We all dined with

Violet and went to see *Zig Zag* at the Hippodrome. George Robey was wonderfully amusing. Esmond loved it.

Saturday, 19 May:
Esmond rode early with Violet. He is still dreadfully in need of sleep and I mind his refusing to have a long morning in bed, as it is such an effort for him to wake up even after 9. I go into his room several times before I have the heart to rouse him. This means his having to rush off without giving himself time to swallow any breakfast.

He and I lunched with Ruby and Rowland then went to the Gaiety and were much amused by 'Theodore and Co.' Going to a play with Esmond adds enormously to one's enjoyment as his intense appreciation of the jokes is so infectious. We had tea with Violet at Carlton House Terrace.

Sunday, 20 May:
Not a very nice day, but we hired a little Ford car and after luncheon Esmond and I picked up Victoria, Vere Pryce Jones and little Alan and went to see Hever. It's a wonderful place full of priceless possessions. Walked around the gardens and sent for Engledew who was our coachman in Canada for six years, he is now with Lord Astor. He was so pleased to see Esmond, though he didn't recognise him at first, not having seen him for ten years.

Monday, 21 May:
Esmond went up to London with the early train in order to ride with Violet. I followed later. Dined at Claridges with Esmond and went to *London Pride* which we both thought excellent. Esmond went to Edward Stanley's small dance for the Prince of Wales, Claudie Hamilton, Walter Dalkeith, Humphrey de Trafford and a few other friends.

Tuesday, 22 May:
Esmond rode with Violet. I went to the Mall in order to meet them, returning to Carlton House Terrace where we lunched. Shopped with Esmond. Went to Barrett to order a travelling toilet case designed by a brother officer called Pretyman. Esmond dined at the Carlton with Violet, Lord Claudie Hamilton and Cynthia Cadogan, and went to the *Maid of the Mountains*.

Esmond's diary:
Sat in Rotten Row with Mother under the Hawthorn trees, now in full bloom. Chatted to Prince of Wales.

They lunched with Elizabeth Kenmare, part of Mary's circle of friends which included Ettie Desborough. She had sent three sons to war; her middle one, Dermot, had been killed in 1915, her eldest Valentine had nearly died of his wounds and her youngest, Gerald was still at the front. Esmond was taken that evening to the theatre in a party which included Bridget Coke, whom he had seen at Le Touquet and also at Edward Stanley's dance on the 21st. He then continued on to another gathering, but the only girl he knew there was Irene Curzon. He bumped into Fuzzie Baillie, Philip Cary and Arthur Howard, who had been wounded in February.

> Thursday, 24 May:
> Esmond and Eileen went to Miss Vacani to learn the Two Step, Fox Trot etc. I went to look on. Esmond enjoyed himself immensely and made me dance too. We lunched with Violet. Eileen and Francis gave a little dance for Esmond – about 60 guests were invited. It was a huge success, they danced until 3.45 a.m. There was a jazz band. Everything was so well done. Excellent supper and champagne.

Esmond's verdict on the party, which included the Prince of Wales and the Duchess of Sutherland, over from France, was: "Rather too many men to start with but it was great fun."

> Friday, 25 May:
> Esmond rode when he woke up which was pretty late. I met him after lunch at the dentist and we went to have tea with Violet. Esmond had changed at Carlton House Terrace after riding so we left the house carrying his boots and breeches. There was not a taxi to be had.
> Esmond having been away for seven months had not realised how impossible it has become to get about London with no motor cars, a dearth of taxis and overcrowded buses. At first it seemed to amuse him to see me struggling to effect an entry into a bus, and though it appealed to his sense of humour to find that I usually had to stand holding on to a strap, swaying to and fro with the sudden jerks, erratic motions and unexpected halts, with passengers climbing past me and treading on my toes, his tender solicitude for my comfort made him privately hate this new condition of things, which I and hundreds of others are experiencing for the first time. It makes me realise with shame that I have always accepted my luxurious life as a matter of course, and have never sufficiently considered the great majority who face the rough the tumble of their daily task without a murmur.
> Esmond has always had a tremendous feeling for people whom Providence has placed in less favoured surroundings. His thought for others has often been a lesson

to me. He thinks that a little discomfort for a certain class at home is not a bad thing; he feels so strongly that no one in this country can even faintly imagine all the horrors of warfare. He has often said "I believe there are many people who do not remember that a war is going on."

During these days, I have rarely alluded to the sufferings at the front, being anxious that I should, for the short time he is at home, try to dismiss all the misery from his mind

Saturday, 26 May:

Went early in a taxi with Esmond to collect necessary things forgotten till the last minute. He went on to fetch Violet to go out for their last ride. I met Elizabeth Kenmare in the Park and we sat in Rotten Row and watched the riders. Felt very proud of Violet and Esmond on John's lovely polo ponies as they cantered past us.

Esmond went on to another show and a party given by the Duchess of Westminster.

Sunday, 27 May:

Went with Esmond to the 9 o'clock Communion Service at Lancaster Gate. Sat in the Park together and watched the church parade. To Ruby at Wimpole Street for lunch. Violet fetched us with Larry, and we went and sat on the grass in the park opposite 'The Magazine', above the Serpentine. I think we were all acting a part, pretending to be happy, as the last day of Esmond's leave has come. How the time has flown. Photographed Esmond outside 95 with Vi and Larry and the motor.

Ruby, Rowland, Violet and Larry came to dinner at 95 with Esmond and me. Everyone played up, a lot of champagne was drunk, and everyone laughed a great deal. After dinner Esmond tried a variety of records he is taking out with a new gramophone for the Battalion. He was perfectly wonderful, the life and soul of the party.

In a scene reminiscent of the morning of 30 October 1905, when the Mintos said farewell to Esmond before departing for India, Mary described their last moments together:

When I tucked him up in bed that night, and kissed his soft, boyish cheek, while saying my good-night prayer, it seemed to me that the years had stood still, and that he was the same little child who had always turned to me in his joys and sorrows. I could hardly realise that he was now a soldier, trusted by his men, proud of the responsibility, and enduring with a smile all the horrors and hardships of warfare.

Monday, 28 May:

Sat with Esmond while he dressed and had his breakfast. Watched him put on his identity disc with the little charm that Eileen gave him '*Que Dieu vous garde*'. Said good-bye to him in his room, in another second he was rushing downstairs. I would have given all the world to call him back for one last kiss. Violet was at the door in her little motor, waiting to drive him to the station at 7.15 a.m. I stood on the balcony and watched him through my tears as he looked up and waved his hand to me till the car whirled him out of sight, leaving me alone with only the memory of all we had said and done together.

Dramatis Personae

Lady Irene Curzon, 1896-1966. Eldest daughter of Lord Curzon. Succeeded as Baroness Ravensdale. Created Life Peer 1958. Unmarried.

de Trafford, Capt. Sir Humphrey, MC, DL. 1891-1971. Oratory/Coldstream Guards. Distinguished racehorse owner.

10

Return to the Front

I don't think the fear of one's self being killed enters one's head, it's the responsibility for the men under one's charge which does.

Esmond

Ypres was one of the few Belgian cities to remain in Allied hands for the duration of the War and The Ypres Salient, the frontline that curved around the town, was the scene of some of the fiercest fighting; it was the most treacherous part of the British front. The Germans operated from high ground on three sides. They were in well-prepared defensive positions organised around a network of concrete bunkers, known as pillboxes, defended with masses of wire and nests of machine guns, which inflicted heavy casualties on Allied troops. In the extraordinarily wet summer of 1917, the rain simply drained down from the enemy trenches into British ones below.

In preparation for the offensive some 4.5 million shells were fired from 3,000 guns by the British. These breached river banks and destroyed the delicate drainage system turning the terrain into a quagmire from the outset. Transport became a real problem and, with horses and mules sinking into the mud, heavy trucks were the only means of conveying soldiers and equipment.

The main objective of Third Ypres was to remove German forces from the dominating ground on the southern face of the Salient and prevent them from exploiting the weakness of the French Army, where morale was at a perilously low ebb after the reverses suffered during the Nivelle Offensive. The whole sector was pivotal for the British Army in terms of bases and lines of communication. Furthermore, the seizure of Roulers, the German transport hub, was also very appealing.

Another reason for breaking out of the Salient and pushing forward across the plain to the Belgian coast was to destroy or capture the German naval bases at Ostend and Zeebrugge. Increased activity by German submarines posed a significant threat to the British war effort and caused real hardship at home. At the same time, France put pressure on Britain to mount an offensive in anticipation of Russian withdrawal from the war, and pre-empt the re-deployment of German forces from the Eastern Front.

29 May, diary:
Left Folkestone at 9.45 a.m. yesterday and managed to get a cabin on the boat. Reached the Battalion at Corbie about 9.30 p.m. after lunching at Etaples and dining at Amiens.

I passed my Platoon's billets in Corbie and, immediately they saw me, they cheered me, which was nice of them. And Leitch helped me to carry the gramophone.

30 May, letter to Mary:
My Darling Mother, this is just a line to say I arrived all right last night. I can't say what a glorious ten days the leave was. I never dreamt I could have so much enjoyment in such a short time. It makes such a difference having all that splendid time to look back to. Coming back seemed just like going back to school again.

The Battalion move tonight by train on a twelve hours' journey, and go to that part of France where once Lord Lancaster of the Orgies lived so much.[1] I had only to carry my luggage about a mile from the station when I met some of my Platoon who came to the rescue. The gramophone is having quite a success and is hard at work now.

31 May, diary, St Omer:
Entrained at Corbie which we left about 1 a.m. and reached St Omer at 1.30 p.m. where Cavan met us. Marched on to Brandinghen, Flanders, not far from Cassel, which we reached about 5 p.m.

1 June, letter to Eileen:
Everyone was so wonderfully kind and I don't feel I thanked either you or Francis half enough for the dance or play. I am one of those awkward blokes who finds it very hard to say all one feels.

We are in really very comfortable billets: a bed and sheets, the first I have had since coming out here. The houses extraordinarily clean and the people most obliging. We have our Mess in an Estaminet and there are three daughters of the house. I asked them to come and dance to the gramophone. They said they would be delighted to 'assister' but that the Curé had forbidden them to dance 'pendant la guerre'.

3 June, diary, Brandinghen:

After Church Parade the whole Left Half Battalion, minus Milne and Pretyman, motored in 'Michael' to Cassel for lunch and on to Mont des Cats. We saw our guns giving the Huns an intense bombardment along the Pilkem and Messines Ridges, a wonderful sight. Left Flank dined with us – a most amusing evening.

4 June, diary, Brandinghen:

This evening was the XIV Corps Eton Fourth of June dinner; a great success! About 250 there: twelve Generals, including Cavan, Gough, Matheson, Jeffreys, Gathorne Hardy, John Ponsonby and George Paynter.

We all signed our names, and afterwards there was the usual speech making, and Cavan took 'Absence'. All the old songs were sung. The Generals sat together, and it was really too funny seeing the ten of them standing on the table with their champagne glasses in their hands singing *Floreat Etona*. The CO in great form, ragging more than anyone else! The proceedings ended by Gough being carried out on our shoulders, as were all the other Generals in turn. Motor buses took us back to our Battalions.

Yesterday we had some aquatic sports between us and the 1st Battalion. They were held in a very dirty canal and were quite fun. Geoffrey Feilding was there and asked after the whole family. John Dyer, John Ponsonby, Valentine Castlerosse, John Cobbold, Pat Bradshaw, Romilly and many others there.

7 June, diary, Brandinghen:

The 2nd Army push started today with great success. Messines and Wytschaete and 5,000 prisoners taken so far.

8 June, diary, Brandinghen:

On picquet. Very hot. The 2nd Army Battle, so far, a great success. I see Humphrey de Trafford is engaged to be married. It was one of the little romances I was watching with deep interest when I was on leave.

9 June, diary, Brandinghen:

The 2nd Army have taken 7,000 prisoners and about 30 guns. Very few casualties. The Huns apparently expected us to advance another mile and massed accordingly. But when we gained objectives we dug ourselves in and awaited the counter-attack; hence the few casualties.

10 June, diary, Brandinghen:
Church Parade. Milne went on leave. Douglas Haig rode past this afternoon. Had tea with Arthur Penn. To bed early for once.

10 June, letter to Mary:
I am getting this letter taken home for me. The censor is now so strict that one can hardly mention the word war. We are told all our letters are being opened, and if anything is found in them, a Court Martial. It is very stupid, as of course in spite of all these precautions, information is being given away by those going on leave.

We are at present near St. Omer and not very far from Cassel. We were in reserve for the last battle, but it has been such a success that it is improbable that we shall be used now, and I expect our show will be later, when or where I don't know.

Everyone is awfully optimistic. This last battle has gone like clockwork, they say the best thing we have done. Perhaps we are at last beginning to learn by experience. Apparently, the Huns expected us to advance a mile further than we did, and massed there accordingly – for once we had the sense not to go beyond our objective.

Please do not ever quote this letter. I am sending a film home with instructions to the Kodak Company to send it to you, and please forward it to me.

12 June, diary, Brandinghen:
The idea is that we are to take the Pilkem Ridge; if so I believe our Battalion is in Brigade Reserve, which is really the worst job, as we shall get all the shelling whilst we are consolidating, and the counter-attacks too.

13 June, diary, Brandinghen:
Very hot. An amusing story that is going about here is that my late chief went to the Corps Commander's Conference in a pair of very light shorts and a blue helmet!

Motored to St Omer and went over the whole of the 23rd Veterinary Hospital and tried to change some of our crocks for better horses. Afterwards we dined at the Piccadilly, Dick Farmer, Ally Boyd, Prix (Priaulx), Jollyboy (Pretyman), Victor Perowne and self.

14 June, diary, Brandinghen:
Douglas Haig walked past our billets today. He spoke to every officer he saw.

The Coldstream Band came over and played. A great dinner in the evening; all left flank plus Ross and Dick Farmer.

16 June, letter to Mary, Cormette:

We are all being rapidly reduced to a mass of pulp, never do I remember it being so hot anywhere before, and when we have to do a certain amount of marching, it is even worse. Yesterday we marched here about 12 miles to do Musketry. The heat was intense and one sweated through one's tunic. Today we have been shooting all day really rather successfully and my Platoon was the best average of the Company.

Did I tell you that Gamble, the son of your friend, is now General Feilding's ADC?

I see by the papers that your … and … are bucking up a bit, and really seem to be showing themselves a little more.

This last reference, with omissions for the censor, was to the King and Queen who were stepping up their morale raising efforts, visiting towns and hospitals around the country, and safeguarding their public image by changing the family's German titles to British ones – Windsor replaced Battenberg and Gloucester and Cambridge replaced Teck. In her diary of May, written during Esmond's leave, Mary had recorded a conversation with another courtier, Lord Islington, in which he had told her that a recent royal trip to the North of England had not been a great success and there was concern about growing revolutionary feeling.

In his letter of the 16th, Esmond also recalled that it was a year to the day since he had arrived at Minto, for that precious weekend with the family.

18 June, diary, Herzeele:

Paraded at 5.30 a.m. for the Range. Left at 1 p.m. in busses for Herzeele. Very hot and dusty. The same old story; no proper billets for the Left Half. We have, however, found quite nice billets for ourselves and we have a combined Mess again. Sharing a billet with Ally Boyd.

The Brigade was put to work constructing a replica of the area identified for the planned future attack. A similar operation had taken place a year before in June 1916.

19 June, diary, Herzeele:

Started digging training ground, trenches, canal and river to represent the Yser Canal and the Ypres Lys over which we are apparently to attack. The Brigade is digging as far as possible a facsimile of the trenches over which we are to attack; the front is 700 yards, and the objective I believe, 1,700 yards.

21 June, diary, Herzeele:
On fatigue all day. The attack is not till about the 14th and we are to take the last objective, according to present arrangements. RF (Right Flank) and F (Company) in front and G (Company) 'Moppers Up', and Left Flank in Brigade Reserve.

23 June, diary, Herzeele:
Watched Brigade, minus our Battalion attack over prepared trenches; went off quite well. Wynne-Finch, Tony Maynard and Victor Harbord dined.

29 June, diary, Herzeele:
Practised the attack all morning. The attack is rumoured to be a combined sea offensive. The Americans have landed in France, they say 40,000.

30 June, diary, Herzeele:
Wet day. Motored to St Omer to see Peter Gilpin who is in hospital; the roads alive with Transport. The French are to attack on our left; the French 1st Corps being next to us.

Esmond sent his mother a copy of the *Eton College Chronicle* with an account of the Fourth of June dinner; he wanted her to keep it for his scrap book. In a letter written on 1 July he gave her their new position and this time, in contrast to any communication before his last leave, he was open about the dangers they faced. He had walked up to Woesten with Pretyman and had met some French soldiers of the 1st Corps who had given them a sobering account of their experiences. The French Army by now was beset by widespread disaffection, indiscipline and mutiny, following the failure of the Nivelle Offensive in the Spring.

1 July, letter to Mary, Brandinghen:
We moved up here this morning and are now north of Ypres. We are, according to present arrangements, to be here for a fortnight. We are on carrying fatigues, which is none too pleasant a job, as I believe they shell the back areas a bit. We are not for the trenches for a bit, but I believe the frontline is the quietest place just now. There is a great change in this district since I was here this time last year.

Today we talked to some French soldiers who are near us. They had been in all the Champagne fighting and talked with some bitterness about the casualties they had there.

Mary's diary of the time revealed her concern. "Esmond writes from north of Ypres. They are being heavily shelled. They have had three months out of the trenches, but this present anxiety is very hard to bear."

1 July, diary, Coppernollehoek Woods:
Left Herzeeleat 7.30 a.m. for Coppernollerhoek Woods, about 4 miles behind the lines and north of Poperinghe, near to Woesten, where we are in bivouacs.

After nearly four months in the back areas we are once more up forward well surrounded by guns. We have been training ever since we left the Somme in May for what is supposed to be the attack; from the sea to Armentieres we believe is the area. The whole of this area is swarming, and the French, who are attacking on our left, have their 1st Corps and Iron Corps still to come.

Our attack is the Pilkem Ridge, which entails the crossing of the Yser Canal and the Ypres Lys. The former has little water but impassable mud. This difficulty is to be met with the patent mats. The Ypres Lys, which is about 12 feet wide, is deep; we haven't yet been told what the secret is for dealing with this.

The Cavalry are all on their way up here and I believe the Navy are going to bombard from the sea. The Artillery is going to bombard for 10 days before the attack.

2 July, diary, Coppernollehoek Woods:
On picquet. Walked over to see the G2 Naval Gun which is on the line near here. It is a most enormous thing, range about 20,000 yards.

Fatigues are mostly from 10 p.m. to 3 a.m. We are laying cables, carrying to the frontline; pushing trucks and making tracks. At night, the Bosche shells the roads a good deal, and the Transport has to gallop down the road between the shots.

A few shells have come near here; I think they are trying for the Railway and the G2 Gun.

Fatigues were frequently interrupted by shell fire and high casualties. Between 1 and 23 July, nearby Canada Farm Cemetery was filled up with the bodies of guardsmen killed preparing for the great battle.

3 July, diary, Coppernollehoek Woods:
Fatigue today. Lunched with a Royal Engineers Officer. He used to be the Manager of Barnham and Baillie's Circus [sic] in the States! I am not sure that he did not mistake me for one of his seals, as he only gave me two sardines to eat![2]

The Divisional General came round and told us that the King and Queen are coming to inspect the 2nd Brigade on July 6th.

The Russians have started an offensive and taken 10,000 prisoners.

4 July, diary, Coppernollehoek Woods:
Poor Jollyboy, the best that ever breathed, killed at 1 a.m. at Boesinghe on fatigue while carrying gas from Boesinghe to the frontline, the biggest loss the Brigade could have had. The Huns put up a barrage in Boesinghe High Street where they were waiting for the remainder of the men to return from the frontline. The shelling lasted about 30 minutes and it was the last shell but one that did for poor Jollyboy. Priaulx was sitting next to him; a piece of shell hit him on the back, another bit bent the buckle of his Sam Browne and a button of his jacket, but he was none the worse. He turned around to look at Pretyman who just groaned, being killed instantly.
16 other ranks also killed and 9 wounded that night.

Frank Pretyman's death was a blow to Esmond who told Mary on 7 July: "He had been out since the beginning of the war and had transferred to us the same time as I did, and we were at Wellington Barracks all the time together, and again at Tadworth. The funeral was yesterday when *The Flowers of the Forest* was played."

In the same letter, having read about his uncle, Lord Grey's decline in the papers, Esmond commiserated with his mother over her brother's illness. He knew how much it would be affecting Mary who had been up to see him in Northumberland, on her way to Minto. Despite being gravely ill, Uncle Bertie had taken the trouble to send Esmond some books, including Donald Hankey's 1916 best seller *A Student in Arms*, which he loved and urged his mother to read: "Do get *A Student in Arms*, it is wonderfully true. I have only read half the first volume so far, but the chapters on *The Beloved Captain* and *Discipline and Leadership* are excellent."[3]

On the same night as Pretyman was killed, the 2nd Grenadiers made a raid.

5 July, diary, Coppernollehoek Woods:
The Grenadiers crossed the Canal all right. But the raiding party of two Platoons later returned in their entirety, having seen no Huns without their two officers, Basil Blackwood and Gunnis, and one Sergeant. It looks very fishy, as if the men had "run".
There are any number of civilians in this district, most of whom I am sure are spies, as usually the Huns don't shell much near farms occupied by civilians. The whole district is alive with troops; where there are not men there are guns or tanks. The difficulty in the attack will probably be getting our own people over our Reserve lines where the Hun barrage will drop.
They say the French losses in the Champagne attack, for which Nivelle got the sack, were 100,000!

The Camp was shelled a bit today; luckily no casualties for our Battalion but the Coldstream had five. One shell scuppered a Grenadier football match.

On fatigue tonight at Elverdinghe. They shelled us quite a bit but the men were splendid as usual.

6 July, diary, Coppernollehoek Woods:
Rode into Poperinghe with Ally Boyd and Paton, 4th Grenadier Guards.

Two Bosches attacked our 'sausages', burnt one, and killed all five men coming down in parachutes. A really sporting Hun.[4]

Gas alarms went tonight.

7 July, diary, Coppernollehoek Woods:
A lot of air fights today. We saw one of our planes bring down a Bosche; he dived at him from above and set him on fire, the whole thing came down a burning mass.

8 July, diary, Coppernollehoek Woods:
A wet morning. Went to Church in the evening. On night fatigue; Ally in charge, burying cable near Boesinghe and Guvvy Farm. They shelled us quite a bit but, luckily, we had no casualties. We left here at 9 p.m. and got back at 4.30 a.m. They shelled round here whilst we were out.

The King was at the 5th Army HQ on the Lovie yesterday. I believe the Bosche put a shell into it just as he arrived. The rumour is that he has ordered them to move their HQ further back.

9 July, letter to Mary, Coppernollehoek Woods:
Stayed in bed till late as it was 5.30 a.m. before I was undressed. Ned Grosvenor came over in great form. He says we got none of the 20 raiders over London on Saturday, but those we got belonged to another formation protecting a patrol.[5]

Dined with the 4th Grenadiers; Cecil Keith, Jack Pixley and Eddy Hay were there – he is their Intelligence Officer.

10 July, diary, Coppernollehoek Woods:
Rode to Poperinghe with Knollys and got a bath. Dined again with the 4th Grenadiers; Rupert Farquhar and Eddy Stanley. We played "21".

11 July, diary, Coppernollehoek Woods:
No fatigues. The Bosche has attacked at Nieuport on a 1,400-yard front and advanced 600 yards. Two Battalions, the North Hants and the 2nd/60th, being literally cut to pieces. The 2nd/60th has only one officer and 30 men left – according

to reports, they were taken prisoner, but escaped by swimming the Ypres Lys [Yser River].

We are now this side of the Canal and the Germans on the other side. They started bombing at 4 a.m. yesterday and attacked at dusk after blowing up all the bridges.

The Allied line ran between the Yser Canal, which was 70 feet wide in places, and Boesinghe, where the Battalion had its HQ. The 2nd Scots Guards were in the 3rd Guards Brigade of the Guards Division and on the extreme left of the line, in close touch with the French. Boesinghe was a popular target for the German artillery, making it one of the most dangerous spots on the Western Front.

12 July, diary, Coppernollehoek Woods:
Wood, my late groom in the Yeomanry, came over. He is in the 9th Royal Scots and is now a Lance Corporal with a Military Medal.

On fatigue tonight pushing trucks to Boesinghe. Relieved Fuzzy Baillie at 11.30 p.m. He had had four killed and six wounded. I luckily had no casualties, but we had a good deal of shelling. The 29th Division were raiding at 2.30 a.m. so it was essential to be clear of Boesinghe by then.

13 July, diary, Coppernollehoek Woods:
Got back this morning about 4 a.m. Had a demonstration of a practice crossing the Canal. Everyone there; Army Corps and Divisional Commanders and CREs (Commanders Royal Engineers) and several French officers.

Claudie Hamilton told me that the Huns had knocked out 27 of 55 of our heavies in the last week.[6]

14 July, diary, Coppernollehoek Woods:
Was sent for by Commanding Officer as a Sergeant reported me for cursing him and unloading his trucks on Thursday night. I told the Sergeant I would report him for incompetence, so he has got his in first! Their exhibition was a disgrace. I have had to send in a report, and I expect I shall have to go up before the Brigadier.

The bombardment for the attack starts tomorrow and we have all dug slits as we expect a certain amount of retaliation.

15 July, diary, Coppernollehoek Woods:
Church this morning. On fatigue tonight in charge of fifty men of Left Flank. Peter Gilpin in charge of another fifty. Work consisted of filling and laying sand-bags in a house at Zonnerbloom. The whole place is alive with guns; 135 heavy

batteries in Ypres alone, one gun to every seven yards of trench. Stacks of ammunition are everywhere.

The Bosche put a shell over which set some Verey lights off, which then set fire to another house. The Hun thought he had got a dump and shelled for all he was worth. It was less than 100 yards from where we were. One of our men was killed, but the Welsh, who were on their way up to the line, must have had ten or twelve casualties. A piece of shell made a hole through my Sam Browne belt.

The Germans have been shelling a good deal, particularly from 9 p.m. to 1 a.m., and it was most unpleasant being on these fatigues. The worst part of being in the trenches is the going in and coming out, which we have to do every night, and sometimes twice a night. And the Germans are not sparing with their shells.

I don't think the fear of one's self being killed enters one's head, but as Hankey in *The Student in Arms* says, it's the responsibility for the men under one's charge which does. They are the most wonderful example of cheerfulness and calmness.

There have been a good many aeroplanes about lately, flying in very large formations, 20 and 16.

16 July, diary, Coppernollehoek Woods:
The bombardment started yesterday. It is surprising how little one hears. We went to see a Battery this evening. You can see the shell quite plainly leave the barrel of the gun, quite slowly like a cricket ball.

17 July, diary, Coppernollehoek Woods:
The Battalion is probably going to do a raid when we go into the line on the 21st. The CO has warned me and Victor Harbord to be the officers. We go in two parties; each party has two mats and consists of about 25 men. The object of the raid is to get identification: to find out what the Ypres Lys is like, how strongly the line is held, and to kill as many Huns as possible. The whole of my Platoon volunteered for it, which pleases me.

I am awfully glad I have been chosen, and only hope all will go well.

Trench raids, under cover of darkness, were a brutal feature of trench warfare, and the risks of failure were high. However, they were vitally important as they were a means of getting information about the enemy's wire, positions and troop movements while gaining control of no man's land. Taking prisoners was an essential part of intelligence work. It was for combatants who, with blackened or masked faces, had no qualms about using heavy entrenching tools, medieval-looking, spiked maces, brass knuckledusters and daggers, sometimes all at once, in close quarter fighting. Only a small number were selected, from those who volunteered for these perilous expeditions, but they were supported by larger covering parties. On a typical raid, soldiers would crawl along, on all fours, across a corpse-strewn no man's land, trying to avoid detection. The German barbed wire entanglements, which had been strengthened over many months, would take a while to traverse, before the raiders, adrenaline pumping through their veins, would storm the enemy trenches, attacking at will with their arsenal of weaponry. At the sound of a whistle, they would retire immediately to the allied lines.

The following extract from the poem *Night Patrol*, by Arthur Graeme West, describes the gruesome obstacle course that formed the initial part of a raid:

Over the top! The wire's thin here, unbarbed
Plain rusty coils, not staked, and low enough:
Full of old tins, though – When you're through all three,
Aim quarter left for 50 yards or so,
Then straight for that new piece of German wire;
See if it's thick, and listen for a while
For sounds of working; don't run any risks;
Our hands on the topmost sand-bags, leapt, and stood
A second with curved backs, then crept to the wire,
Wormed ourselves tinkling through, glanced back, and dropped.
The sodden ground was splashed with shallow pools,
And tufts of crackling cornstalks, two years old,
No man had reaped, and patches of spring grass,
Half-seen, as rose and sank the flares, were strewn
With the wrecks of our attack: the bandoliers,
Packs, rifles, bayonets, belts, and haversacks,
Shell fragments, and the huge whole form of shells
Only the dead were always present – present
As a vile sickly smell of rottenness;
The rustling stubble and the early grass,
The slimy pools – the dead men stank through all,
Pungent and sharp; as bodies loomed before,
And as we passed, they stank; then dulled away
To that vague factor, all encompassing,
Infecting earth and air. They lay, all clothed,
Each in some new and piteous attitude
That we well marked to guide us back.[7]

17 July, diary, Coppernollehoek Woods:

The bombardment was much heavier today and the Hun must have been having a bad time.

The CO and Brigadier have both taken my side as regards the Coldstream Report, and I don't think anything further will come of it.

Rode with Ally, Tommy McDougal and the CO. Later I rode over to see Ned Grosvenor. He lives in the most luxurious quarters for these parts.

18 July, diary, Coppernollehoek Woods:

The Hun gave a two-hour gas bombardment on Brigade HQ tonight. We get regular gas alarms which means putting on helmets. The other night a signal went, so the Roman Catholic padre of a certain battery rushed for his helmet and sat in it for two hours. What he thought was the gas alarm was not at all, but a horn blown to clear the level crossing for a train! But not funny when one knows how horrible a gas helmet is to wear

The 4th Grenadiers went into the line tonight and are to raid tomorrow.

19 July, Coppernollehoek Woods:

Detailed men for the expected raid. Nothing is certain till the result of the Grenadiers' raid tonight is known.

An intense bombardment further north. We are certainly giving it to the Huns now! Today they have retaliated but little. They keep most of their shelling for the nights when they know our working parties are out.

20 July, diary, Coppernollehoek Woods:

We were shelled today, three or four falling in the yard of the Farm in which HQ are billeted.

Hopwood, the CO and his 2nd I/C of the 1st Coldstream were killed in the cross line this afternoon coming back from inspecting the frontline. The bombardment becomes more intense each day.

21 July, Coppernollehoek Woods:

Practised the raid today; Left Flank and G Company cross on two mats from 20-25 yards apart and work outwards as far as 60 yards. F Co and Right Flank do the same 220 yards to our right.

Rode into Poperinghe to get torches for the raiders.

The Bosche has got some new gas which blinds you. There were over 1,000 cases of this yesterday around Ypres. But they hope they may be able to see after five days. They put stuff in the shell which paralyses the muscles of the eye so that you can't open it. As they send it in shells there is often no time to put the gas helmets on. Our new gas I believe goes straight through the Bosche helmets, and it is supposed to kill them, which I think is much more humane.

The Germans were using "mustard gas" for the first time. It was a powerful corrosive which, when discharged from shells, could penetrate through clothing. In addition to producing in its victims some of the usual symptoms of gas poisoning, such as blindness, vomiting, difficulty in breathing and bleeding from the nose, it raised painful blisters on the skin. Leaflets reminding soldiers not to delay putting their masks on were widely circulated in the trenches:

> In a gas attack
> There are only two crowds
> The Quick and the Dead
> Be quick & get that Gas Mask on!

Horses and mules passing over ground infected with the gas were similarly affected, their skin excoriated where it was thinner and less densely covered with hair.

Wilfred Owen's famous poem, *Dulce et Decorum Est*, vividly depicted the effects of a gas attack:

> Bent double, like old beggars under sacks,
> Knock-kneed, coughing like hags, we cursed through sludge,
> Till on the haunting flares we turned our backs,
> And towards our distant rest began to trudge.
> Men marched asleep. Many had lost their boots,
> But limped on, blood-shod. All went lame; all blind;
> Drunk with fatigue; deaf even to the hoots
> Of gas-shells dropping softly behind.
> Gas! GAS! Quick, boys! An ecstasy of fumbling
> Fitting the clumsy helmets just in time,
> But someone still was yelling out and stumbling
> And flound'ring like a man in fire or lime.
> Dim through the misty panes and thick green light,
> As under a green sea, I saw him drowning.
> In all my dreams before my helpless sight,
> He plunges at me, guttering, choking, drowning.
> If in some smothering dreams, you too could pace
> Behind the wagon that we flung him in,

And watch the white eyes writhing in his face,
His hanging face, like a devil's sick of sin;
If you could hear, at every jolt, the blood
Come gargling from the froth-corrupted lungs,
Obscene as cancer, bitter as the cud
Of vile, incurable sores on innocent tongues,
My friend, you would not tell with such high zest
To children ardent for some desperate glory,
The old Lie: Dulce et decorum est
Pro patria mori.

Esmond went to Boesinghe Chateau to see Lt Col Orr Ewing to review arrangements for the Raid; there he was informed that he would be in sole charge of the Raiding Party. Victor Harbord, having been gassed, was not well enough to accompany him, his lungs were badly affected and he had no voice.

22 July, diary, Boesinghe Trenches:
We left Camp about 9 p.m. to relieve the 4th Grenadiers in the line (along the Ypres-Yser Canal). I was in charge of 68 Raiders, 17 from each Company, and we were at Paradon and Roger Farms. We got in all right but, as soon as we were in, the Bosche began shelling us very badly.

The Huns put a barrage down on Bridge Street which caught a fatigue party of the 1st Grenadiers, killing one officer and about 25 men. All these had to be carried to Paradon Farm. At the same time the Huns got a direct hit on the house in which were No 12 Platoon. Fergusson, the Orderly, was buried, and seven were wounded. Everything was chaos.

The relief was completed before 11 p.m. but I was out till 2 a.m. with Corporal Caldwell, who was quite excellent, to look for any wounded who were left behind and help bring them to the Dressing Station. We only had three stretchers, which added to the difficulty. Those that could hobble we helped along on our shoulders, and we got them from Paradon to the Dressing Station by degrees, where Corporal Smith did the bandaging.

23 July, diary, Boesinghe Trenches:
About 2 a.m. they started putting gas shells over, which meant all of us putting on our gas respirators. During the night, we must have been bombarded by between 12 and 15 of them. They had shelled the X line where Perowne was with 9 and 10 Platoons since the relief. He came down to us at 4 am, the first opportunity he was able to get communication through, for he had had a 7-hour gas bombardment.

His eyes were bad then and later on he had to go to hospital. At 10 a.m., Knollys decided to bring back the Platoons to Paradon Farm. They were all gassed so badly, several of them quite blind.

Menzies, Ferryman and Tony Maynard had to be stretchered off; Milne relieved Perowne.

I met two Platoons coming out of the line, some of them totally blind; all their eyes dreadfully swollen and inflamed. They told me they had left three men behind who were stretcher cases and who were afterwards brought down. They have all had to go to hospital. Later on, Menzies, Ferryman and Tony Maynard, gassed and totally blind.

Our casualties from gas and wounds are now 140-150 men; Victor Harbord and Green have also gone down gassed, and 21 more men were sent down today. The gas is composed of mustard and phosgene, I believe, and paralyses the muscle of the eye. So, if one is bad, one cannot open them. The Medical Authorities say the after-effects are the worst; the blindness they hope will only last 10 days. But there is some irritation in the gas which affects the lungs and is very liable to give one pneumonia.

The Bosche has been shelling a good deal today, particularly Boesinghe and Bridge Street, but I think we gave a great deal more to the Huns. I went up to the frontline at 7 p.m. and it was wonderful to watch our shelling.

24 July, diary:
Behind Paradon, and only about 50 yards from the billet is a Battery of 4.9 Field Guns. Yesterday and today they were practicing their "Creeping Barrage" so the noise was tremendous. And when our Guns are not shelling the Huns are, or the French are bombarding on our left.

The Raiding Party left Paradon by Companies at 15 minute intervals at 6pm, owing to the heavy shelling the Huns had been giving Bridge Street and Boesinghe. I saw the first Party leave Paradon and then I left for Marguerite Farm to arrange with the Artillery for co-operation if necessary. It was decided that on my sending up a Golden and Silver Rocket, the Batteries would fire at the rate of two rounds per gun per minute on Baboon Support. This signal was only to be used in case of emergency or in the event of a counter-attack.

Orr Ewing's Raid Orders had the following objectives: to find out the condition of the German trenches and the location of any strong points; to reconnoitre the Yser Canal and ascertain what difficulties would be encountered crossing it and to kill as many of the enemy as possible, while taking a prisoner for interrogation. He recommended a short bombardment by Trench Mortars to keep the enemy's heads down, together with overhead machine and Lewis Gun fire to deaden the noise of the mats being put down.

The enemy lines were to be entered in four places on a front of about 300 yards. The first two parties would be 20 yards apart, as would the third and fourth parties, with a distance of 260 yards between nos. 2 and 3. Each party consisted of: two Matmen; one NCO and six men making up a Covering Party; two Bayonet men; one NCO and three men as 'Moppers Up'; and two men acting as sentries over dug-outs.

The canvas mats, fitted to wire netting and wooden slatted frames, were supplemented by light bridges built out of wooden piers with a foundation of petrol tins. Two entire Companies of the Divisional Pioneer Battalion, 4th Coldstream Guards, were trained to lay the mats and bridges. Once the mats were in position, the Covering Party, led by an Officer, would cross first and establish itself on top of the German *Baboon Trench*, so named after the trench map reference letter B. It would then be followed by the Matmen who remained on the enemy side of the Canal. Next to cross and jump into the enemy trench, would be the Bayonet men, closely followed by sentries over Dug-outs, and Moppers Up. In great detail, Esmond described the raid and the hours leading up to it:

25 July, diary:
Zero hour was to be 12.5 a.m. and we were to be over there no more than 20 minutes. The mats had to be put down by the 4th Coldstream at 2 minutes before midnight.

It was wonderful to see our Guns shelling before the Raid; one line of black smoke and mud flying into the air.

At 10.30pm, I went round with the Coldstream officer to see if the mats were in position ready to be put down. As we went along the line the Hun put over several Gas shells so close that they very nearly choked me. I put on my respirator, but had to take it off again for coughing and sneezing. Each man had a Rifle and Bayonet and two Bombs. The Covering Party had three Mills Grenades, and the "Moppers Up" had three Phosphorous Bombs for Dug-outs.

At the X line, I found Sergeant Smart in command of G Party held up by the shelling. Milne was there too with a fatigue party. He had been blown up by a shell twice trying to get through the barrage, and was left for dead by the men. He was blown into the air by the first shell. And when he was getting up he was knocked down by the second. Wonderful as it may seem, he is none the worse for it.

I decided not to stop there but to make my way round by Hunter Street with my Orderly. It was a long way around, which entailed walking down Boesinghe High Street, the most unhealthy place of all. However, we reached Battalion HQ safely.

I then went straight up to the Canal Bank where I found they had all arrived safely; went around with Victor, who was looking dreadfully bad, to see where the mats were to be put down; Left Flank and G Company 20 yards apart, and each Company to work 60 yards outwards. Right and Right Flank were to be 260 yards to the right, their mats 20 yards apart and to work the same way as G and LF.

The French were raiding on our left, and we had to make arrangements as to where to meet before the Raid. We decided to be at a certain concrete emplacement the other side of the Canal, and that we and they should clap our hands three times to show who we were. Anyone heard there not clapping their hands would be shot.

I went into the French area to see where they were going to cross, a full 600 yards down, and round the curve of the Canal, and imagine my surprise when I saw that they were bridging the Canal then, despite what had been agreed, and that some of them had already crossed. The French officer showing me round rushed off and crossed too, but I could not possibly follow him as I had an Orderly and two Sergeants with me. The French apparently saw one Hun go into a concrete emplacement and, as they had no bombs they came back and said they would deal with him in the evening!

I got to the middle of the Canal, up to my waist in mud and water, when it was passed back to me that the mats were too short and sank considerably and that we could not get across. It would have been useless to have tried to struggle on with no mat. So, I decided to take the whole lot back and to cross on the Left Flank mat, 20 yards further down.

Owing to the darkness we missed the mat, but afterwards found it. It was getting late, so I sent the whole party back to our own trench and crossed myself with Sergeant Smart and two men. I found Left Flank, who had met no Germans, and had been as far as the arranged rendez-vous with the French who never turned up. Covered by the Covering Party, I then went on with two to reconnoitre the Yper Lys [Yser Canal], about 20 yards beyond. It could be crossed anywhere.

Baboon Trench was blown to smithereens by our shelling, and clearly untenable. Poor devils, they must have had a bad time as there was practically no trench left! The concrete Dug-outs and Machine Gun emplacements (were) very much damaged. I am sure the Huns hold this trench at night by patrols, and it is just a matter of luck whether one runs into them or not.

We were there for over 20 minutes. We, alas, met no Huns! The greatest disappointment to us all – we had so hoped to collar a prisoner or two.

After the Raid, we returned, drenched to the skin, to Coppernollenoek Woods, about 4.30 a.m. without any incident; the Coldstream, who were raiding on our left, had 8 casualties and, I believe, never got near a German trench!

Two hours after the raid was over two weedy Huns came in and gave themselves up to Right Flank. I so wish we had found them in the trench, it would have been so much more satisfactory!

The CO has been most awfully nice about the Raid, saying we found out all the information asked for.

His conduct was relayed to the Brigade Commander, Henry Seymour, who wrote to Francis Scott on the 26th:

Esmond did a first-rate raid last night. They had bad luck in a way as the Huns had cleared and they met none at all, though the raiding party stayed 20 minutes in the Hun's trench, and an NCO penetrated a further 200 yards. Norman Orr Ewing tells me Esmond is the best boy he has got, and the fact that he chose him for the raid proves it, for it was of great importance to get information.

The information gained from Esmond's raid was the game changing moment for Feilding. The German frontline, it emerged, was barely detectable. British bombardment had rendered it completely untenable and the enemy had withdrawn from it to positions 500 yards in the rear of the Yser Canal. With the memory of Messines fresh in their minds, the Germans had panicked on hearing sappers tunnelling in the canal banks. The canal was a formidable obstacle and neither side had so far attempted to cross it.

The Guards Division had been due to launch their attack on 31 July from 500 yards on the near side of the canal. However, on the strength of Esmond's information, Feilding was able to order some of the Guards Division across the canal, in broad daylight with no artillery bombardment or covering fire, to seize the opposite bank in the early hours of 27 July, four days ahead of the main assault. They were ideally placed, holding a line 1000 yards beyond the canal.

26 July, diary, Coppernollehoek Woods:
There was very heavy firing all last night. The Battalion came out this afternoon. Just before they left, the Huns got a direct hit on Paradon, killing four left flank men.

Our casualties for the four days are five officers and 150 Other Ranks. The majority of the men and all the officers gassed. Green and Fuzzie Baillie have now gone down gassed and 21 more men were sent to hospital today.

The advance of the Guards Division on 27 July made it plain to German observers that the long-expected offensive was about to be launched and the German guns were continually active thereafter.

27 July, diary, Coppernollehoek Woods:
The Hun is supposed to have gone back to Langemarck, but rumours are flying everywhere.

All our Gas cases have been evacuated; they are rather frightened of the after effects as it may go to their lungs.

Knollys was *hors de combat*. Esmond would have to take his turn as Company Commander. Several of Esmond's friends lost their voices. Victor Harbord became very depressed as he still could not speak after several days.

In the evening, we were bombed. They got the 1st Brigade Transport, about 300 yards from us – 80 horses killed, 3 men killed and many wounded, besides 15 Welsh Guards wounded. I think they were trying for the railway; very good shooting if they were.

We went out to help to collect the wounded. We had to order an awful lot of horses to be shot there and then. I hate being bombed.

The Grenadiers came over to our Mess afterwards.

Among the Grenadiers was the Prince of Wales who, as Esmond told Mary, was making himself fairly visible. David was the name by which he was known in family and close circles:

David has been going about an awful lot, he is constantly seen up at Battalion HQ in the line. It would be everything for him to get a wound, and if he continues to go where he has been lately he stands a very good chance of it.[8]

27 July, letter to Mary, Coppernollehoek Woods:
The men who came on the raid were the most splendid lot, all volunteered for it, of which nine were from my Platoon. We had absolutely no casualties during the raid; in fact, it could not have been quieter. Douglas in my Platoon was wounded very badly Sunday night, his knee, as far as I could see, smashed, and another one (sic) in his abdomen. He worked at Minto and lives at Yetholm and is the father of six children. I am writing to Mrs Douglas, but would so like you to go and see her, but I must find out first if he is dead. He was marked 'Dangerous'. Once they go to the Field Ambulance it is awfully hard to get hold of them again and find out how they are.

Three days later he wrote again to say that Douglas had died: "I have of course written to his wife; such a difficult letter, having to break the news to her. When you return to Minto, or if Violet is there, will you go to see Mrs Douglas?"

29 July, diary, Coppernollehoek Woods:

Very wet. Green has gone to hospital feeling the effects of Gas.

Apparently, the Hun gave up 1,000 yards because our shelling made their trenches untenable and cut a whole lot off. We intercepted a message yesterday saying the ground was to be got back and that the Huns had a Divisional relief last night. Consequently, our Guns never stopped firing all day and all night. There is a 12-inch gun which fires from here, and several 8-inch which they were shelling yesterday, so they must have had it badly.

The main 'biff' according to present plans, is to be on Tuesday (31st), about 3 am.

Owing to the Gas casualties Mike Malcolm, I and probably Ally Boyd are now the only ones to be in reserve. None of the Companies can spare any officers; three a Company to go in; and of course, because of the casualties, no men can be left out. I wish I was going in. I simply hate being left out, but I suppose we shall go into the next attack, which is believed to be eight days after the first.

Owing to our heavy shelling we cut the Huns off and have been able to advance about 800 yards, which is just everything, enabling us to bridge the Canal before we start.

30 July, diary, Coppernollehoek Woods:

The Battalion left at 9 p.m. for the attack at 3.50 a.m. tomorrow, Ally, Mike Malcolm, Drummond and myself left out. It was awful seeing them go off. I do hope it will be a success with few casualties. Some of them I don't think really wanted to go, but I would honestly have given anything to have gone with my Platoon.

So high was the risk of a battalion being wiped out in an attack, that a nucleus of officers and NCOs was always left behind to ensure a sufficient number survived to carry on the work.

The great offensive opened on 31 July. Four days of heavy rain followed, prompting Crown Prince Rupprecht to describe the weather as "our greatest ally"; for Foch, however, the combination of "Boue et Boche" created the conditions for disaster. The left wing of the attack, which included some of the Guards Division, achieved its objectives, but the right wing failed completely.

Approximately 160,000 British troops died on the Ypres Salient out of a total of 410,000 casualties over a period of just over three months. With bodies of men and animals rotting in the mud and stretcher bearers unable to reach the wounded, the scenes were hellish. Many of the survivors would not enjoy a peaceful night's sleep for the rest of their lives.

31 July, diary:
The attack was launched at 3.50 a.m. behind the most wonderful creeping barrage; shooting with liquid fire; Field Guns – 4.5 and 6 inch to a depth of 1,000 yards. All objectives were taken with practically no casualties.

Joseph Chambelayne and Kit Cator wounded and Fuzzie very slightly and has not gone to hospital. All objectives taken. The Huns showed no fight, and just gave themselves up.

The Battalion casualties, as far as we know, were about 50, very few of whom were killed. The Battalion was relieved in the evening, and back in camp at Zonnerbloom less than 24 hours after they started.

Drummond and I spent the day at the Casualty Clearing Station at Canada Farm waiting for the wounded to come in – a dreadful occupation. Wonderfully very few came in. But five Officers of the 1st did come in. An awful lot of Bosches were brought in an ambulance, poor devils, some had had no food for four days. The organisation was wonderful; treated exactly the same as our own men. They had not arrived five minutes before they had tea and sandwiches.

Poor John Dyer was killed at Advanced Divisional HQ this afternoon by the last shell they sent over there. He was one of the nicest fellows out here, and had been out since the first battle of Ypres.

The weather deteriorated very quickly with heavy rain rendering the trenches more unpleasant than ever. Rats and trench foot were a major problem. Despite constant shelling, men were digging new trenches at dusk, while others caught up on sleep or acted as sentry to repel any attack. The deluge continued for four days and nights causing the banks of the Steenbeek and its tributaries to overflow.

1 August, diary, Decouck Farm:
Pouring rain! It has rained for 48 hours and everything is soaking. Went to see the Battalion. The Brigadier told us that we are to attack again in four days. The Brigade casualties for the last attack were only 369.

Kit Cator's wound is rather bad and is causing some anxiety. He is to be operated on tonight. A piece of shell entered between the shoulder and a small bit into the lung.

Mary was to be with the Queen, for which she left Minto and went to stay with Eileen and Francis at their house in Lennox Gardens. She wrote to Esmond on 1 August:

I am thankful not to be alone either at Minto or Lancaster Gate. Eileen is so beloved and sympathetic. I am so proud darling of a letter Francis read me from

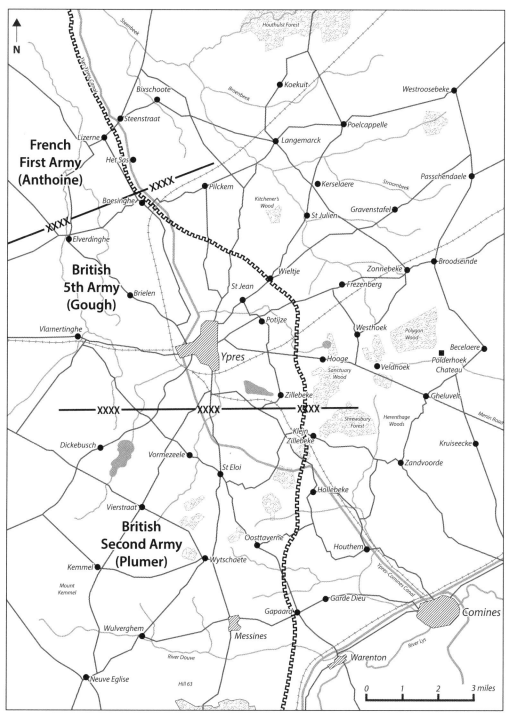

Map 2 Ypres Salient, 30 July 1917.

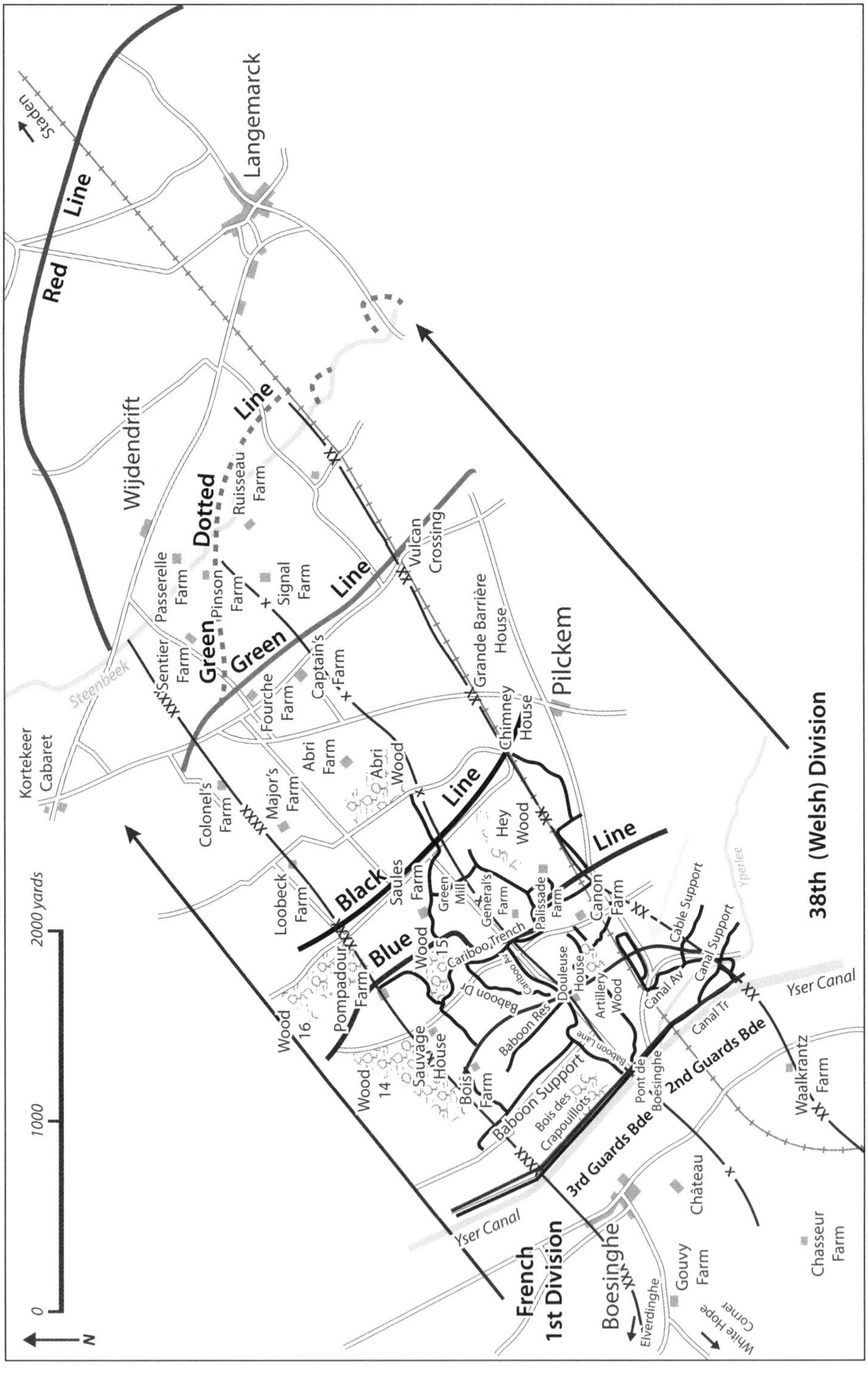

Map 3 Guards Division advance, 31 July 1917. The 'Blue', 'Black', 'Green', 'Green Dotted' and 'Red' lines denote operational objectives. The final Red Line objective was not captured on that day. Thus Esmond Elliot was mortally wounded whilst defending a section of the Green Dotted Line.

Lord Henry Seymour…It makes me so happy thinking how proud Father must be. I am sure you have inherited his wonderful influence with the men as I know they all adore you.

2 August, diary, Zonnerbloom:
Pouring rain! The details moved up to the Battalion today. Wilfrid Ewart, and Hamilton have joined, the former to G Company.

Wilfrid Ewart described the scene that confronted him on arrival at the bivouac where Esmond was: "There are a few stunted wind-blown trees, a few husks of buildings scattered about, a landscape that is intersected by ditches, mud-tracks, pools of stagnant water; in the foreground the ghost of a great church tower set amid wind-riven poplars; for the rest, a mere waste of nondescript weed-grown fields, grey and colourless as the sky – and mud, mud everywhere."

2 August, letter to Mary:
We have Billy Wynne Finch going on leave tomorrow and I am enclosing this film. Could you send me another writing case like the one I got from Asprey, and a waterproof case to keep it in? It has rained for 48 hours and everything is soaked and ruined. I am writing tomorrow.

3 August, diary, Zonnerbloom:
Pouring rain! Rode over to the baths. The minor operation we were warned for has been definitely postponed and we go into the line tomorrow night.

   I have just had a letter from poor Victor Harbord. Very confused as he still can't speak.

3 August, letter to Mary:
I am writing this in bed, as just lately it has been more or less impossible to write during the day. I can't say how sorry I was to get your letter about Uncle Bertie. The papers' accounts implied that the operation had been unsuccessful. I do hope that he is not suffering. It must be too awful for you all seeing him get weaker and weaker. I cannot say how sorry I am. He will leave a tremendous gap.

   It has rained without stopping for the last three days and the whole country is under water, as bad as the Somme last winter.

   Everyone seems to be pleased with the Division's part in the attack, and everything went without a hitch. The barrage I believe was wonderful, starting with liquid fire which lightens up the whole sky. We who were left out about three miles behind could see but little except the flares of the guns and we could hear the tremendous noise. It was wonderful having so few casualties in the Battalion, about 60 in all, of which only 7 were killed and 9 missing. Our 1st Battalion had rather a bad time, I believe, and had 8 officer casualties.

Since crossing the Canal on the raid ten days ago neither of my watches has been the same and both are constantly stopping. Could you get me a luminous wrist-watch?

We go into the trenches tomorrow, the new bit of line recently won. If it goes on raining, we stand a good chance of drowning. The men are simply wonderful and never complain. They are only in bivouacs and, as it is raining continuously, they can never be dry. Their thoughtfulness is amazing. A man in my Platoon came back from leave today, the first he had had for 20 months and, in addition to his kit and rifle, he brought back for me, as a present, twelve records for my gramophone. The more one gets to know them the more one likes them. This is the only reason I don't mind going into the trenches, as they are always at their best there.

I got this morning a new Sergeant in my Platoon, and find he comes from Lilliesleaf. The world is small.

Dramatis Personae

Uncle Bertie, Captain the Rt Hon. the Earl Grey, Albert, GCB, GCMG, GCVO, PC. 1851-1917. Harrow/Cambridge. Brother of Lady Minto, he had been one of her friend Ettie Desborough's suitors. He succeeded Lord Minto as Governor General of Canada 1904. He died shortly after Esmond.

Caldwell, Corporal T, later Sergeant, MM. Scots Guards.

Douglas, Private William. Scots Guards. KIA 23 July 1917.

Drummond, Lt. Gerald, MC. Harrow/Scots Guards. 1898 – KIA 3 September 1918.

Gamble, Lt. Ralph '*Freddy*', MC. 1897 – KIA 22 August 1918 Moyenville. Eton/ Coldstream Guards. On leaving Eton before joining the Army he spent the summer of 1915 in La Panne, Belgium, as a private tutor to Prince Leopold, heir to the Belgian throne, who was due to go to Eton. Esmond's parents were friends of Sir Reginald and Lady Gamble in India. They exchanged letters after their sons were killed.

Gough, General Sir Hubert, GCB, GCMG, KCVO. 1870-1963. Eton/16th Lancers. Tirah Campaign. Boer War. Wounded. Mentioned in Despatches eight times. Commanded 5th Army 1916-1918.

Green, Lt. WW. Scots Guards. KIA 12 October 1917.

Gunnis, Lt. Fitz. KIA on a night raid across the Yser Canal 4 July 1917. Grenadier Guards. Mentioned in Despatches.

Hamilton, 2nd Lt. George. Uppingham/Scots Guards. KIA 26 November 1917 Cambrai.

Hay, Lt. Lord *'Eddy'*. 1888-1944. Eton/Oxford/Grenadier Guards. Killed when a V1 flying bomb landed on the Guards Chapel on 18 June. As a Lieutenant-Colonel, he was commanding the Grenadier Guards and had just finished reading the lesson and was walking back to his seat when the bomb exploded.

Hopwood, Captain Edward Byng George *'Byng'* Gregge-Hopwood, DSO. Eton/ Coldstream Guards. Commanding Officer 1st Coldstream Guards. Mentioned in Despatches twice. KIA 20 July 1917. The fourth CO of the 1st Coldstream to be lost.

Leitch, Corporal, later Private at his own choice. Scots Guards. Esmond's orderly.

Malcolm, Lt. MAJ. 1898-1976. Eton/Scots Guards. Wounded. ADC to King George V. Later Sir Michael Bt.

Matheson, General Sir Torquhil, Bt., KCB, CMG. 1871-1963. Eton/Coldstream Guards. Boer War. Wounded. Mentioned in Despatches ten times. Commander 20th Infantry Division and Guards Division for final months of the war. Inherited the baronetcy in 1944 when his three elder brothers and his three nephews predeceased him.

Menzies, Lt. Archibald. *'Eastern'*. George Watson's/Scots Guards. Worked in Shanghai and Kobe. Badly gassed 23rd July 1917. 1887 – KIA 25 November 1917 Cambrai.

Nivelle, Robert. 1856-1924. *'The Butcher'*. French Artillery General. Promoted to Commander-in-Chief of the French armies on the Western Front in December 1916, largely because of his persuasiveness with British and French political leaders, and his fluency in English (his mother was British). Very stubborn, he was responsible for the disastrous offensive at the Chemin des Dames, which led to serious mutinies in the French army. He was replaced in disgrace by Philippe Pétain in May 1917.

Paynter, Brigadier-General Sir George, KCVO, CMG, DSO & Bar. 1880-1950. Eton/ Scots Guards. Commander 172nd Brigade. He was Mentioned in Despatches five times. Boer War. He twice won the Grand Military Gold Cup. As only a Captain, he was a very popular and efficient Commanding Officer of the Second Battalion in 1914 after loss of many Officers. He oversaw the Christmas Day truce and negotiated with a German commander to bury the dead of both sides. In March 1916, he was injured at Neuve Chapelle but recovered and later in the year appointed to command a Brigade. He was injured again in October 1918 and sent to the military hospital at Highclere Castle to recover. While there, he recovered sufficiently to be caught *in flagrante delicto* with a pretty nurse who was sacked forthwith by the Countess of Carnarvon. In 1927 Paynter became an Equerry to the King.

Smart, Sergeant P, MM. Scots Guards. Mentioned in Despatches.

Wynne-Finch, Captain WH, *'Billy'*, MC. 1893-1961. Eton/Scots Guards. Had been Adjutant of 2nd Battalion for 14 months. Wounded twice. Mentioned in Despatches twice. Brought Esmond's Kodaks back to Mary on 2 August 1917.

11

His Final Role

All my thoughts now seem one big prayer.
                    Mary Minto, unopened letter, 3 August 1917

On Saturday 4 August 1917, the third anniversary of the declaration of war, the 2nd Battalion Scots Guards went into the line again. Esmond was selected to command G Company for the next two days in the trenches on the Western side of the Steenbeek stream. In this role, he was preferred over Wilfrid Ewart who was three years his senior; he felt uncomfortable about this, fearing it would hurt Ewart's pride and he asked Knollys to reconsider it. However, his conduct in the raid ten days before had convinced his CO Orr Ewing, that he was the right choice. Although he had commanded the Company several times before, it was a huge responsibility for a young man of 22 to take on; under 'ordinary' conditions, a Company Commander would be a much older, more seasoned soldier, but with such a high casualty rate among officers, many CCs in 1917 turned out to be young subalterns, like Esmond.[1]

Between 1 and 4 August, Mary wrote Esmond four letters; in them, she made no attempt at concealing her anxiety. On the 31st, she told him, she had heard the sound of guns all day, drifting across the Channel: "How awful that noise must have been close by."

Friday, 3 August, Mary's letter to Esmond:
We know this attack began on Tuesday 31st. I felt sick at heart till this information came. I am thanking God from my heart tonight my darling, all my thoughts now seem one big prayer. I see before me such days and days of anxiety – I don't quite know what to do.

Saturday, 4 August, diary, Steenbeek Line:
Came into the trenches tonight; myself in charge with Ewart and Milne.

Relieved the 1st Battalion, who went away before the relief was anything like completed. They did not know where the troops on the right and left were and I was forced to go out and get this information for myself.

Trying to find the 38th (Welsh Infantry) Division I walked into a Bosche patrol; they challenged us, but I could not hear what they said until the third time they said "Was ist das?" They fired at us and we retired sending out a Patrol to deal with them.

Later I went out to see where the Patrol was, when Smith got shot in the back, I think by the 38th Division. They are quite 250 yards behind us and were actually holding behind us a bit of the ground we were responsible for.

There was a great deal of confusion over where the line was. G Company was about four hundred yards in advance of the French and they were being shelled by their own people. Esmond called for volunteers to go back and inform them of their position, so that he could give a message to HQ. He went to check on them with Smith who became the unfortunate casualty of friendly fire. They were crossing a railway line which was on higher ground and they showed up, unidentified figures on the horizon. Esmond had no time to dwell on this appalling incident and his narrow escape from death; he had to inform HQ on their position as a matter of urgency. The firing then stopped and the line was clarified.

Ewart remembered the pandemonium in *Scots Guard*, his personal account of time in the Regiment: "There was a terrific and unceasing bombardment from the Bosches. We got badly shelled by our own people all through Sunday, and this, following the Bosches' bombardment of the night before, gave us a very worrying time."[2]

Sunday, 5 August, diary, Steenbeek Line:
We have had to dig pretty hard, as there was hardly any trench. We are now in touch with Left Flank on our left.

Sent Milne home, as we only have a small captured blockhouse for Company HQ, to hold two.

Were shelled the whole day by the enemy and frequently by our own side. The most intense bombardment at Langemarck from 2 to 3 p.m. I have never seen the like!

The Huns flew up and down our lines from 2 to 3.30 p.m., very low and unmolested!

They got a direct hit on our trench this morning with a "dud", burying Sergeant Harris.

In the relative privacy of the blockhouse, Esmond tapped Ewart for news and gossip from London. With the continuous booming and banging of the batteries in the distance, intermittent shellfire and aerial bombardment, the two men also talked about their hopes and plans for the future.

Meanwhile in London, Mary was staying with Eileen in Lennox Gardens. She knew that Esmond was going to see action that day and was very uneasy. She attended a Service of Remembrance at Westminster Abbey for the anniversary of the start of the war and sat next to the King.

> Sunday 5 August, Mary's diary:
> Was at Buckingham Palace at 9.40 to go with the King to the Service at Westminster Abbey – we drove there in open carriages. The service was very lovely and the Archbishop's sermon began well, but was too long. He reviewed the last three years and this trial which England had passed and bade us to be of good courage. Walking to the cloisters I found myself next to Lloyd George who was humming a tune. I said how I wished this was the last year of the war, he said now that Russia has collapsed this was very unlikely.

On her return to Knightsbridge, Mary attended a Communion Service at St Simon Zelotes and, in the evening, she visited a third place of worship, Holy Trinity Brompton. She was restless and beside herself with worry. "A terrible dread has taken possession of me which I can't throw off", she wrote in her diary.

That Sunday night Esmond's Battalion was due to be relieved by the 1st Battalion, the Grenadier Guards. During the relief, at around midnight, the Germans began to attack both bridgeheads across the Steenbeek, in front of their trench; they were only a hundred yards away. Ewart included this attack in a long novel he wrote straight after the war, *Way of Revelation*. The book was praised by the historian Cyril Falls for "the author's sincerity and the power with which he described what he had seen: the characterisation of the hero is indeed brilliant…the scenes in France have hardly yet been surpassed."[3] The two protagonists, Adrian Knoyle and Eric Sinclair, were based on Ewart himself and on Esmond.

The attack on the bridgeheads was described in detail:

> Eric maintained an air of detached interest in the proceedings and presently strolled off, saying that he was prepared to take up his position on the road which divided the trench-sector in half and whence the whole field of action could be surveyed. Adrian jumped down into the trench with his men. German machine guns from half-a-dozen hitherto unsuspected points now began to reinforce the

crackle of the rifles, the collective sound being a deep metallic bass. The bullets, though high, were evidently directed point-blank at the trench itself, the idea doubtless being to keep the defenders' heads down. Here and there a man sank back shot through the head or chest. Coloured signal-rockets went up singly from behind the German lines. At a word from Eric the white spiral of the British SOS shot up from the company-headquarters. A sound of faint shouting could be heard to their left. Now and then stray shells burst near. Through the tremendous din Eric's voice could be heard giving cautionary orders, as it had so often been heard on the field-range, and his slight figure could be seen by every man in the company silhouetted against the moon above them. Eric's voice could still be heard. "Steady! Wait for the word! Take aim when you fire! Don't waste your ammunition! Aim at the foot of the wire in front! Wait for the word, and then all together!"[4]

After giving the men their orders Esmond left the trench at around one o'clock on Monday morning to report back to HQ. As he crossed the moonlit road with his orderly, Patrick, heading for the shelter, a bullet struck him in the left upper arm. It pierced his side, just below the armpit, travelled through his lung, shattering two ribs, and exited his upper back. A second round killed Patrick outright.

"Mr Elliot is bowled over!" a voice was heard, shouting above the noise of the guns. Esmond's orderly, Milne, heard this and rushed in the direction of the road, only to find him being carried back to the trench by Sergeant Lindores. Esmond was conscious, but going into shock because of the pain; still, he had the presence of mind to tell Ewart to take command of the Company. His orderly, Leitch, bandaged him as best he could whilst they waited for the stretcher bearers, then he and Milne went with him to the 1st Grenadiers regimental aid post.

Knollys later gave Francis Scott an account of what happened:

> They bound up his wound and gave him a little morphia, lifted him on to a stretcher and put a pad under his back. Esmond said: 'Never mind my arm, it's my side and my back.' They carried him down to the 1st Grenadiers' Dressing Station which was the nearest and easiest for access. The road was very rough but he never complained. He apologised for giving them so much trouble; he never said he was in pain. He was given a little brandy in the trench, but he hardly touched it, and Milne got him some Perrier water to moisten his lips. On arrival at the Clearing Station, the doctor, Captain Grant, examined the wound; it had bled through the first bandage.

Just before he was given another dose of morphine, he felt Milne trying to remove his identity tag. He resisted, pleading: "Don't take that off, it has my lucky charms on it." Along with the *Que Dieu Vous Garde* medal, given to him by Eileen, there was a disc with the image of the Virgin Mary, bought for him by his mother when they visited Lourdes in 1914, and which she had waited until the time of the raid in July to send him. Knollys continued:

> After the doctor had bandaged him, the stretcher bearers came to carry him to the Base Hospital but, seeing he had got very pale, he said: "Don't move him just now. Leave him for a bit." Esmond said: "I'm very tired, I think I'll go to sleep." Those were his last words. A few minutes later, the end came quite peacefully.

The night had passed and he died at about 4.15 on Monday morning. His body was left with the Grenadiers until the Battalion came out of the line later that day. Asked to report back to the rear, Milne, who had been with him at the end, returned to Esmond, for he couldn't bear to leave him unattended. Later, the Scots Guards 2nd Battalion MD, Davidson, retrieved Esmond's body and carried it by himself till help came.

Two days later, on Wednesday, 8 August, Esmond's body was taken to be buried in the little cemetery at nearby Proven. The rain had ceased and, at last, it was sunny, but with a freshness in the air. It was peaceful for once in this corner of Flanders, with its rolling corn and hop fields interrupted by the occasional farmhouse. All his Battalion and most of the 1st Battalion attended the funeral. Many of the Divisional officers and senior commanders, including Generals Feilding, Ponsonby and Seymour, were there. He was lowered into the earth, wrapped in a Union Jack, and the pipers played *The Flowers of the Forest*, the lyrics to which his ancestor Jean Elliot had penned, in recollection of Flodden.

Esmond was to rest far from his beloved Borders, in a landscape so very different from the heather-clad hills and tall crags around his home. Removed from the breast pocket of his tunic at the Clearing Station was an opened envelope containing the last communication from his mother, dated 1 August:

> Someday this terrible war may be over and please God we will have the joy of walking over loved haunts at Minto, every stone of which we love so much. I am sure you must so often picture the peace and beauty even when you are in the midst of all the horrors of war and long for a respite in that awful din of battle, which must be so overwhelming in horror.

A year later to the day, the Battle of Amiens began, the One Hundred Days Allied offensive which would eventually force Germany to surrender.

Dramatis Personae

Davidson, Dr. J.W. MD 2nd Bn. Scots Guards

Ewart, Lt. Wilfrid, 1892-1922, in Esmond's battalion. Blind in one eye, he entered the regiment by way of a favourable medical arranged by his cousin, the Master of Ruthven, a Major in the Scots Guards. Ewart's brief time with Esmond near the Steenbeek, was something he never forgot and it influenced his thinking when he wrote *Way of Revelation* which was published in November 1921. It became an instant bestseller thanks to its remarkable, authentic descriptions of battle and the characterisation of the two protagonists based on Ewart and on Esmond. The two hadn't known each other for long, so Eric would have been drawn from the impression made by Esmond on his new friend during the twenty-four hours they spent together in the blockhouse, when they were both in mortal danger, together with memories of fellow officers. Eric's final moments were identical to Esmond's and, like Esmond, he was of delicate build, "Nevertheless, the small frame is wiry and the heart vigorous and great. Nor is a quick intelligence lacking in one whose patronymic is coupled with an Empire's statesmanship."[5]

Soon after finishing the novel, Ewart suffered a nervous breakdown which prevented him from doing any more writing; after several months, he was able to begin work on a history of the Scots Guards commissioned by the Regiment. Whilst travelling in Mexico, he was killed by a stray bullet watching New Year celebrations from the balcony of his hotel. *Scots Guard* was published posthumously in 1934 and dedicated to the memory of four brother officers, including Lt. Hon. G.W.E Elliot.

Grant, Captain J C B, RAMC. Attached to 4th Grenadiers. MC, Mentioned in Despatches. A short while before attending to Esmond at the Clearing Station, Captain Grant, had been very gallant when a working party had got shelled; this hadn't gone unnoticed and Esmond had remarked on what a splendid, brave fellow he was to Knollys.

Harris, Sergeant, Frederick. Scots Guards. 'Buried' by a shell the day before Esmond was killed but survived. Later POW.

Lindores, Sergeant Scots Guards. Esmond's Platoon Sergeant, who carried Esmond back to their trench when he was hit. Later wrote to Lady Minto saying "We have lost our idol".

Smith, Corporal, Scots Guards. KIA by friendly fire the day before Esmond died.

Esmond's Grave

Plot 3, Row D, Grave Number 2, Mendinghem British Military Cemetery, Proven (the casualty clearing station established just prior to Third Ypres). Proven is five miles NW of Poperinghe on the road to Bergeus. Casualty Clearing Station – those who died on the operating table, or awaiting treatment, were buried outside. These instant graveyards now form the basis for numerous Commonwealth War Graves Commission cemeteries. Mendinghem is one of a local trio. The remaining two are Dozinghem and Bandaghem, the names humorously coined by British troops to sound Flemish. The 2nd Scots Guards erected a small picket fence round Esmond's grave which was marked by a wooden cross and several officers placed flowers by it.

12

Aftermath

The friends who leave us do not feel the sorrow of parting, as we feel it, who must stay lamenting day by day.

Henry Wadsworth Longfellow

Soon, very soon, our brief lives will be lived. Soon, very soon, we and our affairs will have passed away, uncounted generations will trample on our tombs. What is the use of living if not to strive for noble causes and to make this muddled world a better place for those who will live after we are gone?

Winston Churchill

It fell to Francis Scott to inform Mary of Esmond's death. At 9 a.m. on Tuesday 7 August, he received a telegram from Geoffrey Feilding: "Tell Lady Minto that Esmond Elliot was killed Sunday." The news was broken to her shortly afterwards at Lennox Gardens. Bishop Bury came to console her: "I am stunned. I can't believe it. God help me to pray", she wrote in her diary. Poignantly, she received a letter that afternoon from Esmond, penned on 1 August.

That night, accompanied by Eileen, Mary left London for Minto. Violet hurried over from Meikleour, the house she and John had on the Tay, and was ready to meet her mother off the train early on Wednesday morning; she had had to break the news to Larry. Her elation at the prospect of joining her husband in Paris for his long-anticipated leave, had now turned to despair as she faced the loss of her adored younger brother. As they had done at the time of Rolly's death, the family gathered together in the Borders: "The future for us all without him is dark indeed," Mary wrote in her diary.

On 10 August, another message arrived from Esmond, this time as an enclosure to the letter he had sent to Aunt Louisa in December 1916:

My dear Aunt Louisa, Today I go to join our 2nd Battalion, and as the Division is in the line, I shall be sooner or later of course going into the trenches. I am an absolute fatalist, and always feel everything happens for some reason, but though a fatalist I do think one should at the same time be prepared for all possibilities, and this is why I am writing to you … If anything should happen to me I should like darling Mother to have some little message of love from me…I wish I had the power to tell you what Mother and the family have meant to me. No life has been happier than mine, and whom have I to thank for it, but her, the family, and you all…It is so hard to write, with half a dozen people in here talking and playing Bridge, so please excuse this, for it is not half I meant to say.

Dated 11 December 1916, Monday night, Esmond's farewell letter read:

My beloved Mother, I am writing this tonight, the evening before I go up to join my Battalion as I should like you to have some little message of love from me if anything should happen to me. I don't think you or the family ever realised what you have meant to me. Your love for me and my love for you and the family, but particularly for you, has made my life the happiest there has ever been. Everything that has brought most enjoyment into my life has always either been done with you or one of the others. I do hope that, if you ever think of me, you will remember some of the gloriously happy times we have spent together and I do ask you from my heart not to sorrow for me. I have never felt happier or more contented than I do tonight, something I can't explain, and it is this which has prompted me to send you this little line, as I feel I am perhaps in the near future going to join father and so many of those who have met that glorious death out here.

I go to the Battalion remembering that I shall have great responsibilities and that I am father's son, and whether I fail or whether I succeed in carrying out what I may be given to do, I promise you it will always be of my best. I have no wishes, except for you to tell the family how happy I am and to thank them for all the love they have given me. Tell them I am gloriously happy and not to sorrow for me.

Look after Nana, the best friend I have ever had, and tell her that my love for her today is the same as it was when I was a little child. And for you my beloved Mother, no words of mine can say what you have meant to my life. I love you as I have loved no one else, and I can say no more. Don't sorrow for me. I am gloriously happy and with what joy it will be when we meet again! Goodbye and God bless you. Your ever devoted, Esmond.

"Such a wonderful letter to possess when my heart has got more accustomed to this anguish," Mary wrote in her diary. Unquestionably, it was her faith that upheld her now and the kindness of everyone around her. Esmond's last communication of 3 August, a long one, with a post scriptum dated the 4th, reached her on the 11th.

In the days that followed, as she prepared for a small memorial service for her 'beloved Essy' at Minto Church on 18 August, Mary was inundated with telegrams and letters of sympathy; by the end of the month, she had written over forty acknowledgements.

Tributes, together with accounts of his last hours, began to pour in from the Army. This 'first wave' of condolences, universally laudatory and heartfelt, reassured her that her boy had done his duty. Geoffrey Feilding wrote to her on the morning of Esmond's death:

> I feel perfectly miserable at having to write to tell you about poor little Esmond's death which took place in the middle of last night... He is a great loss, loved by everyone, both Officers and men. Only a few days ago his Commanding Officer was telling me that he was quite their best boy. He led a very good raid into the German trenches a fortnight ago, and did it splendidly, with all the coolness of an older man and the dash of a boy.
>
> I cannot tell you how we all sympathise with you, knowing what he was to you, and I am more miserable than I can find words to express. I feel however that he died loved by everyone, without an enemy in the world, and as charming a boy as could be found anywhere, always brave and cheerful.

Also written on 6 August, was a letter from Henry Seymour to Francis Scott:

> There was no more gallant boy in the world...it is such cruel hard luck, just a damned stray bullet. We all loved him and we miss him terribly. Pray God we catch some Huns tonight.

John Ponsonby wrote to Mary just after Esmond's funeral at Proven on the 8th:

> Esmond had already made a name for himself as a fearless leader. It has been pretty bad lately, all our very best boys have been taken. And now we have lost Esmond, one of the best boys that ever joined the Brigade of Guards ...

His Company Commander, Erskine Knollys wrote on 7 August; he was greeted with the news of Esmond's death when the Battalion came out of the line:

> As a Company officer, he was more to me than anyone has ever been, and since the day he joined G Company till the last, any good work that may have been

done was due chiefly to his untiring energy and loyalty to his Company and me. Two days before they went into the trenches, his platoon had asked to be allowed to give him something to show their appreciation for all he had done for them, and throughout the Battalion he was truly loved and this makes his loss so keenly felt by the men as well as Officers. I have lost one of the best friends I have ever had and I wanted just to write and tell you this. I am sorry to say I was not with the Company at the time. Esmond had command himself since I had been left out of the trenches.

Two days later, he wrote again:

> The funeral was yesterday and I went over today to make arrangements that every-thing should be done in the way of looking after the grave. Things will never be the same without him, and if ever anyone did good by personal influence and example, it was he, and it is an influence that will last and become intensified by the sacrifice he has made.

Knollys had Esmond's papers and belongings and, rather than sending them on through the usual channels, he came over to England with them and gave them to his uncle, Sir Henry Knollys, to pass on to Mary. Henry Knollys knew Esmond as a child – he had accompanied him on his trip to India – and was part of the Court circle. In a note to his uncle, Erskine said:

> He is a very great loss to me as a friend… I think he was the most loved Officer, and this is not too strong a word to use, that I have ever known. His own platoon worshipped him, and he knew every man individually. If he had lived, he would have been one of the finest soldiers in the regiment.

Whilst recovering at Lady Ridley's Hospital for wounded soldiers in Carlton House Terrace, Colonel Bertram Romilly, a distant cousin of the Mintos, sent his condolences: "I was terribly grieved when I heard of Esmond's death. He was a born soldier and, had he lived, would almost certainly have risen very high in his profession."

Not knowing the Mintos, Jack Stirling felt more comfortable writing to Kitty Drummond:

> He was such a splendid boy and how they all adored him – so many of them lately – the older ones – have said "If only Esmond Elliot gets through.

I was round his Company, (he was commanding at the time) with Copper Seymour, our Brigadier a few minutes before, and he had just been congratulated on what splendidly good work his Company had being doing in the line.

With a mixture of desolation and frustration he concluded:

We all feel Esmond's death as badly as one can feel anything in this cursed war.

Written in the same bleak vein was the Prince of Wales's note, sent without delay on 7 August:

I can't tell you how much I feel for you, for I know what he was to you … it was a great shock to hear yesterday that he had been killed, and it's such cruel luck, as he was kept out of the battle of 31 July with several other officers of his Battalion to act as reinforcements. It was a real victory last week, but all the casualties, and particularly this one, sicken one of the whole business and almost make one forget about the success of the operations.

In a letter dated 11 August, Norman Orr Ewing, his CO, told Francis Scott:

Esmond was a splendid fellow. I have never had a better Officer since I commanded a Battalion, or seen one either for that matter. Everyone was fond of him, and the men would have done anything for him. He was a born leader and in sympathy with his men all the time. I know he always put their welfare in front of his own. As you probably know he commanded a most successful raid a few weeks ago, and got his men back without a casualty.

Tom Ross, the Quartermaster, was swift to write to Larry, 7 August:

Never did anything during the whole of the war touch my feelings or hit my heart more than the death of young Elliot. His charming manners, innocence, quick and accurate brain, keen and highly efficient soldierly qualities won for him the admiration and respect of everyone who came into contact with him. I always pictured him as too good for this war, but a great and brilliant Statesman. To make a long story short, if I were told that if I were killed Esmond would live after this war I would die happily as many times as you like. But oh, it is not to be. Why do our best go first?

Larry also received a long letter from Wilfrid Ewart dated 9 August, which provided him with the details of his brother's last day: "during a rather trying twenty-four hours we spent together in the line, I grew to like and admire him enormously."

Rolly's former ADCs resurfaced and sent their condolences. General Jelf, who had been on the Viceroy's staff in India wrote on 17 August: "Everyone had such golden opinions about your dear Esmond and General Seymour, whom I relieved in the line last night, was in deep distress over it, and so of course is everyone who knew him."

Much later, Mary received a message from Evie Gibbs, who was in a prisoner of war camp at Schwarnestedt near Hanover. Written on 18 September, it read:

> My first thought when I heard of it was what 'His Excellency' would have felt; I think he would have thought more of the magnificent splendid death than of the sorrow of his loss – he himself had so often been within the narrowest margin of the same death, and felt so tremendously the splendour of it, that he would have been proud of giving his son in that way. I know you will feel all this too, but it can only in a small degree lessen your heartache and the crushing feeling that you will not see him again here. I think I know what a joy Esmond was to you, and how your heart was wrapped round him. He would have gone far, such a heart as he had would have carried him on and on…his death is the most glorious we men can have.

Harry Graham, on Rolly's staff in Canada, wrote fondly of the 'Commodore', 11 August:

> the very thought of whom evokes such happy memories in my heart. Only the other day I was looking at that photograph in which the ADCs were shown retrieving that adventurous little figure which had dashed off to review the troops on the Plains of Abraham, and I recalled those glorious days when we were all so happy together and so united in our devotion to that beloved little boy. I know well what his loss must be to you, what hopes you must renounce, what dreams you must lay down; and I also know you well enough to know that the sacrifice you are called upon to make will rouse no bitterness – only pride – in your heart.

St. John Brodrick, John Morley's predecessor as Secretary of State for India, was another name from the past to express his sadness, 15 August:

> There is no half way house in such a sorrow. He would have grown up just like Rolly – brave – gallant – sympathetic, and would have been the joy of your life.

The warmth of the letters Mary received from the men in his platoon were astonishing and confirmed that the bond Esmond had felt with them was real and reciprocated. She wrote in her diary: "These messages brought a sense of healing and comfort, for these brave young soldiers are still holding out the flag of hope which Esmond too has held, and which remains flying in token of his victory."

Private Milne, the batman reluctant to be parted from Esmond's body, sent a letter on 9 August:

> As I have been your late son's servant while in France I am taking the liberty of writing you these few lines to console you in the great loss you have sustained. A braver officer nor a better master could not be found. The Company in which he served had I know the greatest admiration and love for him, not only for his gallant conduct but for his kindness to them in hundreds of different ways. I was with him up to the last and he behaved splendidly. A hero through and through and one to be proud of.

Platoon Sergeant Lindores, who rushed to Esmond after he was wounded and carried him back to the trench, wrote on 21 August:

> It is at the general request of the NCO's and men of No. 12 Platoon that this letter is written.
> We desire to express to you and yours our sincere sympathy in your very sad loss. You have lost a son, we an officer, a gentleman, a comrade in arms. Beloved by all, ever ready to sympathise with us in our troubles, we mourn his loss.
> As a soldier he lived, and as a soldier he has gone to his last resting place. We have lost our idol, for we had set him on a pedestal in our hearts. He came to us and claimed our affections so that, now he has gone, we miss him more than words can tell.

These were powerful words for Mary, giving her strength to carry on. She was deeply touched by the outpourings of admiration and love for Esmond from people she didn't know and she resolved to make contact with them and their families later on.

On 14 August, she fulfilled Esmond's request to visit Mrs Douglas, living close by at Yetholm, the grieving widow of Private Douglas killed in the build up to the raid. A mother of six children, she had been completely dependent on her husband; Esmond had dreaded informing her of his death, but he had done it with great tenderness and she showed his letter to Mary.

On 17 August, the eve of Esmond's memorial service, Mary went quietly to Minto churchyard where she placed a heart-shaped wreath of roses next to Rolly's Celtic cross. On a card, she wrote: "For my Beloved Esmond. With all my heart's love from his devoted mother." On a separate wreath of laurels, she added the following message: "For my brave and gallant darling boy with the devoted love and pride of his adoring mother." And, quoting the poem by Maurice Baring about Julian Grenfell, which Esmond had sent her at Christmas in 1915, she added: "And you will speed us onward with a cheer and wave beyond the stars that all is well. I thank God for my memories of you."

The next day, at three o'clock in the afternoon, a small service was held in the churchyard; several men from the parish who had also perished in battle were remembered along with Esmond. Their bereaved families, tenants and employees of the Minto estate, stood next to Mary, her four remaining children and her sister Victoria. A few friends joined them together with some Officers from the Lothians and Border Horse Yeomanry. Also present was Esmond's old nanny Harriet Ward, Nana, remembered with such affection in his farewell letter.

As at Proven, the mourners listened to *The Flowers of the Forest* and the *Last Post*. In the distance, came the faint rumble of thunder, which grew steadily louder and more frequent, until it threatened to subdue the pipers and buglers of the Highland Light Infantry. It was an eerie reminder of the booming guns Mary had heard in London just a fortnight before. Forks of lighting flashed at length against a leaden sky until eventually the rain came down, the "pitiless rain", as she called it. The full extent of her loss had not fully sunk in: "I could not myself realise that we were holding a service for my beloved Essy."

Major Walter Scott, from the Lothians, writing from Macedonia, echoed this disbelief: "Of all the sad things in this war, this news of Esmond is the worst I have heard. We all loved him, and loved him dearly. I shouldn't think anyone was better loved by everyone who knew him than Esmond was. I can hardly believe he is dead. It does not seem possible, he was so splendid in every way and I, for one, admired him beyond any words." Another Major in the regiment, Robert Stormonth Darling, remembered Esmond's perceptiveness and presence: "he had a wonderful knowledge of human nature for one so young, and that was how he got the best of out of his men. When I told my Sergeant Major the sad news today, he just stopped dead and said 'Oh No Sir! Surely that's not true.' He is a Hawick man and thought the very world of Esmond."

He added that Esmond had written two letters from France when he heard of his father's and brother's deaths:

> In writing of the latter, he ended by saying 'The only thing is that he died a soldier's death, which is the best death of all.' And now he has fallen. I ask you to forgive my writing to you. But I was very fond of Esmond and felt it was the only thing I

could do. And it shows you, though you knew it, that there are many, whom you really do not know, who loved Esmond.

Major Scott Plummer wrote to say that when Esmond left the Lothians in Haddington to join Feilding in France, his men felt a pang: "When he left us the first time to go to France they found out when he would be leaving and all went down to the gate to give him a cheer. It was a small incident but it struck me at the time as being so spontaneous and such a touching tribute to his influence with them that I think you may like to know about it."

Letters arrived promptly from Esmond's brother officers, people whose names Mary had seen mentioned in diaries and letters home.

On 8 August, Ally Boyd wrote:

> Dear Esmond, he was absolutely the best. He was the kindest and cheeriest fellow I have ever met. We all simply loved him. It seems that the best always go – I shall never forget him. Esmond was by far the most popular officer amongst both officers and men that I have ever seen out here. He never thought of himself, but was always trying to do something for someone else.

Echoing Ally Boyd's sentiments regarding Esmond's selflessness were the memories of the Battalion Chaplain, Rev. Macrae, 11 August:

> I shall never forget how, one evening after a long march we arrived at a very cold dreary hut in the midst of a mud swamp and were all shivering with cold, he insisted on my taking his fur coat and wearing it until my own arrived. I did not want to take it but he and another Officer, with boyish glee, forced me into it. It is a proud memory now. He was always doing kind things to the men of his Company and they simply adored him.

Arthur Kinnaird wrote on 8 August: "Everyone in our 2nd Bn is heartbroken at Esmond's death as they all loved him. I always thought that he was one of the most attractive people I have ever met." Kinnaird himself was killed three months later at Cambrai.

From his oldest friends, who had been at school with him, came intensely emotional letters, validating the line from the *Boating Song* that nothing in life would sever the chain around them that was Eton. Eddy Hartington, who left at the same time as Esmond and was due to share rooms with him at Cambridge in 1914, put it very simply:

11 August:
I was fonder of Esmond than of anyone in the world, and indeed no one could know him as well as I did without loving him.

His loss is by far the worst which I personally have had since this terrible war began.

Esmond's spirit was so fine and pure and wonderful that the world will be a poorer place without him. But one can be confident that, whatever the hereafter may be, nothing can be more certain than such a fine thing cannot pass away utterly.

On 15 August, James Stuart wrote: "From among my friends there is no one I could have been sorrier to lose. He would be a great loss to anyone who knew him well, and I always hoped to be able to look upon him as my greatest friend."

On 21 August, Ned Grosvenor wrote:

Just before the push I saw a good deal of Esmond, thank God. We used to meet and talk things over, just like the old days at Eton, and our friendship was forged to an unbreaking strength. His unfailing spirit, that wonderful charm and splendid courage was a tonic to me. The ghastly news was brought to me by two of his brother officers who walked miles to tell me. I could not eat or sleep that night. At dawn a sort of peace came to my tired brain, as if Esmond was speaking, and he seemed to tell me that he was so happy, and in wonderful peace.

He had had this sensation on the day of the funeral at Proven and had placed a small bunch of flowers on Esmond's grave. "I will go every week and see that his grave is properly cared for and looked after", he promised Mary.

Victor Cazalet, who had lost a brother earlier in the war, sent Mary the following lines on 16 September:

I knew Esmond so well at Eton, and always connected him with Bob Wendover, as they were such good friends.

He always seemed to me to possess just the qualities I should like to have most myself, modesty and charm of manner, and that perfect unselfconsciousness which must have endeared him to all. However, he has gone to join a worthy company, with Bob where he will find a rest and happiness unknown to us – and his memory can but live to brighten and lighten the pathway of those left behind.

Victor Perowne seemed more than any other friend to be traumatised by Esmond's death. He had crossed over with Esmond as he returned from the trenches practically blinded after a prolonged gas bombardment, on the eve of the raid. They had said goodbye to each other on the 28th at Paradon Farm and then, because of his injuries, he was taken to England where he lay for three weeks in hospital. His mother, who knew how much he admired Esmond, kept back the news of his friend's death. Victor's sight was just returning when another friend came to visit him; upset at recent losses and unable to conceal the truth, he told him about Esmond. The shock was so great that any progress Victor had made was completely reversed. At first, he wrote quite formally to Mary from the Prince of Wales Hospital in North London on 13 August:

> I was at Eton with him, although rather junior to him, and know how highly everyone thought of him – and I also could discuss India with him. I have never known someone so unalterably cheerful under trying circumstances – he was as brave as a lion and we all loved him. We were together so much, and I cannot tell you how much I feel for you in your loss.

Several letters were later exchanged with Mary, a correspondence encouraged by Victor's mother. It became clear that he found it helpful being able to talk about Esmond and what their friendship had meant to him and just as Victor's openness of heart was immensely comforting to her, so her readiness to console him in his grief was vitally important to him. He was intelligent and articulate and able to express his feelings, but he was still very young, only twenty, and it was hard for him to come to terms with such a loss.

In the autumn, Mary invited Victor up to Minto and asked him to contribute his recollections to the record she was preparing of Esmond's life. He wrote a detailed chronological account of their time together in G Company which gave him plenty of opportunity of offering a complete picture of Esmond's character.

They had first met at Eton in 1911 and although Victor was two years below him, Esmond's facility with recollection meant he instantly remembered him when they came across each other again at Maltzhorn Farm in December 1916. After that, they were inseparable. Because of their difference in height, they were called "The Long and the Short":

> I think that his influence was all the greater because it was entirely unconscious. There was never anything of the 'talker' about him. He was always so modest and self-effacing and always thought of others. Well as I knew his great affection for his home and his devotion to his mother, he never mentioned them, except casually.

He never talked or thought of himself at all, and was never happier than when doing things for others.

Victor's story contained many humorous anecdotes which typified Esmond's approach to life and, although reading it must have been very painful for Mary, she found consolation in the confirmation that his contagious cheerfulness and kindness were not simply reserved for the family. His ability to tell a funny story and his skill at mimicry, honed in the classroom in Ottawa with Mademoiselle de Jaffa, would have people in stitches, so much so that they were able to forget briefly the horrors of war. He would remain calm and collected in the most trying of circumstances even when he had been on night-time fatigues with no break.

> When in the trenches, up to their waists in mud, and frozen with cold, Esmond made such light of it that it helped others to bear their discomfort cheerfully. He would always do the disagreeable thing himself, or take the most uncomfortable place. His unselfishness was a great example, and made many think more of others than they had ever done before.
>
> I think Esmond had had such a beautiful full life and there was nothing to regret in it. Wherever he went, he left it happier than before and he was unconscious too of the good effect he had on others. He was so broad-minded, there was nothing of the prig about him. I always felt I could have such trust in him, the kind of person you can always turn to in a difficulty and I think everyone felt the same.

Victor's memory of Esmond's resilience, common sense and coolness under pressure, would remind Mary of some of the qualities she prized in Rolly. Like his father, Esmond seemed to be a peace-maker too. When they met up at Minto, Victor told Mary that:

> There had been a certain amount of friction and jealousy between the different Companies, but after Esmond had been there a short while, this all changed. He helped others to forget themselves, till unconsciously they took their cue from him, and the whole atmosphere was different. 'G' Company and Left Flank became not only friends but messed together.

Esmond took the trouble to understand the various characters and their foibles, teaching Victor the importance of not being judgemental. His friend's example would inspire Victor after the war, as he forged a successful career in the Diplomatic Service. "He sowed the good seed throughout the Battalion, and it will grow and continue to flourish." Of his faith, he said: "He never talked much about religion, but I know he often loved to go to Communion. He never seemed too tired to go, even after an arduous turn in the line."

Concluding his sketch for Mary, Victor summed up the essence of his friend: "He had some inextinguishable flame within him, which I must believe still burns somewhere for our good."

Victor wrote two poems about Esmond in 1917; one of them, entitled *A Dirge*, was included in *The Muse in Arms*, an anthology of British war poetry published by John Murray in November of that year. The other, *In Memoriam*, a more personal composition, recalled familiar scenes and events associated with Esmond:

The bells of Arlee ringing
In the clear month of May,
With birds in gardens singing,
All at the break of day.
The elm trees by the water
Where I walked with my friend,
The happy life and laughter –
Oh! Why had this an end?

White through the darkness, lying
On roofs in Amiens town,
The snow when day was dying,
The churches old and brown.
The tapers dimly burning
Before each silent shrine –
Why is there no returning?
All this was his & mine.

Grim though the evening peering
The ruins of Péronne,
The flaming houses leering
Like souls whose hope is gone.
Through the rain's sullen streaming'
The castle old and wet,
Its towers dully gleaming –
So much I can't forget.

Now, other pipes are playing
The tunes we know so well –

Past me the men go swaying,
And is there none to tell?
Only the sad waves beating
Along the empty shore,
Remorselessly repeating
That you return no more.

When Etonians returned to school at the beginning of the Michaelmas Term, they had to read an extended list of OE casualties in the Roll of Honour kept in a glass case on the outside wall of College Chapel. Their names were read out at the first Evensong service. Hugh Macnaghten wrote to Mary as soon as he learnt of Esmond's death, 10 August:

> I thought somehow that Esmond would have been spared. It seemed impossible that so bright a spirit should be taken, one so necessary to you and our cause, so invaluable as a source of courage and inspiration to others. From first to last, as far as I can remember, he was just perfection. Quite honestly, I can think of nothing in which he fell short of the highest standard of chivalry – I might say Christianity, but that wasn't on the surface, though it was in the heart of him. He could always be trusted beyond the utmost limit which it is fair to trust boys and he never failed one. That is hardly ever true of, even of the best of boys, but it was true of him. And he was the very soul of courtesy, excelling all others but never wishing to outshine … Esmond under all circumstances was happy, and so a true source of delight and happiness to others. God bless him. Wherever he is there must be happiness around him. All this is no comfort, but I know he owed a great part of his dauntless courage to his mother, and it will not fail her now. The thought of his life leaves a radiant happiness which even death cannot dispel. The loss must be crushing, unbearable, but he lives on.

He also forwarded a letter he had received from Tom Cattley, a master who had taken temporary charge of his house in the summer of 1911: "It is a great grief to me to see Esmond Elliot's name in the Roll of Honour. My thoughts go back to the summer of 1911 when you left me in charge of your House, and he was cox of the VIII. I remember saying to him that I hoped he would not become conceited. His answer was, 'I hope you'll kick me if I do!'"

Macnaghten set about writing Esmond's obituary which appeared in the *The Eton College Chronicle* at the beginning of October:

Four years ago at Eton, half in earnest, half in jest, he said: "I should like to be in a battle, just for once: I want to know if I should be afraid." Then he added with a laugh: "I don't think I should be afraid, but I want to know." Very certainly, in courage as in courtesy, he seemed to us here to lack nothing. "Probably the most trustworthy boy in the world," was written of him while still at Eton. His Colonel said of him that he was the best officer he ever had in the regiment and every one said: "If only Esmond Elliot gets through." His modesty was always delightful. When he first steered the Eight, he never walked with any of the crew, going to and from the boat, but always, quite unselfconsciously alone. On being elected to 'Pop' he was genuinely surprised, and said: "Isn't it absurd, I don't want to be in 'Pop'. Of course, I don't mean that I mind." Indeed, he never "minded" anything. Always happy himself, he was a source of happiness to all: instinctively he took the wise view, and did the right thing inevitably. As a cox, he never made a mistake in all his races. As a boy, he had the highest ideals, of which he never spoke and from which he never swerved. Such he was to us: but what was he to those he led out there.

Macnaghten also suggested to Mary that a tribute to Esmond should go on a bronze tablet next to the one which had been unveiled in memory of Rolly, at the instigation of Lord Rosebery, in the ante-chapel of the College. Both designed by Sir Robert Lorimer, they were connected by a scroll inscribed with the words *Pater et Filius*:

Mother, brother and sisters
Are glad amid their tears
As lovingly they recall
ESMOND ELLIOT
One very dear to all, most devoted to his own,
Well known at Eton as the ideal of
Manners and modesty,
Of surpassing skill in steering,
Afterwards when the war began, as
Lieutenant in the Scots Guards,
Bearing himself so nobly
That all others longed that he above
All others should come through safely,
On the day when in his twenty third year
He fell fighting
For his Country
August 6th 1917.

By the end of the war, Eton had lost 1,157 old boys out of the 5,560 who had taken up arms; it was the highest loss of any public school and, indeed, in percentage terms, of any single institution in the country. Three hundred and forty OEs were killed in the Ypres Salient alone. Their families and other alumni set up the Eton Memorial School in Ypres, for the children of those tasked with the rebuilding and rehabilitation of the town and surrounding area.

The agony of losing fifty-three boys from his house eventually broke Macnaghten and he took his own life during Long Leave 1929. He had attained the position of Vice-Provost and was living in great comfort, in quarters which overlooked meadows stretching down to the river, with Windsor Castle in the distance. Yet, overwhelmingly, his surroundings served to trigger painful memories of happier times. In his obituary, he was remembered as having said: "There's only one thing matters anywhere – that's to be loved."[1]

Mary stayed on at Minto in September, but everything reminded her of Esmond. His absence reopened the wound of Rolly's loss. Her diary entry for 21 September: "Walked to the White Rock and tried to think they were with me. Every turn reminds me of my darlings and I love the memories, but they make the coping worse." To add to the grief, her brother Albert Grey, for whom Esmond had shown such concern in his last letters home, had died at the end of August. She was inconsolable. On 30 September, her diary read: "Called at the kennels & saw all the hounds & horses. I kept thinking all the time how enormously Esmond would have enjoyed the expedition. The heartache gets worse & worse without him."

Mary took delivery of Esmond's personal effects and went through them with the children – a harrowing exercise. Esmond had been in the habit of sending home from France anything he wanted to keep for posterity in large brown envelopes addressed to himself at Lancaster Gate; now the things he had kept and carried around with him for emotional, as well as practical reasons, arrived back with Erskine Knollys. In addition to two letters from his mother, one dated 11 October 1916 and the other, 12 December 1916, there was a small brown pocket book containing the 91st Psalm, given to him by his aunt Victoria; an extract from an article cut out of a newspaper entitled *Why are we fighting?* by General Pétain; a copy of the code arranged with his mother in the event of his being taken prisoner; and his leather writing case, spoilt and discoloured by the rain, containing a letter from Uncle Bertie and three unopened letters from Mary, which had reached France after 6 August.

Mary also found photographs of herself and Rolly; Esmond's leather watch strap and a small coin purse; pencils, one or two unused and in pristine condition; a compass, a letter opener, a pad of Truslove & Hanson blue writing paper, his Cox & Co. cheque book and some notebooks.

She added these to a collection of 'papers and little treasures' which she found in his bedroom, such as a 1914 guide to Tours and hundreds of letters, neatly organised and tied up in packets by Esmond on his last visit to Minto, exactly a year before his death. Whilst handling these now sacred objects, she also came across an early glass plate photograph in an oval frame of herself as a young girl.

At the end of September, Mary heard that Sergeant Lindores was on leave in Edinburgh and she decided to meet him. It was the first of many interviews she conducted with people in Esmond's regiment which would form a significant part of her proposed record of his life. Lindores spared her no detail in this painful meeting, but she was grateful to him for the facts.

> 26 September, Mary's diary:
> Lindores said the bullet had made a hole the size of a half crown in his back. It was not bleeding which he knew was a bad sign. He offered him a glass of port wine. Esmond took it & put it to his lips, but couldn't drink it. Then they took him away to the Grenadier dressing station as the Scots Guards station was being shelled and he died about 3 hours afterwards. Lindores couldn't leave his post and couldn't go with him.
>
> He told us how they all worshipped Essy. He came among them so much & always saw that their food was good. He came every morning while they were having breakfast. He knew every man and no one was ever so cheery. When they were under fire he would keep up their spirits by some light-hearted remark.
>
> One day they were sitting in a wood and bullets kept on rattling over their heads. Esmond remarked that the shooting wasn't good enough to get them – just to cheer up the men.
>
> He said his grave had a white rail round it and was very well tended. He was buried in the clothes he was in, just removing his belt, with the Union Jack over him.
>
> He said they would never have anyone like him again. It seemed impossible to believe we were talking of my darling Essy. I told him how much I valued his letter.

Mary recorded that many of Esmond's brother officers, when home on leave, offered to come and see her and each one of them told his own story simply "with genuine sorrow and regret". The affection they felt for Esmond seemed to take away any shyness or embarrassment at meeting her in such difficult circumstances, and she found the experience very comforting.

23 October, Mary's diary:

Major Jack Stirling came to see me; he is 2nd in command of the Scots Guards
& saw Ess the night he was killed. He says everything possible was done to save
him – that he really died of the shock – that Essy had to cross the road going from
one trench to the other. He said his loss is tremendously felt, that it is given to few
people to have an influence on his whole generation. He had never known the loss
of an officer affect the whole Regiment in such a way, nor had he seen someone so
universally mourned.

Esmond's influence will live, he said, for years. You'll find long after the war is
over these Scotsmen will go back to their homes & tell about the wonderful boy
who came to them & showed them what could be achieved by goodness.

When John Buchan wrote his 1924 biography of Lord Minto, it was Stirling's tribute
to Esmond he chose to include.

At the end of October Mary was back in London and she saw Chamberlayne,
Knollys and Ally Boyd. Chamberlayne informed her: "There is not one of us who
would not have laid down his life to save him. We all realised that he was head
and shoulders above anyone else. We hoped he had a big future before him, as he
was fitted to hold any position in the world." She couldn't help herself when she
remarked: "Chambelayne was wounded in the push. Oh! How lucky!! It is so hard
not to be envious."

On 29 October, Mary recorded a visit she made to Erskine Knollys at the Sister
Agnes Hospital in Belgravia. They had a long talk and he gave her more details of
Esmond's final moments:

He evidently adored Esmond. He said Esmond had very frequently taken risks,
he was so tremendously brave. But on this occasion, he was only doing his duty.
He thinks he didn't suffer much. They gave him morphia when they tied up his
wound. He knew all about this, as he had asked the doctor exactly what he should
do if the men were badly wounded. If morphia is administered, an M is put on their
forehead with an indelible pencil so that the doctor should know they had already
been given some.

Two days later, Ally Boyd came to see her at Lancaster Gate. Mary's diary,
31 October:

He was one of Esmond's great friends. He had the Left Company. He said much
the same as the others. How his loss was irreplaceable, that he dreaded returning to
France to find him gone. He said nothing would ever be the same without him. He

said he had never seen anyone the least like Esmond. His intense modesty in spite of his unusual capacity was so immensely attractive. He was worshipped by all. He seemed utterly unconscious of the devotion he inspired in everyone.

Ally noticed that "he was so anxious not to push himself forward, that it was quite difficult at first to make him go out riding or walking with any superior Officer." He always thought he wasn't wanted. Ally said he asked him once if he had rowed in the Eight at Eton. Esmond simply said "no" & it wasn't for weeks afterwards that Ally discovered he had coxed the Eight for 3 years running.

Ally said he was quite regardless of danger. He would never order anyone to take a message if it was fraught with danger. He always insisted on going himself. At first, he used to go about alone, not even taking an orderly. He said: 'Why risk two lives instead of one?' But his Captain insisted he should always have someone with him.

Both Ally Boyd & Captain Knollys told me the raid, which he carried out so successfully, would have ensured his being given the MC. He was gassed that same night himself which made him very sick & giddy. In spite of this he crossed the river up to his neck in water & got into the Hun trenches where he was for half an hour. He carried out the whole plan just admirably. Ally said his cheerfulness under the most trying circumstances was so helpful. Everyone came to him to be encouraged. He never was cast down. He used to say: "If I get through this show …" But Ally didn't think he anticipated anything happening to him. He used often to say how much rather he would be killed than lose an arm or leg.

Ally himself came all the way from Devonshire to see me. He said: "That's the least I could do." I feel I now know all the Officers he was with for the last 7 months of his life. They have this intense devotion to him which makes such a link between them & me.

Mary's meetings were a great comfort throughout the autumn, but there was one day she was simply dreading, 13 November – a day on which, for as long as she could remember, her beloved Esmond would think about her and send her loving birthday wishes. She escaped to Ireland to stay with Louisa and it was there that she received a message from Violet written on the 11th; thoughtful and sympathetic as ever, she knew precisely what her mother would be feeling:

Letters take so long to Ireland that I am writing today in the hope that this may arrive on your birthday. It takes with it all my love darling and I shall think of you so much. Anniversaries hurt so much and this one with so much of the sunshine and happiness of your life gone will be horrid. I know how you will miss that darling boy's letter of love and wishes, but he will be near you, very near.

She sent her mother a little diamond cross: "I hope my little present will arrive safely…I showed it to Margaret who said with tears in her eyes 'it will remind her of Jesus's Mother who gave her precious boy'."[2]

John and Violet were expecting their first child, conceived just after Esmond's death, and Violet ended the letter on a note of hope, telling her mother that she was beginning to feel the baby moving. With the cross came some leaves from Esmond's grave, which she had asked Ned Grosvenor to pick for her. On the day of her birthday, at Mary's request, Ned placed a wreath at Proven: "I put your wreath just below the Cross; I think that is where you would have liked it … I have given instructions for his grave to be very carefully looked after."

Mary received many letters and visits from old friends, some of them in the same tragic circumstances. Ettie Desborough who had written the day after Esmond's death: "I had so prayed that he might be saved for you, your wonder boy," went up to Minto in October. "We sat up talking together till 2.30 a.m. She has suffered so dreadfully that no one understands better all the anguish I am going through which seems to get worse and worse", Mary wrote in her diary.

Another grieving mother, Pamela Glenconner, whose son Edward Tennant had been ADC to Feilding with Esmond, wrote: "The sense of the community of suffering upholds us in our sorrow, and the spirit animating his self-sacrifice places us securely above the desolation of grief. We know, as do those many other parents who share the same loss, that his has not been a life cut off or wasted, but a life fulfilled." Both Ettie and Pamela published tributes to their sons in 1916 and 1919.[3]

Evie Devonshire, Eddy Hartington's mother, who knew Esmond well, because he had been to stay at Chatsworth, wrote: "There was something about his bright, joyous nature that was wonderfully attractive, and that did everyone good who came into contact with him."

Frank Pretyman's parents wrote a long letter at the end of November thanking Mary for Esmond's photographs of their son's grave and enclosing Esmond's own words of condolence sent to them in July: "We can at last offer you the deep sympathy which we have for so long felt for you…You have thought of us kindly, just as your gallant boy did, and as every scrap of paper they put their hands to becomes sacrosanct, I enclose a copy of the dear fellow's letter." Frank was their second son to die in the war, their elder boy having fallen at Gallipoli.

In 1918, just after the war was over, Mary wrote to and received a letter from the parents of Ralph Gamble, a friend from Eton with connections to India through the Foreign Office. Sir Reginald Gamble was out in Peking when his son, in the Coldstream Guards, was killed in September:

You have been through much sorrow and have lost your own dear son, and can realise what Ralph's death means to us – he was just the pride and joy of our lives and the light seems to have gone out. There is little for us to look forward to in this life, but we know that the splendid boys who so willingly and heroically made the supreme sacrifice for the glorious cause would have us carry on as bravely as possible, and not sorrow as those without hope.

Furthermore, Sir Reginald wanted Mary to know that Esmond had made an impression as a fine soldier:

When I wrote last year on hearing the sad news of your son's death I mentioned how highly Ralph had written about him. Some little time ago we met in Shanghai an officer who had served with the Guards in France, where he had been terribly wounded, and he told us that four young fellows had been marked out as the most promising, of whom Esmond Elliot was one. I think you would like to hear this as it does help one to know that others appreciated those we love. Only one of the four has been spared.

Early in 1918, Mary heard from the lady poet whom Esmond had befriended on the ship to India in 1906, and written to her from school:

I am glad now I sent them for I hesitated, fearing to hurt you more. They are so like him, so natural and unspoilt by the world – be comforted he has gone back to God with his beautiful boyish soul as fair as it came. When I met him, I was broken down with long years of nursing and a life of sorrow and among a crowd of selfish, worldly, hard men and women, that dear little boy of eleven understood and comforted me…All my heart goes out to you. I shall never forget him. He has been spared the sorrows of life, and you will meet him again.

Hearing that the men of Esmond's Platoon would appreciate a photograph of Esmond, as a keepsake, Mary arranged for copies to be made of his Bassano portrait, taken in October 1916. She ordered small prints which they could put in their bibles and larger ones which she framed and sent to their homes to await their return. The letters of the mothers and wives of these men, who were grateful to receive a little memento of their much loved officer, were kept by Mary and included in the record of his life. There was one from Private Smart's mother whose other son was seriously wounded and in the Military Hospital at Craigleith; one from Sergeant Major Nicole who had received the photo of Esmond from the post girl on the platform at Melrose Station, as he boarded the train to London for his return to the front;

and one from Sergeant Gill, recovering in hospital in Leeds, who said "I can safely say that there wasn't a man who wouldn't have laid down their life for him, for he was such a grand officer". Finally, there was one from Mrs Fraser, written on 4 January 1918: "My husband told me months ago, when he sent me some verses about Lieutenant Elliot, to be sure to keep safely any photograph or writing which might reach me about him. I am very proud to have it, and will assuredly keep it safely in the hope that my husband may return and see it." She went on to explain: "Lady Minto will be sorry to hear my husband, 15787 Alexander Fraser, 12 Platoon, G Coy 2nd. Scots Guards, has been missing since 25 November." The addition of his rank and number suggested she had given up hope of seeing him again.

With Violet's help, Mary took just over a year to complete her account of Esmond's life; a prolific chronicler of her own 'doings', she put her diary on the back burner. She was busy throughout 1918, talking to all sorts of people who had come across Esmond, each of whom had their own story to tell. Along with recollections, came poetry, prayers and assorted sayings which reflected him in some way and remembered his sacrifice. However painful, it was a cathartic exercise for her. He had 'belonged' to other people, not just to Mary and the family, and they had treasured him. It made his mother feel that his brief life was as full and as well-lived as it could have been. "It has been a wonderful satisfaction to me to record each episode and to live over again with him those joyous twenty-two years," she wrote in her Introduction.[4]

Violet helped Mary to organise Esmond's photographs, pasting them into the master copy of the record and annotating them. Mary in return compiled a small book of prayers and poems for Violet, which included lines from the last stanza of a poem by Robert Service, a Scotsman who had travelled widely in Canada:

> They've told me the truth, Young Fellow My Lad:
> You'll never come back again:
> (Oh God! the dreams and the dreams I've had,
> and the hopes I've nursed in vain!)
> For you passed in the night, Young Fellow My Lad,
> And you proved in the cruel test
> Of the screaming shell and the battle hell
> That my boy was one of the best.
> So you'll live, you'll live, Young Fellow My Lad,
> In the gleam of the evening star,
> In the wood-note wild and the laugh of the child,
> In all sweet things that are.
> And you'll never die, my wonderful boy,

While life is noble and true;
For all our beauty and hope and joy
We will owe to our lads like you.
         Young Fellow My Lad from *Rhymes of a Red Cross Man*, 1916

Occasionally, as they collaborated on this project, mournfulness would be leavened on hearing amusing anecdotes concerning Esmond. Violet shared with her mother a story told to her by Captain Francis Ward who had served in the Scots Guards with Esmond in the Spring of 1917. When Esmond came back from his three days' leave in Amiens, he came in and woke him up in the middle of the night, keeping him in fits of laughter for over an hour whilst he related his experiences. "If another fellow had dared to disturb me I would have killed him, but there was something about Esmond which made him different to the rest of the world."

The war continued to claim more casualties as it entered its critical last phase and another set of anniversaries were like a further twist of the knife, the deepest one coming on 25 April. It was around this time that Mary showed the Queen some of her condolence letters from Esmond's brother officers:

> Thank you so much, dear Mary, for those wonderful letters, how touching they are. You must be prouder than ever of your beloved Esmond when people could write thus of him but – and now comes the but – what a loss to you and posterity that so fine a character should have left this world so young, though perhaps he may be doing some great work in the 'Land Beyond'. Ever yours most affectionately, Mary R

Mary had suggested to the Queen that she should resign as Lady-in-Waiting; evidently, she had found maintaining a brave face during the endless round of royal duties a strain. But the Queen insisted that she stayed on. On 3 May, she wrote: "I think you were splendidly 'courageous' here, and I hope you will not think of leaving me, as I love having you with me in joy or sorrow." The Queen had Mary's interests at heart and knew that if she could continue to feel useful at Court, it would help her cope with her bereavement; accordingly, in the summer of 1918, Mary took a house near Windsor.

Remembering that Esmond had always spoken with gratitude about Miss Dempster, the physiotherapist at Eton, Mary arranged to see her and brought her a copy of the Bassano photograph. "Miss Dempster spoke with warm affection of Esmond. She said he stood out in her memory more distinctly than any other boy in the school." She agreed to write down some of her recollections; remarkably, she produced eighteen pages of notes, described by Mary as being "alive with Esmond's personality".

On 1 June, Violet gave birth to a son, an heir for John, and gave him the name that Esmond was baptised with, Gavin. The baby, naturally, was an enormous consolation for Mary, and she doted on him. As he grew up, he reminded her more and more of Esmond, with his charm, kindness and good sense of humour. The family was overjoyed that, having been so close to the action for so long, John had been spared; however in September, his right leg was shattered by a shell near Cambrai and half of it had to be amputated.

The third most difficult hurdle which Mary had to overcome, in the immediate aftermath of Esmond's death, was when the Armistice was signed on 11 November; amid the sense of relief and deliverance, there was the overwhelming, suffocating sadness at the knowledge that many loved ones would not be returning. 42,000 British officers were killed out of a total of almost 800,000 men from the United Kingdom alone.[5] Over one and a half million would return wounded, of which many would bear lifelong mental and physical scars.

At the end of 1918, Major Mackenzie Rogan, the Coldstream Bandmaster visited Mary and brought his own war diary to show her. There were several entries featuring Esmond, all of which captured his enjoyment of life. With no women to dance with at Ponsonby's birthday celebrations, the officers had to improvise:

> 25 March, 1916:
> General Ponsonby's birthday dinner. Among others Lt. Elliot, ADC. A very merry and jovial party. Band played dance music. Young Elliot and the General insisted on my taking a turn, so I danced right merrily with young Elliot to the tune of the 'Sunshine Girl'. I had not danced for 20 years. I felt Elliot's personality. He has a charm which I have never felt equalled.

> 29 June 1917:
> Played at 2nd Scots Guards concert. Had dinner with officers. On my left, next to me, my good friend, whose friendship I had the privilege to enjoy at Poperinghe, the Hon. Esmond Elliot. He is a charming boy, and has all the kindness and charm of manner of his father, Lord Minto, whose portrait occupies a most prominent place in my house.

> 6 August 1917:
> Have heard many of my friends are killed, amongst them that dear and charming little gentleman, Elliot of the Scots Guards. I had dined with him the night before he went into the line, and he walked with me before dinner. I promised him I would write a march and call it Michael, after the Battalion car.

Early in January 1919, Mary had a visit from Sergeant Henry Wood, Esmond's groom in the Lothians. Just two years younger than Esmond, he had accompanied him to France when he was ADC to Feilding. Unable to follow him into the Scots Guards, Wood transferred to the Royal Scots. In April 1917, he won the Military Medal for gallantry. Mary recorded their conversation:

> Wood told me of his devotion to Esmond how patient he had been with him when he first taught him to ride. He alluded to his wonderful influence with the men. He went on to say: "I have had a good deal of experience now, and have been under many officers of all ranks, Generals and Colonels, but I have never seen one to touch Mr Esmond for coolness under fire. He'd just ride along in a light-hearted way, watching the course of the shell that had whistled close over his head. He'd wave his hand to it and say Good-bye as he saw it fall, and do the same to the next one."

Esmond's steady nerve soothed the men under his command. Wood continued:

> I never seemed to mind the danger if I was with him, but he just inspired us all. One morning he and General Feilding were out in a tremendous bombardment; he rode in as cool as could be and said; "Wood, we've had a lively morning of it". It was the same when a shell burst in the Orderly Room where he was sitting, covering him with splinters and dust, and which killed anumber of people in the yard outside. Nothing seemed to trouble him. I know, as long as I live, I shall never see his like again.

In June 1919, Mary made her first visit to Flanders and the Somme accompanied by Geoffrey Feilding. It was a reflection of his strong attachment to the Mintos and fondness for Esmond that he offered to be her guide. Tours were offered by companies straight after the war, enabling people to visit their loved ones' graves, but it wasn't until later that the majority of people could afford to go thanks to charities, set up specially for the bereaved. Feilding spent three days showing Mary a few of the important locations where Esmond had been, but not where he was wounded. Much of the countryside was like a churned-up wasteland.

> 6 June:
> General Feilding drove me through Elverdinghe to Boesinghe, over the Canal on the Pilkem Ridge where Esmond carried out his raid. The desolation of the country is indescribable; nothing but vast pits caused by the shells. We drove past Hell Fire Corner to the high ground of the Hooge, along the Menin Road to Lille, and slept at the Hotel Royale.

On 7 June, they drove to Chateau d'Esquelbecq, Esmond's first port of call in February 1916, where the Guards Division had its HQ. It belonged to a Monsieur Bergereau who showed Mary the room which Esmond had occupied. He told her that, when the General and his staff arrived, he confused Esmond with the Prince of Wales, whose kit bags labelled with his name were waiting for him at the chateau. Only when he saw the two of them together, did he realise his mistake.

> 8 June:
> Motored by Douai to Cambrai; passed Bourlon Wood; climbed down into the deep trenches of the Hindenburg Line; crossed the Canal du Nord; drove to Bapaume, now a complete ruin: saw the Sailly-Saillisel Line, where Esmond had a desperate time in the trenches defending a place called Paltz and Potsdam in March 1917; on via Péronne to Cartigny and Amiens.

Feilding took her to Mendinghem Cemetery at Proven where she saw Esmond's grave enclosed by a little white picket fence; there she planted some bulbs and seeds: snowdrops, violets and forget-me-nots. She had herself photographed by his wooden cross. On the drive back to Boulogne, she noticed the profusion of crimson poppies across the fields.

Later in the summer of 1919, Mary met Quartermaster Tom Ross, who suggested she visit an exhibition of paintings of memorable battlefield incidents by an artist acquaintance of his. When looking around the show, she was astonished to find a painting in which Esmond featured as the central figure – it was the first picture she saw. Subsequently, Ross was able to tell Mary the story behind it – a scene dating back to February 1917:

> When the Germans retired to the Hindenburg Line in 1917, they had for over two years stored up a colossal supply of ammunition of all calibres. This had to be got rid of and, in consequence, for three days prior to the retirement, they delivered the severest bombardment on record. During this period, G Company occupied the Outpost Line in front of St Pierre Vaast wood; 'Paly Posts', with HQ under Knollys and Chamberlayne; 'Potsdam' and communication trench posts under Esmond. The Company carried in four days' rations at a time, but these were often lost on account of the mud falling in, and also the very severe bombardment. No man could show himself by night, without drawing the enemy's fire. This picture shows Esmond carrying two petrol tins of tea to his Platoon, which occupied the Bombing and Lewis Gun Posts in 'Potsdam' and the communication trench. He was up to his knees in mud and in full view of the enemy. The tea was prepared by his servant 800 yards in the rear. This is a very rare occasion where an Officer is

seen unaccompanied by an orderly. His actions were described in different words by
his men. But they meant that the splendid courage which he displayed was of the
nature which leads only to a Victoria Cross or the grave.

In October, Mary returned to Belgium with Violet. They spent the first night at
Poperinghe and went to Proven the following day; the forget-me-nots planted in
June were growing well. Mary tried unsuccessfully to find the Steenbeek. In dense
fog, they found their way to a cemetery near the Menin Gate, where Charlie Mercer
Nairne was buried and, on arrival in Boulogne, before sailing back to England, they
visited Julian Grenfell's grave.

In August of the following year, Mary was at last able to locate the spot near the
Steenbeek where Esmond was shot. With the help of Major Pope, whom Mary had
known in Canada as a boy, and accompanied by Eileen, "we found the concrete pill-
box and the shallow trenches which we knew had been hurriedly made on the day of
the advance, 5 August. Major Pope paced the exact distance from the river, the spot
where Esmond crossed the road." Mary continued: "It was a beautiful evening, calm
and still, and wild flowers and ferns grew all around in profusion: masses of rusted
iron and shells, pieces of guns, stacks of ammunition and old helmets half buried in
the ground, all told of the terrible struggle which had taken place, and how fiercely
every inch of ground had been contested." She wanted to be alone. She sat down by
the side of the road and contemplated her son's final moments. Finally, she picked
up a shell case outside the blockhouse to take back home.

Mary returned several times to Belgium. She combined two visits, in 1926
and 1930, with a journey to France with her good friend and cousin, Elizabeth
Kenmare, who wished to see her own son Dermot's grave at Vermelles; Elizabeth
remembered seeing Esmond in London during his last leave. Her eldest boy,
Valentine Castlerosse had written to her on the day of Esmond's funeral: "Alas,
the very best fellows have been killed. I think Esmond Elliot's death has affected
everybody most. He was extraordinarily popular and a wonderfully fine fellow.
His CO, Norman Orr Ewing was talking to me about him the other day. He told
me he thought he was the best Officer he had ever seen, and Norman is not as a
rule profuse in praise."

Having taken receipt of Esmond's 'British War and Victory Medals' in April
1922, Mary prepared to accompany the King and Queen on their official visit to the
battlefields and cemeteries, known as the King's Pilgrimage, in May. Frank Fox, an
Australian journalist and author wrote a book to accompany the trip, its opening
line stressing that: "It was our King's wish that he should go as a private pilgrim,
with no trappings of state nor pomp of ceremony, and with only a small suite." It
included a poem by Rudyard Kipling, who had lost his only son at Loos, and some

spectacular photographs. Douglas Haig was there to meet the King, as were Foch and Pétain. During this visit, Mary made a 225-mile round trip from the royal palace at Laeken to visit and lay flowers on Esmond's grave.

Mary took Larry to Proven in 1925 and a photograph taken of her beside the grave, now with its new headstone, showed a much-changed woman; once radiant and engaging, she appeared beaten down. Larry had married in 1921 and was now raising a family at Minto with his Canadian-born wife Marion. Mary kept a pied à terre in London, not the imposing, stucco fronted end of terrace house in Lancaster Gate, too full of memories of Rolly and Esmond before the war, but a much smaller, newly-built house in Chelsea Park Gardens. She made her permanent home at Hydon End, near Hambledon in Surrey, situated half-way up a hill and surrounded by a beautiful garden. There she could be within easy reach of the Palace and also Violet and her growing family in Kent. In her bedroom, she had a table dedicated to Esmond, on which she placed many things he had given her over the years, together with more recent tokens of love from the front, including the broken crucifix he had found in Mametz Cemetery.

Esmond's wooden cross at Proven was replaced by the Imperial War Graves Commission standard Portland stone headstone in 1923 and the cross was bought back to the Borders to hang on the wall next to the family pew in Minto Church. In her dealings with the IWGC, Mary soon discovered that the ages of the fallen were rarely recorded on the memorials, which she considered ill-judged. She asked for this rule to be changed and met with opposition on the matter, the Commission claiming that if they did this for everyone, it would be a huge undertaking. After three years of fruitless negotiation with the Commission, during which she expressed her views very strongly in correspondence with officials there, she engaged the support of a number of influential people, including the Queen, the Prince of Wales, the Archbishop of Canterbury and Douglas Haig and wrote a long and impassioned letter to *The Times* on 25 October 1921, which included the following paragraph:

> Surely the age at which the soldier is killed or dies on Active Service belongs to his military career … It appears that only 20 percent of the headstones already completed record the age, the absence of which removes all individuality, reducing the headstones to a dead level of monotony. Would anyone in private life fail to chronicle at what age their child died? The whole current of thought is altered by reading the age on a tombstone; the record three score years and ten produces a sense of completeness and repose, whereas the boy cut off in early youth, with the promise of the future unfulfilled, cannot fail to strike a chord of sympathy in every heart. In life youthful achievement counts for something, therefore why not in death? To future generations it will be an inspiration to read that old and young

alike rallied to their country's aid. They will be proud to know that the VC was hardly more than a boy; that colonels and even generals were often under 30, and that veterans of 50 served as 2nd Lieutenants.

She managed to sway public opinion with it and the Commission was swamped with letters of support for Mary; eventually it had to concede the point and the ages of the dead were thereafter recorded on their headstones.

Mary began a correspondence with Fabian Ware, the visionary behind the Commission, and compared notes on horticultural matters, an important aspect of the organisation's work. She was keen to mitigate the desolate aspect of Mendinghem, in the middle of flat countryside, surrounded for miles by fields of corn and hops, and she suggested that a hedge be planted behind the Cross of Sacrifice to provide, amongst other things, a shield from unappealing farm buildings nearby. Because of one mother's interference, the little cemetery now filled with over 2,300 war dead, gained a more peaceful and intimate feel.

Her wishes were followed to the letter on his headstone. In front of Elliot, in place of his initials, it bore Esmond; it gave his regiment, the date he died, his age, the line from Revelation, "I will give thee a crown of life", and, crucially, the fact that he was Rolly's son.

Mary's last visit to Esmond's grave was with Violet in July 1936; the roses from Minto, planted years before, had grown tall, and the violets were still blossoming. She lived for another four years, kept busy by her family, her writing and her royal duties. Among Violet's papers was found a Christmas card, written by Mary in 1939 to one of the sisters in the Lady Minto Nursing Association. It had been returned to Violet in the 1960's because it was thought she might like to keep it as a memento of her mother. Instead of a traditional Nativity scene, the front of the card showed a nineteenth century watercolour of the Procession of Boats at Eton on the Fourth of June.

Esmond was commemorated at home in the Borders in two significant ways. In addition to a new ward for the cottage hospital in Hawick named after him, for which the Prince of Wales laid the foundation stone, it was decided in 1921 to erect a memorial in Minto churchyard to the men of the area who gave their lives in defence of their country.[6] A well-known Galashiels born sculptor called Thomas Clapperton, who had been at the front himself, was chosen to create a statue of a soldier, representative of all the fallen, wearing a helmet, puttees and greatcoat, on guard with rifle in hand. His face was modelled on Esmond. The statue was placed near the tall cross marking Rolly's grave on a pedestal of rock taken from the Minto Crags, bearing the inscription:

THE FLOWERS OF THE FOREST ARE A'WEDE AWAY. OUT OF DARKNESS, THROUGH FIRE, INTO LIGHT. REJOICE, WE HAVE CONQUERED.

On Sunday 18 September 1921, in front of a large gathering, the statue was unveiled by Earl Haig. An article in the local paper described the scene:

> Lord Haig addressed the congregation, and there were few, I think who can have gazed unmoved upon the man who won the war for us, and won it not only by fine soldiership, but by generous self-abnegation, and whose life, now his campaigns are over, is given to caring for the welfare of those who served him so well. Speaking simply and straightforwardly, with no touch of rhetoric, but with such weight as no other speaker could have commanded, he paid his tribute to the fallen.

The paths of the Haigs and the Mintos were to cross again with the marriage of the Field Marshal's daughter Irene to Violet's son, Gavin Astor, just after the Second World War.

Following the memorial's unveiling, Mary had the statue turned one hundred and eighty degrees from its original position, to face Germany, maintaining that "a British soldier never turns his back on the enemy."

Dramatis Personae

Cazalet, Captain Victor, *'Teenie'* MC. 1896-1943. Eton/1st Life Guards. Friend of Esmond at Eton. Called 'Teenie' as he was only 5' 3". Later MP for Chippenham. A godfather of the actress Elizabeth Taylor, there were rumours that he was her natural father. He was killed in a B-24 on take-off from Gibraltar with Polish Prime Minister, General Sikorski, on their way to visit Polish forces in the Middle East.

Devonshire, Evie, Duchess of. 1870-1960. Married to 8th Duke of Devonshire, she presided over four English houses and one Irish castle. Mistress of the Robes to Queen Mary 1910-1916. Her husband was then appointed Governor General of Canada. Mother of Lady Dorothy Cavendish, who married Harold Macmillan.

Jelf, General Rudolph, CMG, DSO. 1873-1958. Eton/60th Rifles. ADC to Viceroy of India June 1907-March 1910.

Kinnaird, Lt The Hon Arthur, MC. Scots Guards. Born 1885, KIA 27 November 1917 Cambrai. One of his platoon received the VC for trying to carry him to safety under fire.

I vow to thee, my country, all earthly things above,
Entire and whole and perfect, the service of my love;
The love that asks no question, the love that stands the test,
That lays upon the altar the dearest and the best;
The love that never falters, the love that pays the price,
The love that makes undaunted the final sacrifice.

Sir Cecil Spring-Rice, British diplomat
and Old Etonian, 12 January 1918

Appendix

Mary Minto's Introduction to the Record of Esmond's Life

When this record of Esmond's life was commenced I thought it might possibly be printed, hence the formal allusions to members of the family. Our absence in India during five years of Esmond's boyhood left only his correspondence to guide me, but I realised that nothing I could write could possibly give his true personality in the same way as his own letters, which I have tried to link together, stating facts as briefly as possible, in order to keep an unbroken sequence. The record has become so intimate that I have decided to have only two copies typed, one for myself and one for my children. Esmond hated any form of publicity; he disliked seeming to pry into the private concerns of others, and he certainly would never have believed that anyone outside his own family could possibly care to read his private letters.

It has been a wonderful satisfaction to me to record each episode and to live over again with him those joyous twenty-two years. "What a lot of happiness one can get out of life" he once wrote home from the front. Happiness was the mainspring of his being, and although we have been deprived of his earthly presence, we can still feel the power of his influence, and try to realise the radiance that must now surround him on his promotion to the "City of the Sunlight".

Mary Minto, February 1919

Esmond's name is commemorated on the following War Memorials:

The House of Lords War Memorial.
The House of Lords Illuminated Memorial Book.
Minto Church War Memorial.
Memorial Tablet with his father in in the ante-chapel Eton College Chapel.
Colonnade Memorial at Eton College.
The plaque in the Cloister at Eton College commemorating the 53 old boys of
    Macnaghten House who were killed in action.
Macnaghten War Memorial Library, Eton College.
The Brass Memorial Tablet in St George's Church, Ypres, of Old Etonians killed in
    the Ypres Salient.

Notes

1 Family & Early Life.

1 Mary, Countess of Minto, *India Morley and Minto*, 1935.

2 Mary, Countess of Minto, *Record of Esmond's Life*, 1919.

3 John Buchan, *Lord Minto, A Memoir*, 1924.

4 Margot Asquith, *Myself When Young*, 1938, a collection of short autobiographies of notable women, including Coco Chanel, Amy Johnson and Sylvia Pankhurst.

5 Panshanger, in Hertfordshire, later owned by Ettie Desborough.

6 Minto, *Record*.

7 Ruby Cromer, *Such Were These Years*, 1939.

8 Minto, *Record*.

9 Cromer, *Such Were These Years*.

10 Minto, *Record*.

11 Buchan, *Lord Minto*.

12 Cromer, *Such Were These Years*.

13 Cromer, *Such Were These Years*.

14 Buchan, *Lord Minto*.

15 Minto, *Record*.

16 Minto, *Record*.

17 Buchan, *Lord Minto*.

18 Minto, *Record*.

2 India

1 Lord Minto's Journal.

2 Maler Kotla: A Muslim majority state. In 1947, when there were riots in the Punjab, Maler Kotla remained an oasis of peace.

3 In 1806, the 1st Lord Minto had protected the rights of the Phulkian States from the encroachments of Ranjit Singh, who wished to extend his territory across the Sutlej. It was the support of the British which allowed these four princely states to survive.

4 Loyn, David, *Butcher and Bolt* (London: Hutchinson 2008).

5 Lady Minto's Nursing Association. Lady Curzon had begun a movement to provide an extensive nursing association across India, but had run out of funds. Mary Minto took up

the challenge in 1906 appealing to the public in Britain and India to start an endowment fund. Thus, the scheme was founded. Violet was on the Committee and Queen Mary was the Patroness. It was rolled out initially in six provincial states and was staffed by fully qualified European nurses.

6   Over £2.5m in today's values.

3 Eton

1   Knox, Ronald, *Patrick Shaw-Stewart* (London: Collins, 1920).
2   Minto, *India, Minto and Morley*, 1935.
3   Miss Dempster's Notes, 1918.
4   Minto, *Record of Esmond's Life*, 1919.
5   Minto, *Record*.

4 Prelude to War

1   This refers to the celebrity Lina Cavalieri, 1874-1944. A former Italian opera singer, she ran a cosmetic salon in Paris when Esmond was there. In 1910, she had married Robert (Bob) Winthrop Chanler, an eccentric designer and muralist and one of the famous 13 Astor orphans. With other members of his family Bob had committed his brother, Archie to a mental asylum. When Bob married Lina Cavalieri, having signed a pre-nuptial agreement effectively giving her his entire fortune, Archie sent him a telegram: "Who's looney now?".
2   The repatriation of bodies was stopped in 1915 and thereafter all soldiers were buried where they fell or, if they died in casualty clearing stations and hospitals, in the nearest war cemetery.
3   Ego Charteris, Lord Elcho, heir of Lord Wemyss, Eton and Trinity College, Oxford. Captain in the Royal Gloucestershire Hussars. Based in Egypt for the Dardanelles Campaign. KIA 23 April 1916, aged 32. His younger brother Ivo, KIA 17 October 1915 aged only 19, after only 5 weeks in France.

5 Staff Officer

1   Zotos: anti-seasickness pills.
2   Little pocket book *Short Daily Prayers* given to Esmond from his Aunt Victoria in 1916.
3   Vauban, Sebastien Le Prestre de Vauban. 1633-1707. Marshal of France. Foremost military engineer of his age. Designed fortifications; advisor to Louis XIV on defence of France's borders.
4   "It's prohibited!".
5   Stellenbosched: Stellenbosch was a military base, used as a 'remount' camp, during the 2nd Boer War; officers who had not distinguished themselves at the front were sent there. The term caught on to indicate suboptimal performance on the part of a soldier.
6   Esmond's tooth had been loosened by a cricket ball at Eton.
7   Randall Davidson 1848-1930.
8   Lord George Scott.

6 Joins the Scots Guards

1   Interview with Brian Johnson 1986, published in *The Grenadier Gazette*, 1988.

2   Always leading from the front and by example, Guards officers inspired their men to be fearless and prepared for sacrifice. The Germans had a healthy respect for the Guards and their iron discipline.

3   Deccan Horse, or 9th Horse, cavalry regiment of the Indian Army which could trace its formation back to 1790 when it was called Asif Sah's Irregular Cavalry.

4   G Company – The 2nd Battalion Scots Guards Senior Company was known as Right Flank with the tallest men. Then there was F and G Companies and Left Flank. The Guards aroused admiration but also envy among less distinguished regiments.

    The five foot regiments of the Guards Division often served together. The Grenadiers were nicknamed *Bill-Browns*, the Coldstream *Coalies*, the Scots *Jocks*, the Irish *Micks* and the Welsh *Taffies*.

7 The Diggers

1   The *Mona's Queen*. Between January 1915 and April 1919, she was continually employed as a Troop Transport from Southampton to France carrying almost half a million troops. She earned the rare distinction of sinking a German Submarine, by avoiding a torpedo and ramming its bow with her paddle floats. For this act "great brilliancy", as it was described on a commemorative postcard, her captain and crew were suitably rewarded.

2   Bruce Bairnsfather. Famous British cartoonist famous for *Old Bill* published weekly in the Bystander during WW1. 1887-1959.

3   "Qui hi": Anglo-Indian summons for a servant.

4   Rumpelmayer, patisserie and coffee shop.

5   Lloyd George who had recently replaced Asquith as Prime Minister.

8 Platoon Commander

1   The letters were hugely appreciated and some of them were published as *Eton Letters 1915 – 1918*, privately printed by Spottiswoode, Ballantyne & Co Ltd, The Savile Press, Eton (1920).

2   Limber: a two wheeled cart or trailer used for carrying ammunition.

3   By Major E. de Stein (60th Rifles).

4   Le petit taquin – "the little tease."

5   The Lewis gun was a relatively portable machine gun designed by an American for the Belgians. Nicknamed the "Belgian Rattlesnake" by German troops who came up against the weapon in 1914, it was adopted as the standard issue British Army machine gun by the end of 1915.

6   "Don't get angry – just stop and think."

7   British Summer Time was first introduced in 1916.

10 Return to the Front

1   Lord French was a tenant of George Gordon Moore's at 94 Lancaster Gate, across the terrace from the Mintos. Moore, an American, threw lavish parties with modern jazz bands and plenty of champagne. They would be attended by young officers and he would provide them with young beauties for company. According to Diana Cooper, they became known as the "Dances of Death", because they were often the last parties enjoyed by the officers, before being killed on their return to the front.

2   Barnum and Bailey's Circus, founded by Phineas Taylor Barnum (1810-1891) in 1870, a travelling circus and museum of freaks.

3   *A General's Letters to his Son* by H.S Smith-Dorrien, 1917; *Private Spud Tamson* by R.W. Campbell, 1916; and *A Student in Arms*, by Donald Hankey 1916. *A Student in Arms* was an instant best-seller; most of the essays are religious in nature and, in tone, vary from being enthusiastic and rousing to reflecting disillusionment.

    Donald Hankey was 2nd Lt. in the Royal Warwickshire Regiment, killed in action near Le Transloy on 12/10/16. He was buried where he fell, but after the war his grave could not be found, so his name appears on the Thiepval Memorial.

4   Sausages: barrage balloons.

5   By 1917, Zeppelins were replaced by long-range bombers and on 7 July, London was attacked by 22 Gotha GV aircraft. They targeted the City and the East End and 57 people were killed.

6   Heavies: heavy large calibre guns and howitzers.

7   *The Night Patrol* by Arthur Graeme West, from *Diary of a Dead Man*, 1916; KIA April 1917. The tins in the third line refer to empty cans which were hung outside trenches to act as an alarm if the wire was disturbed.

8   Prince of Wales, known as David to his family and close friends.

11 His Final Role

1   A Company Commander was in charge of approximately 200 men, made up of four Platoons. Typically, he would get very little sleep as he would be visiting his troop's positions, continually receiving messages and casualty reports and giving orders. The life expectancy of a subaltern in trenches was only six weeks. Officers were twice as likely to be killed as the men. By 1917 casualty figures were so high that most company commanders were not more than twenty years old. It normally took 10 years to reach this rank before 1914.

2   Ewart, Wilfred, *Scots Guard*, 1934.

3   Cyril Falls, *War Books: A Critical Guide*, 1930.

4   Ewart, Wilfrid, *Way of Revelation*, 1921.

5   Ewart, Wilfrid, *Way of Revelation*, 1921.

12 Aftermath

1   Among the 53 fallen in Macnaghten's House were the Lawrence brothers, Oliver and Michael, very close in age and contemporaries of Esmond. The sons of General Sir Herbert Lawrence, Douglas Haig's Chief of General Staff from the beginning of 1918, they both perished on the Western Front. A.R. 'Ronnie' Backus, in the VIII with Esmond at Henley in 1913, survived being buried alive in 1915, shot at on the Salient and then again on the Somme, only to be mown down by a lorry as he was returning to his Battalion on his bicycle after a dinner. Rupert Farquhar, also a rower, in the year below Esmond, won an MC and was also killed in Flanders in September 1917. Four years older than Esmond, 'Billy' Congreve, killed by a sniper on the road to Longueval in July 1916, was the first infantry officer in the Great War to win all three gallantry medals, the MC, DSO and VC. Mentioned in despatches four times.

2   Margaret Petty-Fitzmaurice (1910–2003), married Lieutenant Colonel Ririd Myddleton, Coldstream Guards.

3   Glenconner, Pamela, *Edward Wyndham Tennant – A Memoir*, 1919; Grenfell, Ethel Anne Priscilla, Lady Desborough, *Pages from a Family Journal 1888-1915*, Eton College 1916.

4   See Appendix I.

5   See Anthony Morton, *Sandhurst and the First World War: The Royal Military College 1902-1918*, 2014.

6   Violet and John paid for the Esmond Elliot Memorial Ward at the Hawick Hospital to be built. The Prince of Wales laid its foundation stone in 1924 and it was opened by Violet two years later.

Select Bibliography

The National Archives (Kew)

WO 95/912: XIV Corps War Diary.
WO 95/1222: 3rd Guards Brigade War Diary.
WO 95/1223: 2nd Scots Guards War Diary.

Published Sources

Major-General Sir Allan Adair, *A Guards General: The Memoirs of Major-General Sir Allan Adair* (London: Hamish Hamilton, 1986).
Simon Ball, *The Guardsmen: Harold Macmillan, Three Friends, and the World They Made* (London: Harper Collins. 2004).
Mark Bence-Jones, *The Viceroys of India* (London: Constable, 1982).
Brian Bond, *Survivors of A Kind: Memoirs of the Western Front* (London: Continuum, 2008).
John Buchan, *Lord Minto: A Memoir* (London: Thomas Nelson, 1924).
David Cannadine, *The Decline and Fall of the British Aristocracy* (London: Penguin, 2005).
Hugh Cecil, *The Flower of Battle: How Britain Wrote the Great War* (Hanover, New Hampshire: Steerforth Press, 1996).
Alexandra Churchill, *Blood and Thunder: The Boys of Eton College and the First World War* (Stroud: History Press. 2014).
—— with Andrew Holmes & Jonathan Dyer, *Passchendaele: 103 Days in Hell.* (Solihull: Helion, 2017).
Norman Cliff, *To Hell and Back with the Guards* (Braunton: Merlin, 1988).
Damian Collins, *Charmed Life: The Phenomenal World of Philip Sassoon* (HarperCollins, 2016).
Duff Cooper, *Old Men Forget* (London: Rupert Hart-Davis, 1953).
Ruby Cromer, *Such Were These Years* (London: Hodder & Stoughton, 1939).
Richard Davenport-Hines, Ettie, *The Intimate Life and Dauntless Spirit of Lady Desborough* (London: Weidenfeld and Nicholson 2008).

Henry Dundas, *Scots Guards: A Memoir* (Charleston, South Carolina: Nabu Press reprint of 1921 edition).

Anthony Eden, *Another World: 1897-1917* (London: Allen Lane, 1976).

Brigadier-General Sir J.E. Edmonds, *Military Operations France and Belgium 1917, Vol. 2* (London: HMSO, 1948).

Richard van Emden, *The Trench: Experiencing life on the Front Line, 1916* (London: Corgi Books, 2002).

—— *The Quick and the Dead: Fallen Soldiers and Their Families in the Great War* (London: Bloomsbury, 2011).

Wilfred Ewart, *Way of Revelation* (London: Forgotten Publishing, 2012). Note: Ewart based one of this novel's two main characters, *Eric*, on Esmond Elliot.

—— *Scots Guards in the Great War* (London: John Murray 1925). Note: Ewart, who served with Esmond Elliot and was with him when the latter was mortally wounded, wrote the first two chapters before his accidental death in Mexico City on New Year's Eve 1921-22.

—— *Scots Guard on the Western Front, 1915-1918* (London: Rich & Cowan, 1934). Note: Ewart dedicated the book to the memory of four brother officers killed during 1914-18: Esmond Elliot, Lieutenant Sir Edward Hulse, Lieutenant A.R.W. Menzies and Second Lieutenant L.A. Jarvis.

Cyril Falls, *Military Operations France and Belgium 1917, Vol. 1* (London: Macmillan, 1940).

Sir Frank Fox, *The King's Pilgrimage* (London: Hodder & Stoughton, 1922)

Pamela Glenconner, *Edward Wyndham Tennant, A Memoir* (1919)

Stephen Graham, *A Private in the Guards* (London: Macmillan, 1919).

Ethel Anne Priscilla Grenfell, Lady Desborough, *Pages from a Family Journal 1888-1915* (Eton College, 1916).

Donald Hankey, *A Student in Arms* (London: Andrew Melrose, 1916).

Cuthbert Headlam, *History of the Guards Division in the Great War, Vols. 1 & 2* (London: John Murray, 1924).

Pat Jalland, *Death in the Victorian Family* (Oxford University Press, 1996).

Miles Jebb, *Patrick Shaw Stewart: An Edwardian Meteor* (The Dovecote Press, 2010).

S. Leslie, *Letters of an Old Etonian: July 1914 – January 1917* (London: Blackwell 1919).

John Lewis-Stempel, *Six Weeks: The Short and Gallant Life of the British Officer in the First World War* (London: Weidenfeld and Nicolson, 2010).

Peter Liddle (ed.), *Passchendaele in Perspective: The Third Battle of Ypres* (London: Leo Cooper. 1997).

—— (ed.), *Britain Goes to War* (Barnsley: Pen & Sword, 2015).

Nick Lloyd, *Passchendaele: A New History* (London: Penguin-Viking, 2017).

Michael LoCicero, *A Moonlight Massacre: The Night Operation on the Passchendaele Ridge – The Forgotten Last Act of the Third Battle of Ypres* (Solihull: Helion 2014).

Anabel Loyd, Vicereine, *The Indian Journal of Mary Minto* (Academic Foundation, 2016).

David Loyn, *Butcher & Bolt: Two Hundred Years of Foreign Engagement in Afghanistan* (Hutchinson, 2008).

Oliver Lyttelton, *The Memoirs of Lord Chandos* (London: Bodley Head, 1963).

Lyn Macdonald, *They Called it Passchendaele* (London: Michael Joseph, 1978).

Harold Macmillan, *Winds of Change 1914-1939* (London: Macmillan, 1966).

Margaret MacMillan, *Women of the Raj* (London: Thames & Hudson, 1988).

H. Macnaghten, *Eton Letters: 1915-18 by a Housemaster* (London: Spottiswoode, 1920).

Chris McCarthy, *Passchendaele: The Day-by-Day Account* (London: Arms & Armour Press, 1995).

Mary, Countess of Minto, *India, Minto and Morley 1905-1910* (London: Macmillan, 1935).

Nicholas Mosley, *Julian Grenfell: His Life and The Times of His Death, 1888-1915*, (London: Weidenfeld and Nicolson, 1976).

Randall Nicol, *Till the Trumpet Sounds Again: The Scots Guards 1914-1919 in Their Own Words, Vols. 1 & 2* (Solihull: Helion & Company, 2016).

Anne Nelson (ed.), *For Love and Courage: The Letters of Lieutenant Colonel E.W. Hermon from the Western Front 1914-17* (New York: Random House, 2008).

Juliet Nicolson, *The Great Silence: Britain from the Shadow of the First World War to the Dawn of the Jazz Age* (New York: Grove Press, 2011).

An "OE", *Iron Times with the Guards* (London: John Murray, 1918).

Peter Oldham, *Pillboxes on the Western Front: A Guide to the Design, Construction and Use of Concrete Pillboxes, 1914-18* (Barnsley: Pen & Sword, 2011).

E.B. Osborne (ed.), *The Muse in Arms* (London: John Murray, 1917).

Peter Parker, *The Old Lie: The Great War and the Public Schools Ethos* (London: Bloomsbury, 1987).

Robert A. Perry, *To Play a Giant's Part: The Role of the British Army at Passchendaele.* (Uckfield: Naval & Military Press, 2014).

Sir Frederick Ponsonby, *The Grenadier Guards in the Great War 1914-19, Vols. 1-3* (London: Macmillan, 1920).

Anne Powell, *Bim: A tribute to the honorable Edward Wyndham Tennant, Lieutenant, 4th Battalion Grenadier Guards 1897-1916* (1990).

Robin Prior & Trevor Wilson, *Passchendaele: The Untold Story* (New Haven, Connecticut: Yale University Press, 1996).

A.C. Rayner-Wood, *Twenty Years After: The Letters of an Eton Housemaster* (London: Spottiswoode, Ballantyne & Co, 1939).

David Reynolds, The Long Shadow: The Great War and the Twentieth Century (New York: Simon & Schuster, 2013).

Eugene Ryan (ed.), *Haig's Medical Office* (Barnsley: Pen & Sword, 2013).

Anthony Seldon & David Walsh, *Public Schools and the Great War* (Barnsley: Pen & Sword 2013.

Jack Sheldon, *The German Army at Passchendaele* (Barnsley: Pen & Sword, 2007).

Charles Abel Smith, *From Eton to Ypres: The Letters of Lt. Col Wilfrid Abel Smith* (Stroud: History Press, 2016).

Private Len Smith, *Drawing Fire: The Diary of a Great War Soldier and Artist* (London: Collins. 2009).

John Terraine, *The Road to Passchendaele: The Flanders Offensive of 1917 – A Study in Inevitability* (London: Leo Cooper. 1977).

Colonel E.G.L. Thurlow, *The Pillboxes of Flanders* (London: Ivor Nicholson & Watson, 1933).

Jonathan Walker, *The Blue Beast: Power &Passion in the Great War* (The History Press, 2012).

Philip Wright, *For Distinguished Conduct: WOs, NCOs, Officers and Men of the Grenadier Guards Awarded the Distinguished Conduct Medal in the Great War 1914-18* (London: Blurb, 2014).

Philip Ziegler, *King Edward VIII: The Official Biography* (London: Collins, 1990).

Index